Advance Praise for *No Way to Treat a Child*

"Naomi Schaefer Riley brings to the forefront a crucial question, which is foundational to the design of a compassionate and safe child welfare system in the United States. Her analysis and keen insights are more than worth a read. Her dedication and passion for this work continues to inspire me." —**Mary L. Landrieu,** former U.S. Senator (D-LA)

"Anyone who cares about the disappeared children of America should read this book." Naomi Schaefer Riley is one of the few people who will tell the truth about what really goes on in the lives of children who have been removed from their parents' care by the state. These children end up pawns in a great politically-motivated shuffle that often serves only to break their most important attachments; to leave them languishing for permanent placements until the 'right' kind of parent can be chosen by the state; or returned to dangerous situations. Sent from placement to placement—and school to school—they quickly suffer emotional and educational losses that can't be repaired. I don't know of any writer who reports as deeply and writes as honestly as NSR. At the very least, she bears witness to what we've all chosen to ignore. We all have a stake in this situation." —**Caitlin Flanagan,** staff writer, *The Atlantic*

"Harrowing yet full of heart, *No Way to Treat a Child* tells the searing tale of how political correctness is harming the smallest and weakest among us: kids who need homes. Kudos to Naomi Schaefer Riley for trying to change a system that needlessly puts young lives at risk. May her brave book succeed in its mission." —**Mary Eberstadt,** author, *Primal Screams* and *How the West Really Lost God*

"Our beleaguered, blinkered child welfare system has not kept pace with the scientific consensus on healthy child development or the effect of trauma on the young brain. That huge numbers of children are harmed by the status quo is indisputable. The question is why we can't do better. With a journalist's eye for detail and a scientist's command of evidence, Riley describes how a system mired in forms of reckless idealism, disinformation, and bigotry has abandoned its mission to protect the most vulnerable members of our society. This is bracing, powerful stuff, and Riley is not interested in protecting naive feelings; but her provocative call to action should inspire decent people of all backgrounds, faiths, and identities to reform a disgraceful system and, perhaps, to live in closer alignment to the Talmudic saying that, 'Whoever saves one life saves the world entire.'" —**Erika Christakis,** author, *The Importance of Being Little* and foster/adoptive parent

"Naomi Schaefer Riley's book reveals the extent to which abused and abandoned children are often injured by their government rescuers. It is a must read for those seeking solutions to this national crisis." —**Robert L. Woodson, Sr.,** civil rights leader and president of the Woodson Center, author of *Lessons from the Least of These*

"Everyone interested in child welfare should grapple with Naomi Riley's powerful evidence that the current system ill-serves the safety and well-being of vulnerable kids." —**Walter Olson,** senior fellow, Cato Institute, Robert A. Levy Center for Constitutional Studies

"We want the best for kids, especially the most vulnerable kids. But we aren't getting even close, as Naomi Schaefer Riley masterfully and heartbreakingly shows in her gripping book *No Way to Treat a Child.* More than a tale of woe, however, this book shows the way to a better future for the people who *are* our future." —**Arthur C. Brooks,** professor, Harvard Kennedy School and Harvard Business School, and author of *Love Your Enemies* and *The Conservative Heart*

"Riley documents how America's failure to treat abused children as individuals with rights, rather than property of parents, kin, race, or tribe, sends kids to their graves." —**Darcy Olsen,** founder, Gen Justice.

NO WAY TO TREAT A CHILD

HOW THE FOSTER CARE SYSTEM, FAMILY COURTS, AND RACIAL ACTIVISTS ARE WRECKING YOUNG LIVES

NAOMI SCHAEFER RILEY

BOMBARDIER
BOOKS

A BOMBARDIER BOOKS BOOK
An Imprint of Post Hill Press
ISBN: 978-1-64293-657-5
ISBN (eBook): 978-1-64293-658-2

No Way to Treat a Child:
How the Foster Care System, Family Courts, and Racial Activists
Are Wrecking Young Lives

Cover Design by Tiffani Shea

Post Hill Press
New York • Nashville
posthillpress.com

Published in the United States of America
1 2 3 4 5 6 7 8 9 10

In memory of Richard Gelles,
a compassionate man and an uncompromising scholar

*A note on names: Almost all the names of foster children and parents in this book have been changed to protect their identities. On a few occasions, if a child has been officially adopted and is no longer involved with the system, real names are used. In those instances, last names are listed as well.

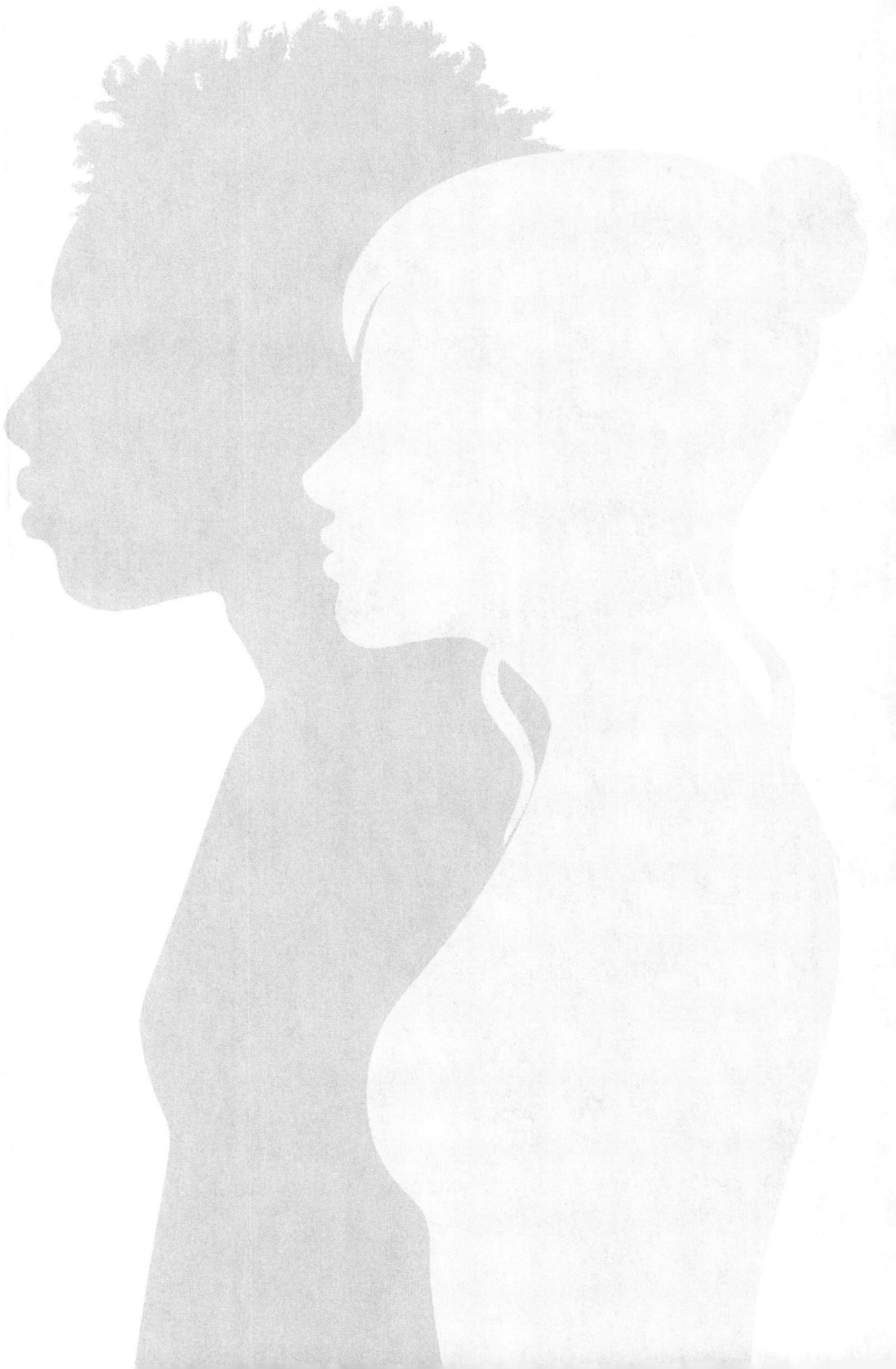

CONTENTS

Introduction: Putting Adults First 13
Chapter 1 - Felicia's Story—Counting Our Failures on the Hands of One Child 27
Chapter 2 - The Ideology of Family Preservation—Sacrificing Child Safety for Family Unity 38
Chapter 3 - Blood May Be Thicker, but It's Not Always Better: The Problem with Kinship Care 61
Chapter 4 - Separate and Unequal: How a Racialized Ideology Is Putting Kids in Danger 77
Chapter 5 - The Problem Is Not Poverty, It's Drugs 107
Chapter 6 - Searching for Justice in Family Court 127
Chapter 7 - The Child-Welfare Cartel: Why CPS Investigators Are Underqualified and Undertrained 145
Chapter 8 - Moneyball for Child Welfare: How Big Data Can Help Fix the System 167
Chapter 9 - It's a Hard-Knock Life in Group Homes—But Possibly Better Than the Alternative 192
Chapter 10 - The Power of Faith: How Religious Communities Are Making Foster Care Stronger 215
Chapter 11 - The War Against Faith-Based Foster Care 236
Chapter 12 - Raising the Bar: Getting Middle-Class Americans to Do Foster Care 250
Chapter 13 - What's Holding Us Back? Changing the Laws and the Politics of Child Welfare 273
Conclusion 287
Acknowledgments 297

INTRODUCTION

PUTTING ADULTS FIRST

I called it. It's not something I'm proud of, but within hours of the announcement of the nomination of Judge Amy Coney Barrett to the Supreme Court in the fall of 2020, some friends were wondering exactly what her opponents might find to attack. I already knew the answer. "The woman might as well be a saint," they told me. "Did you know that she adopted two orphaned children from Haiti?" they asked. Surely nothing in her personal life could be fodder. *Oh*, I thought, *you'd be surprised.*

And there, like some kind of prophetic fulfillment, was Ibram X. Kendi on Twitter: "Some White colonizers 'adopted' Black children," the Boston University professor and author of the bestselling book *How to Be an Antiracis*t, wrote. "They 'civilized' these 'savage' children in the 'superior' ways of White people, while using them as props in their lifelong pictures of denial, while cutting the biological parents of these children out of the picture of humanity."[1]

The idea that white parents caring for black children—black orphans, no less—is a form of colonization is not a new accusation. Indeed, it seems that the United States went almost right from a

1 Ibram X. Kendi, Twitter post, Sep. 26, 2020, 1:04 p.m.

period in which interracial family relationships were illegal—the first official interracial adoption was in 1948—to one in which white adults were criticized as patronizing bigots for wanting to care for children whose skin color did not match theirs.

Malcolm X made the accusation more than a half-century before Kendi. In 1938, Malcolm's mother, Louise Little, suffered a nervous breakdown after her husband was murdered. Six of her children, including Malcolm, were sent to four different foster homes. Malcolm was placed with a white family. In his 1965 best-seller, *The Autobiography of Malcolm X*, which he coauthored with journalist Alex Haley, Malcolm lamented that "Judge McClellan in Lansing had authority over me and all of my brothers and sisters… A white man in charge of a black man's children! Nothing but legal, modern slavery—however kindly intentioned."[2]

It wasn't long after that in 1972, when the National Association of Black Social Workers took up the cause, issuing a statement that took "a vehement stand against the placements of Black children in white homes for any reason." The group called transracial adoptions "unnatural," "unnecessary," and "artificial" and argued that such placements were evidence of the continued "chattel status" of African Americans.[3]

Such views are at odds with the opinions of most Americans, who find interracial families to be either unremarkable or a generally positive development. A Pew Research Center poll in 2017, for instance, found that "roughly four-in-ten adults (39 percent) now say that more people of different races marrying each other is good for society—up significantly from 24 percent in 2010."[4] The

---

2 Malcolm X, Alex Haley, and Attallah Shabazz, *The Autobiography of Malcolm X: As Told to Alex Haley.* (The Ballantine Publishing Group, 1999).

3 Cenie "Jomo" Williams Jr., "Position Statement on Trans-Racial Adoptions." (National Association of Black Social Workers, 1982), https://cdn.ymaws.com/www.nabsw.org/resource/collection/E1582D77-E4CD-4104-996A-D42D08F9CA7D/NABSW_Trans-Racial_Adoption_1972_Position_(b).pdf.

4 Gretchen Livingston and Anna Brown, "Intermarriage in the U.S. 50 Years After Loving V. Virginia." (Pew Research Center, May 18, 2017), https://www.pewsocialtrends.org/2017/05/18/2-public-views-on-intermarriage.

share saying it's a bad thing fell from 13 percent to only 9 percent. A 2017 survey by the Dave Thomas Foundation of potential adoptive parents found that almost half had no preference at all about the race of the child they would adopt.[5] It is hard to express just how remarkable that is, not just in twenty-first-century America, but also in the context of human history. These children will not be their parents' biological progeny, and everyone else in the community will know that.

Nor is it just a sign of racial tolerance. These sentiments are also a measure of the importance that American families place on the well-being of children, even those who are not their own. Of the respondents considering adoption from foster care—obviously a small sample of the population—most did not say that they had a desire to grow their family. Rather, they noted that children needed "good homes," that they deserve a "better future," or that "all children need to know they are loved." Belief in the need to care for our country's most vulnerable children has won over prejudice and even evolutionary instincts.

Unfortunately, our child-welfare system does not seem to have the same orientation. Though many well-meaning people create and carry out the laws and policies that govern child-welfare agencies and family courts, these institutions have been co-opted by a radical and, in many ways, nonsensical ideology. In deciding how to treat children who are being abused or severely neglected, they consider factors that are completely unrelated to and often at odds with a child's best interests. The most obvious of these is skin color.

Children who have substantiated reports of child abuse and neglect are left in dangerous environments because the system is reluctant to be seen as breaking up black (or Hispanic or Native American) families. It keeps children in the foster-care system too long because biological families already have suffered from a rac-

5 "2017 US Adoption Attitudes Survey." (Harris Poll on behalf of the Dave Thomas Foundation for Adoption, February 2017), https://www.davethomasfoundation.org/wp-content/uploads/2018/02/2017-adoption-attitudes-survey-us.pdf.

ist system—so why pile on by severing these family ties? When it removes children and places them in foster care, race often is taken into consideration. And even though there are many more black children who need parents than there are black parents willing to take them in, there are caseworkers and judges who try to keep black children from being permanently adopted by white families.

They do this because they feel sorry for black adults, not because they are concerned about black children. Indeed, as economists Mark Montgomery and Irene Powell concluded after a review of all the longitudinal studies on the subject: "…empirical evidence on transracial adoption suggests strongly that black children adopted into white families suffer no more developmental or adjustment problems than black adoptees in black families."[6]

But our heated racial dialogue in this country is poised to send our child-welfare system over a cliff. The "abolish foster care" movement, which has become a corollary of the demands to "defund the police," is based on the idea that child-welfare agencies are structurally racist and unfairly targeting minority families, even removing their children because of racial bias. They're not. There are reasons for the disparities—like family structure—that have nothing to do with racism. But this accusation has created pressure to leave many children in their homes despite the risk.

If you want to understand how far this dangerous message has trickled down, here's one illustration: In 2020, a *New York Times* reader wrote to the paper's "Ethicist" column to describe a neighbor, "a single mother of color," routinely beating her young children and their "wailing in response." But, the writer notes, "I do not want to involve the police for obvious reasons."[7] In other words, concerned citizens would rather listen to the screams of abused

---

6 Irene Powell and Mark Montgomery, "Transracial Adoption in the Time of Black Lives Matter." (American Enterprise Institute, November 20, 2020), https://www.aei.org/research-products/report/transracial-adoption-in-the-time-of-black-lives-matter.

7 Kwame Anthony Appiah, "What Should I Do About the Abusive Mom Down the Hall?" (*The New York Times Magazine*, December 15, 2020, https://www.nytimes.com/2020/12/15/magazine/what-should-i-do-about-the-abusive-mom-down-the-hall.html.

children than subject a woman to some imagined instance of racism. This is insane.

Hearing consistent cries about how foster care is racist will only discourage good people from reporting child abuse, from going to work for child-protective services (CPS), or from stepping up to become foster parents. The consequences will be deadly.

It is not just race. There are countless other ways in which the system seems to prioritize other concerns over the best interests of the child. Many professionals and policymakers are more concerned with the well-being of the whole family. In this sense, adults—even the ones who severely neglect and abuse children—are seen as victims as well. As a result, the goals of the child-welfare system continue to expand. While many Americans think too many children are being taken from their homes, leaders at both the state and national levels are committed to increasing the number of families the system touches, subjecting them to just the kind of surveillance that critics object to.

In order to serve the whole family—not just the children—the system prioritizes kinship care, transferring kids to the care of extended family, even when those family members suffer from the same dysfunction and even when those family members can't pass a criminal background check. The system is painfully slow, even though these delays can irreversibly affect kids' development. Family courts are stretched thin. They let cases with young children drag on for years at a time. They treat foster parents—even those who care for children for years—like teenaged babysitters. They keep foster parents in the dark about children's needs and what's going on with their biological parents, and they rarely ask for foster parents' input about the day-to-day lives of the children in their care.

The system favors foster homes over institutions, even for children who need a more intensive level of care for a short time. The system favors foster parents without jobs who can turn on a dime to meet the demands of a child-welfare bureaucracy and drives away stable middle-class families who want to help. And the system now seems determined to punish foster families and organizations who are drawn to this work by their faith because child-welfare bureaucracies are more concerned with social engineering and checking the latest sexual-trend boxes than the best interests of the individual child.

In the year 2019, approximately 7.9 million children were reported to authorities as possible cases of abuse or neglect.[8] These represented 4.4 million calls, with each call covering an average of 1.8 children (generally in the same family). Some of those calls came from mandated reporters—teachers, doctors, social workers. But many came from concerned neighbors or relatives. Of those 7.9 million children referred, we know that something was actually going wrong with about 3.5 million of them. (The remainder were "screened out.") That's more than 5 percent of the population of children in the US. Those are the cases that either merited further investigation or received an "alternative response"—meaning there was reason to believe that abuse or neglect was occurring but that the situation was considered low risk. So, the family is referred for various "services," including, say, a drug-treatment program, an anger-management class, or a low-cost childcare program if a parent has been found to be leaving small children alone in order to go to work.

In 2019, there were 656,000 official victims of child abuse or neglect (if you—in the Orwellian categorizations of the federal government—don't count the kids who were, in fact, victims but deemed to be at low risk of being revictimized and so received an "alternative response."). Those included 1,840 fatalities. There has been an increase in the number of reports made to CPS in recent years, an increase in the number of children who receive alternative responses, and an increase in the number of child-maltreat-

8 Associate Commissioner Aysha E. Schomburg, "Child Maltreatment 2019." (The Children's Bureau of the U.S. Department of Health and Human Services, January 14, 2021), https://www.acf.hhs.gov/cb/report/child-maltreatment-2019.

ment fatalities. But there has been a decline in the number of kids classified as "victims," a statistic that authorities tout.[9] Even more strangely, 58,000 children who were classified as nonvictims were placed into foster care.

What is going on here? By reclassifying cases, the federal government is trying to persuade the public that child maltreatment is declining. It's true that different states measure maltreatment differently and, so, the data is imperfect. But the real trend here may be that states are offering more alternative responses to families reported for abuse and neglect. As a result, the number of children classified as victims would decrease even if the number of actual victims is increasing. Because the number of fatalities is small relative to the population, it is hard to reach any firm conclusions about those cases. But one possibility is that keeping more children out of the "nonvictim category" and, therefore, keeping them from more thorough investigations, from more serious interventions, and out of foster care is actually putting more children in danger.

Between 1999 and 2019, the number of "nonvictims" (again, these are kids who have been mistreated but are deemed to be at low risk) almost doubled from 1.52 million to 2.82 million, while the number of victims remained steady, ticking up and down each year between 650,000 and 700,000.[10] There are any number of explanations for the former. There may have been more mandated reports of low-risk cases, for instance. But why has the number of children classified as victims remained so steady? One possibility is that states simply raised the threshold for substantiating a case (essentially, creating a ceiling) or are conducting more cursory investigations where maltreatment is less likely to be revealed.

Child-welfare leaders have figured out that this country has room for about 800,000 kids to be investigated per year and

---

9 "Lowest Number of Maltreatment," The Children's Bureau of the U.S. Department of Health and Human Services, *30th edition of the Child Maltreatment Report.* (January 14, 2021), https://www.acf.hhs.gov/media/press/2021/child-abuse-neglect-data-released.

10 Ibid.

400,000–500,000 kids to be kept in foster care at any one time, and that's it. There are no more resources for child welfare, and the public pressure to keep these numbers down has only been growing. The headlines in child welfare are always about the foster-care numbers, never about actual maltreatment. If foster-care numbers are down, it's seen as a sign of success. If they're up, it's a sign of failure. Unfortunately, things are more complicated.

There are some things we do know for sure about maltreatment.[11] Children in their first year of life are the most likely to be victimized. So are children with disabilities.[12] Black and Native American children are about twice as likely to be victims of maltreatment as the national average. White children are more likely to be victims than Asian children but less likely than Hispanic children. Girls are more likely than boys to die of maltreatment.

It is not uncommon to hear that black children and Native children are more likely to be removed from their homes and that the system must, therefore, be biased. But the picture is much more complicated. If black children are more likely to be victims, then it would be perfectly reasonable for us to remove them at a higher rate. In fact, it is our moral obligation to consider each child's case individually and weigh the best interests of that child rather than trying to make some numbers in an Excel spreadsheet come out even. Unfortunately, the child-welfare system seems oriented around the latter, not the former.

In 2019, 672,594 children were served by the foster-care system; that is, they were legally removed from their homes and cared for by relatives or nonrelatives—sometimes in a group home.[13] Kids

11 Ibid.

12 Roberta A. Hibbard, Larry W. Desch, and the Committee on Child Abuse and Neglect and Council on Children with Disabilities, "Maltreatment of Children with Disabilities." *(Official Journal of the American Academy of Pediatrics,* May 2007), https://pediatrics.aappublications.org/content/119/5/1018.

13 "Preliminary FY 2019 Estimates as of June 23, 2020--No. 27," *Adoption and Foster Care Analysis and Reporting System (AFCARS) FY 2019 Data,* Children's Bureau of the U.S. Department of Health and Human Services, https://www.acf.hhs.gov/sites/default/files/documents/cb/afcarsreport27.pdf.

come in and out of foster care at various points in the year. There were 251,000 children who entered and 249,000 children who exited foster care in 2019. But if you took a snapshot in time, there were 424,000 kids in foster care in 2019, a decrease from 2016 but an increase since 2012 that seems correlated with the opioid crisis. Children spend an average of 19.6 months in foster care, and more than a quarter spend more than two years in care. The children likely to stay in care the longest are older children, children in sibling groups, and children with special needs. About half of children who are removed to foster care are reunified with their biological families. The number is significantly lower for children who are removed before the age of one.[14]

Foster-care systems are run by states—sometimes divided into county systems, with some functions outsourced to private organizations—and funded by both state and federal dollars in approximately equal parts. This money includes stipends for foster parents, money for child-protective services as well as funds for different types of services for families. Family courts also receive both state and federal funding.

The kids who are adopted out of foster care wait an average of two and a half years, but many never find permanent families at all.[15] This is despite the fact that at least a quarter of the children in foster care are eligible for adoption—their parents' parental rights have been terminated. In 2019, almost 17,000 children aged out of the system.[16] And while a number of states have raised the age at which children may continue to remain in care, this policy may only be kicking the can down the road. We can offer them public-housing vouchers and a stipend, but if we are not giving them

14 "Foster Care Statistics 2018," *Numbers and Trends*. (May 2020), https://www.childwelfare.gov/pubPDFs/foster.pdf.

15 The AFCARS Report, Preliminary FY 2019 Estimates as of June 23, 2020, No. 27, The Children's Bureau of the U.S. Department of the Health and Human Services, https://www.acf.hhs.gov/sites/default/files/documents/cb/afcarsreport27.pdf.

16 "Foster Care Statistics," May 2020.

the intellectual, social, and emotional skills they need to succeed on their own, it will not help.

Foster children who reach adulthood with no family connection have a very difficult road ahead. By their mid-twenties, nearly 70 percent of the women are on public assistance.[17] They are more likely to be homeless, to be unemployed, and to be involved with drugs. A survey of California's prison inmates by the California Department of Corrections and Rehabilitation, found that 14 percent had spent some time in foster care.[18] One report found that the costs of letting a single year's cohort age out of foster care without a permanent family were nearly $8 billion.[19]

Meanwhile, children still in foster homes face challenges. Many have psychological and behavioral problems that need to be addressed. Some suffer additional neglect or abuse from foster parents themselves. With a chronic shortage of people willing to take in these kids, states' standards for foster homes are not very high, and the agencies tasked with monitoring and supporting the homes are often understaffed or overly bureaucratized. More than half of the states in this country are operating under federal consent decrees or pending litigation, the result of class-action litigation on behalf of foster kids.[20] But rarely have these agreements resulted in measurable improvement in child maltreatment.

In some ways, this is not surprising. Public (and many private) bureaucracies are inherently problematic; it is not only the child-welfare system that seems Kafka-esque. These systems are incapable of treating any of us as individuals. But our experiences with the IRS and the DMV are limited to a few dehumanizing hours

---

17 Pam Fessler, "Report: Foster Kids Face Tough Times After Age 18." (April 7, 2010, 12:01 a.m.), https://www.npr.org/templates/story/story.php?storyId=125594259.

18 Sarah McCarthy and Mark Gladstone, "State Survey of California Prisoners," *Policy Matters*. (California Senate Office of Research, December 2011), https://sor.senate.ca.gov/sites/sor.senate.ca.gov/files/Foster_Care_PDF_12-8-11.pdf.

19 Annie E. Casey Foundation, "Cost Avoidance: The Business Case for Investing in Youth Aging Out of Foster Care." (May 2013), https://www.aecf.org/resources/cost-avoidance-the-business-case-for-investing-in-youth-aging-out-of-foster.

20 "Can You Share a Summary of Child Welfare Consent Decrees," Casey Family Programs, July 10, 2019, https://www.casey.org/consent-decree-summary/.

a year; those agencies don't make important decisions about the course of our lives. Child-welfare systems are different.

To say that these systems are failing is not to blame the individuals involved. Many child-welfare investigators, caseworkers, lawyers, and judges went into this field for good reason. This is necessary and valuable work, and we want to attract people who are genuinely qualified and committed to it. But from the moment they begin training for these roles, they become part of a system that is oriented around the wrong priorities. Instead of placing the best interests of the children above all else—making the children the "clients," in the words of the late University of Pennsylvania Social Work dean Richard Gelles—the system has settled on serving families.[21] The loudest and most articulate spokespersons for families are the adults, and so we serve the interest of adults, even if they are at odds with the interests of children.

I am not someone who has devoted her life to child welfare. But I have been a journalist for almost a quarter of a century, and, in that time, I have returned again and again to the question of who is caring for vulnerable children in the United States. Early in my career, when I wrote about religion for the *Wall Street Journal*, I regularly came across families who fostered and adopted children both here and abroad who were unlikely to find stable, loving homes otherwise. I marveled at the way these parents talked about God calling them to do things that others—including my friends and I—could never imagine.

A few years ago, I was drawn to the subject of Native Americans. I spent two years traveling to different Indian reservations from Montana to upstate New York. Originally, I just wanted to know why these places were so poor. But as I spent more and more time in these communities, I wondered why they experienced such high levels of child abuse. There are millions of poor parents all over this

21 "Interview: Richard Gelles," *Frontline: Failure to Protect*, https://www.pbs.org/wgbh/pages/frontline/shows/fostercare/inside/gelles.html.

country providing loving, stable homes for their offspring. The vast majority of the poor do not mistreat their children.

The rate of maltreatment for Indian children is 60 percent higher than the national average.[22] In some communities, physical and even sexual abuse are open secrets. Why, I wondered, was no one protecting these children from harm by their parents, relatives, and other community members? And why were officials and private individuals telling the truth about these conditions considered pariahs?[23] Most importantly, why did we have a different set of laws for determining whether these kids were in danger and whether they should be removed from their homes? How could we have a lower bar for the way some kids are treated?

But as I began to look at the subject of child welfare more broadly, I started to see double standards—and a lack of standards—everywhere. How could child-welfare officials decide that it would be safe for black children to remain in a home where they had been abused and neglected but rescue white children in a similar environment. And how could family-court judges sign off on this kind of arrangement? How could foundations with racially-driven agendas be allowed to push agencies and judges into creating and maintaining a separate and unequal child-welfare system? The idea that our society has a higher tolerance for the mistreatment of children—children who happen to look like mine—outrages me every single day.

As a columnist for the *New York Post* for several years, I wrote about some of the most egregious cases of abuse in New York City and how the agency overseeing child welfare seemed to be falling down on the job despite repeated reform efforts. The laws passed at the state and federal level, however well-intentioned and clear, were regularly ignored. All over the country, I could ask the same ques-

22 "Lowest Number of Maltreatment." (The Children's Bureau, January 14, 2021), https://www.acf.hhs.gov/cb/report/child-maltreatment-2019.

23 Timothy Williams, "Psychologist Who Wrote of Abuse Is Punished." (July 30, 2012), https://www.nytimes.com/2012/07/31/us/doctor-who-warned-of-spirit-lake-abuse-is-reprimanded.html.

tions I was asking on Indian reservations. Why did certain parents seem to get a pass for mistreating their children? How was it possible for workers to visit families' homes multiple times and have no sense of the danger that their children were encountering day after day? Why weren't we making better—and faster—decisions about these kids? Why did the entire system seem oriented toward solving the problems and meeting the needs of the adults, rather than the kids?

It is not uncommon these days to hear people talking about how the government is too involved in the lives of families. And I'm inclined to agree. Why are kids being picked up by police for walking to the park alone? Why can't a mother run into the dry cleaners without dragging her sleeping child out of the car too? How does an eighteen-year-old in a relationship with a sixteen-year-old wind up on a registry for sex criminals?

When it comes to parenting my own children, I certainly don't want anyone else intruding. I'm not quite a free-range parent, but I try to give my three children as much independence as possible. I know that letting them bicycle across town and climb trees and stay home alone and use the stove means that they could get hurt. And I wouldn't want to find myself under government scrutiny for making what I consider age-appropriate decisions.

I don't think the government is particularly good at fixing individuals' problems, and I think that in the past half-century, it has probably done much more to hurt families than to help them. And I think there are probably too many kids being reported for abuse and neglect—as we can see from the fact that half of all reports each year are screened out.

But I also think that there are certain functions government must perform, and ensuring the safety of those who cannot protect themselves is one of them. The question is: how can it do that job most effectively without intruding into the lives of families who are doing just fine? It is tempting to take one's ideology—progressive, liberal, conservative, or libertarian—to the field of child welfare, but frankly, it is an issue that requires a more pragmatic approach. And it also requires a little more understanding than most of us have as to what is going on behind closed doors in some families.

In the pages that follow, I try to explain what is happening in the lives of these children and offer some practical prescriptions for how they can be helped. Whether it is deciding which children need attention, whether to remove children from their homes, and where to place them temporarily or permanently if they can't go home, I try to explain where we have gone wrong and what policies are most likely to ensure that at-risk kids wind up in safe, loving, and stable homes. And I try to offer suggestions for how we can find more of those homes, instead of trying to exclude the people who have stepped up to do this vital work. Child abuse and foster care are not something that most Americans have to think about on a daily basis—thankfully—but if they did, I think they would take a similar approach.

CHAPTER 1

FELICIA'S STORY—COUNTING OUR FAILURES ON THE HANDS OF ONE CHILD

In the fall of 2018, when a Colorado foster-care caseworker asked a fourteen-year-old high school freshman named Felicia if she would like to meet Nadia, a thirty-seven-year-old single woman who was interested in adopting her, Felicia replied with a flat "no." She had been in a foster home for two years, and she recalls: "Yeah, I was like, 'I'm done. I don't want it. I'll stay here until my high-school life is over.'" It wasn't clear what Felicia imagined would happen after that, but she thought if she could get to eighteen, then she would figure something out. Felicia recalled: "I was like, 'Whatever.'"

If you want to understand what ails the child-welfare system in this country, you could do worse than absorb the story of how Felicia got to this point and what befell her afterward. Ask yourself: How is it that a bright, attractive girl who was loved and admired by so many of the adults and children she encountered could wind up on the cusp of adulthood, adrift without a real home or a family?

A fashionably dressed, light-skinned, African-American teenager with bright, slightly mischievous eyes, Felicia had no interest in finding a new, permanent family. She had been burned before. Literally, in fact. Along with her older sister, Knowledge, Felicia had been adopted in 2016 by a couple named Adrienne and Chauncy. One day a few months after she moved in, Felicia took a piece of chicken out of the microwave; Chauncy grabbed it and held it against her face. She remembers: "He burned me. And it just hurt, and it hurt. My sister was laughing, but I was crying. And it got in my eye…Oh my gosh. That sucked. Yeah, that really sucked."

That was not the first abusive incident at Adrienne and Chauncy's house, nor was it the last. That happened when Felicia was teasing Knowledge, and Adrienne said to Knowledge, "You really gonna take that? Go show her who's boss." Felicia turned around to go into her room, and, she says, "I just feel this force on the back of my head. I'm like 'Ow,' and I turn around and it's my sister and she's just hitting me." The two wrestled while Adrienne watched from the doorway like a researcher observing animals in captivity. In the tumult, Felicia accidentally pushed her sister down the stairs. "I was like, 'Knowledge, are you okay?' But she just got more angry." Then, Felicia recalls, Adrienne instructed Knowledge to start again. And then, Felicia gets quieter, "my sister beat me up, and I just kind of surrendered and let her hit me."

When Chauncy came home, Felicia expected him to do something—to tell Adrienne to lay off. But instead, he just said, "You shouldn't mess with your sister." And that's when Felicia took her coat and the stuffed animal that she carried everywhere even though she was in seventh grade and went to the door. It was snowing, she remembers, and Felicia called her Aunt Yolanda to pick her up.

Felicia had lived with Yolanda for two years, starting when she was seven. She doesn't remember the exact dates—she wishes she could ask her sister about some of the details of their stay, but Knowledge, who is now sixteen, has run away with her boyfriend. (Felicia says she is in "deep doo-doo" with the police.) "Yolanda,"

Felicia says, "was really strict. We weren't allowed to talk about the bad things that happened because Yolanda—she made it seem like everything was good when the caseworkers were around, but it wasn't good."

Yolanda spanked Knowledge and Felicia regularly and for no reason. She would blame the girls for things they hadn't done. And then, Felicia mentions as a kind of afterthought, there was Yolanda's teenage son, who molested both girls. For a long time, the sisters were afraid to tell their caseworker what happened, "because Yolanda would tell us stuff that really scared us. . . ." She told Felicia and Knowledge that it would ruin her life if they said anything. At one point, Yolanda told the girls that the caseworker already knew, so they didn't have to tell.

At the age of seven, it's hard to know whether Felicia understood how bad her cousin's behavior was. It was not the first time, after all, that she had been sexually abused. Her mother, with whom she had lived until the age of seven, was addicted to drugs and would pimp Felicia to men in return for drug money. Felicia and Knowledge and their younger brother (now in a gang, she says) were also occasionally locked in the basement for days at a time while their mother went out to score drugs. She would leave them only with a box of cereal. To this day, Felicia will not eat cereal or anything that reminds her of its taste.

Once child-protective services understood what was going on in Yolanda's house, Felicia was sent to live with another aunt, Doreen. But by this point, she was out of control. Felicia acknowledges that she was punching holes in the walls and regularly running away. Doreen was overwhelmed and told child-protective services that she couldn't care for Felicia anymore. So, she went to live with foster parents Christy and Dave. They were older—they had been foster parents for twenty-five years already—and had reopened their home to take in Felicia and Knowledge, but only while CPS found her something more permanent. That is when Adrienne and

Chauncy offered to adopt her. After she ran away from them, she returned briefly to Christy and Dave before meeting Nadia.

By the time Nadia and Felicia met for the first time, Nadia had been praying for Felicia for two years. She had seen the girl's face in the Colorado Heart Gallery, the state's adoption website. Nadia initially thought that she wanted to take in a seven- or eight-year-old boy who liked sports (someone like her nephew, with whom she is very close). "I was going to be that soccer mom bringing the oranges, like that was my life's calling." But there was something about Felicia's story that caught her eye.

Nadia, who is six foot six with dark brown skin and dark hair cut in a short bob, has a no-nonsense look about her. She wears little makeup and favors athletic T-shirts and sweatshirts. Nadia comes from a large family, but she says she never wanted to have biological children.

Nadia is a deeply religious person who regularly attends the Mississippi Avenue Baptist Church in Aurora. Several years ago, she made a deal with God. If she reached her thirtieth birthday and had not found a husband, she would adopt a child. "So, thirty came and went, and I was like, 'Well, I didn't really mean thirty, I really meant thirty-five." When she turned thirty-five, she began the process of becoming a foster parent in earnest.

She signed up with an organization called Project 1.27, which takes its name from James 1:27: "Religion that God our Father accepts as pure and faultless is this: to look after orphans and widows in their distress." Since its inception in 2004, the organization has been credited with finding permanent adoptive homes for hundreds of kids who have languished in the foster-care system for years, as well as with finding temporary homes for hundreds more who have since been reunited with their biological families.

By July 2018, Nadia was certified as a foster parent by the state of Colorado. She had completed forty hours of training, including CPR, criminal background checks, and three separate home studies. In some ways, Nadia's home was perfect for Felicia. Nadia had a flexible, well-paying job for a website and was able to work from home. And there were no men in the house for Felicia to deal with. Foster homes can often be a place where children encounter a positive male role model for the first time, but for a girl who has been repeatedly victimized by boys and men, that relationship can be fraught.

In addition to the hours of training, counseling, and home studies that Nadia had to put in, Project 1.27 required that she bring with her at least four people for a four-hour training session. Parenting a teenager without having ever parented before would be difficult no matter what Felicia's background was like, but Nadia realized that things were going to be harder than she imagined. Her caseworker said that Nadia had to change her expectations about how smoothly this process was going to go. In Nadia's defense, she didn't even get the file with the full details on Felicia's background until five months after they met. So, she may not have fully grasped what was going on.

Every time Nadia left the house, Felicia would ask if she was coming back. She would go to the supermarket, and when she returned, Felicia would be surprised. She was used to being abandoned. And then there were other strange things. Felicia cried hysterically one night when Nadia went to bed early and turned off the main lights in the house. Felicia wouldn't brush her teeth until Nadia turned them all back on.

And there were food issues too. Kids who have previously been deprived of food in their homes will often hoard it. Nadia set aside a special cupboard for Felicia that was always stocked with snacks she liked.

Sometimes it was possible to reason with Felicia. But Nadia estimates that Felicia's mental age was about seven. She would throw temper tantrums on the floor of the kitchen. She would occasionally skip through stores. She was "obsessed with stuffed animals." Sometimes she would hop around like a bunny.

Nadia did not discipline Felicia the way that she had been disciplined as a child. She had been trained instead in trauma-informed care, which are behavioral modification methods specifically for children who have experienced severe trauma in their past. There are no physical punishments, and even a "time-out" can be a problem for a child who fears abandonment. Instead, she gave Felicia a lot of choices but was also very clear about boundaries.

"I lay out everything for her. It has been hard, though, because most of my friends have had the chance to parent for fourteen years, not just overnight.... So, there are many times where I'm like, 'Am I doing this right?' or, 'Do I need to ask someone about this?"

And she could not turn to the one person whose counsel and support she most craved—her own mother. Nadia's mom, Nardine, is a small, dark-skinned Caribbean woman with deep wrinkles. She raised Nadia and her brother alone, working multiple jobs after their father left them, never letting his absence get in the way of what she wanted for her children. She has very high standards for her kids, but she is also fiercely protective of them.

That protectiveness may be why she told Nadia that she should simply "send Felicia back." Nardine says, "Personally, I don't care for her." She believed Felicia was manipulating Nadia and the other people around her. She didn't think that Felicia was respectful. When she found out that Felicia had been skipping school, "that kind of threw me off her.... I said, 'Nadia, you need to put your foot down.' And she [did], but not the way I would do it. [I would say] I'm taking that phone, and you wouldn't see it until you're 25.'" She told Nadia, "You don't need that aggravation. You don't need any gray hair in your head."

Felicia had seemed to be adjusting at her new school. She had gotten two As and three Bs during the first semester she lived with Nadia. Felicia said, "I didn't do as well as I would have liked" and worried that any problems with her grades would create a problem when it came time to apply to college. If you tried to reassure her that colleges probably would take her difficult upbringing into consideration, she would say, "Yeah, but I don't want sympathy. Like I want to be let in because I have good grades and I'm super-smart… [not because] I was in foster care…. Like I really hate that when you read my file notes [and say to me], 'Yeah, I know you've had a lot of hard stuff.' Like, yeah, I have, but don't look at that. Look at me because I'm doing what I'm doing."

At moments like this, it was easy to imagine that Felicia had turned a corner, that she had found adults in her life who believed in her, that she was being cared for by a woman who was willing to do just about anything for her, that she was finally being given the proper boundaries a teenager needs and the reassurance that if she violated them, they would still love her. But fourteen years is a long time to live without any of that.

Her behavior problems began escalating—she was regularly skipping school and other commitments and lying to teachers and to Nadia about where she was. She was throwing temper tantrums and cursing and yelling at Nadia that she was miserable and wanted to leave, saying that Nadia was just like Felicia's mother. They tried going to an intensive therapy program together.

Then one day, Felicia ran away. She left school at lunchtime and went to her boyfriend's house across town. Nadia didn't see her again until 9:30 p.m. that night, by which point she had already had to call Felicia's caseworkers and let them know that Felicia was gone. The caseworkers decided it was time to remove Felicia from Nadia's home. "Eight months and one day after she moved in," Nadia says sorrowfully.

Felicia went to stay with some friends of Nadia's for a few weeks—Nadia says there are a number of adults who met Felicia in the past few months who "are still loving on her"—but in all likelihood, her next placement will be a group home. There is no family in the state who has room for a teenager right now. Nadia is heartbroken, "grieving the loss of the unmet expectations," she says. But she also says, "I know our story isn't over yet." She doesn't expect that Felicia will move back in, but she does think that in six months or a year, maybe Felicia will contact her, and they can have a relationship. "Something in me says this is not the end."

For more than a decade, Felicia had been failed by the adults who were supposed to protect her. First, there was her mother, who abused and neglected Felicia and her sister for years without any intervention by her extended family, her teachers, or the authorities. Wanting to keep her with relatives (even though they failed to save her in the first place), her local child-welfare officials decided to put Felicia in the custody of her aunt. That aunt not only beat her and allowed her to be molested by her cousin but also forced Felicia and her sister to lie to authorities. The fact that those same authorities for years failed again to detect how bad the situation was also suggests that their investigations were not very thorough.

And what about Adrienne and Chauncy? How were these two approved to be foster and then adoptive parents? What does it say about a state's screening process or about the pool of foster parents available that an agency was desperate enough to license this couple? What happened when social workers visited their home?

Even when Nadia, a caring woman who came with all the resources and tools needed, offered to care for this child and went through the process of getting certified, it took five months before she was informed about the full extent of Felicia's trauma. Why aren't we transparent with foster and adoptive parents about the problems that children have?

But it wasn't just Felicia's family and the system that failed her. It was also our culture. Taking in at-risk children who are not related to us is still considered odd and an unnecessary burden by most Americans. Though Nadia had plenty of support, the truth is that many family members—like Nardine—don't want their own relatives to take on the responsibilities of foster parenting. Those unrelated children should be someone else's problem.

Finally, there is the fact that Felicia will now be sent to a residential group home only after she has cycled through multiple abusive and neglectful environments. Maybe there was a time years ago when the therapy provided by a family-style group home and the stability and safety of being in one place could have helped her. But now, surrounded in such a facility by other young people who are only in the home as a last resort, it is hard to imagine that she will thrive.

Ultimately, she most likely will age out of foster care; that is, she will never find a permanent home or family to care for her. One hopes that Nadia and the other people who looked after her during those months will have some kind of lasting effect—maybe she will seek them out for support when she is an adult. But the odds are not in her favor. Foster children who reach adulthood with no family connection have a very difficult road ahead: they are more likely to be homeless, to be unemployed, and to be involved with drugs.[1]

Felicia's life did not have to turn out this way, and neither do the lives of the 440,000 kids in foster care today or the tens of thousands more who go in and out of the system each year. Systemic reform will require changes at every level of our society.

Child-welfare agencies are overseen by counties and states. They are staffed by social workers whose decisions are reviewed by state family or juvenile courts, and those decisions are only rarely reviewed by higher courts. While the federal government provides most of the money that funds these agencies, organizations, and courts, Congress does not exercise enough oversight about the quality of services and care that these systems are providing.

Altering the trajectory of young people like Felicia means that the federal government will have to start enforcing the law, making state child-welfare systems work harder and smarter for the billions of dollars that taxpayers send them each year. It will mean family court systems will have to make better and faster decisions about what to do with these kids, ones that do not discriminate based on

---

1 Amy Dworsky, PhD, Laura Napolitano, PhD, and Mark Courtney, PhD, "Homelessness During Transition from Foster Care to Adulthood." (US National Library of Medicine National Institutes of Health, December 2013), https://www.ncbi.nlm.nih.gov/pmc/articles/PMC3969135.

race or allow any adult—regardless of their relation to a child—to mistreat him or her. It will mean that we will have to use the latest data analysis to understand what is going on behind closed doors in some of these families and send in well-qualified, well-trained individuals to help children who are most at risk.

It means understanding that child abuse occurs in different communities at different rates and that our goal should be to reduce it everywhere, not to make the numbers come out even. It means that we will take charges of neglect seriously and understand that substance abuse is not just another lifestyle choice when it comes to parents of young children, but a decision that can have life-altering or life-ending consequences.

It means that private and especially faith-based organizations will need to expand the revolutionary work they have done in foster care in the past decade. It will mean that we need laws to ensure that these organizations can adhere to their religious missions without the interference of activists with other agendas.

It means questioning the assumption that protecting children means reuniting them with their parent or parents or, failing that, with other kin. It means challenging the idea that children's interests are always, or only, served by placing them with foster parents of the same race or socioeconomic background.

And it means that we will have to change the very culture of our communities to accept foster care as a collective responsibility. Even if we cannot host a foster child in our homes, it means that we have to support (financially, emotionally, and spiritually) foster families in our neighborhoods, our religious institutions, and our cities. It means that we will have to regain what was the consensus view in the 1980s and 1990s: that adoption is the best option for some children and that families who take children into their homes permanently should not face knee-jerk accusations of having a "white savior" mentality.

Plenty of problems likely will not be solved in our lifetimes—poverty, racism, international conflict. But in the wealthiest, most enterprising, and most generous country on earth, finding safe, loving, and permanent homes for our most at-risk children should not be among them.

CHAPTER 2

THE IDEOLOGY OF FAMILY PRESERVATION—SACRIFICING CHILD SAFETY FOR FAMILY UNITY

The overarching goal of every institution, from child-protective services to family court to foster-care agencies, is family preservation and, if a child is removed, rapid family reunification. We should never take kids away. But if we do, how can we get kids back home as soon as possible? Kids belong with their families, we are told again and again. But it's become very clear that some kids do not belong there. And pursuing family preservation above all else is destroying children's lives.

Jack was eleven months old when he came to live with Samantha and her husband Mitchell at their home in Brooklyn. In some ways, they live the typically busy lives of working parents with young children. They are upper-middle class, living in an airy apartment in one of the more expensive areas of Brooklyn. Mitchell is an airline mechanic and has served for a number of years on the board of a nonprofit that helps at-risk kids in Barbados, which is where he is from originally. Samantha is from Jamaica but has been in this country for longer than Mitchell. But their lives are also an unending series of court dates and visitation appointments for Jack.

Jack was the youngest of four children born to a mother who was twenty-two. Each child had a different father, and Jack's mother was addicted to opioids. She regularly left the children by themselves. The school reported to the authorities that the oldest child, who was six at the time, was absent for weeks at a time. When the Administration for Children's Services arrived at the home to investigate for the first time, the mother was not there, and the oldest daughter let them in. She didn't know her mother's phone number or when she would be back. Jack was three months old. They waited for over an hour, and when the mother returned, they warned her not to leave the children alone again.

But it happened again. And again. The next time that she was reported for leaving the kids alone for a long period of time, it was a roommate of hers who called the Administration for Children's Services (ACS). Two of Jack's siblings went to live with their grandmother, and the other one went to live with his father. This just left Jack. His father is in a gang and has a history of beating Jack's mother. For almost two years now, Jack has been living with Samantha and Mitchell, and officially ACS still plans to reunify him with his mother.

For the past year, he has had unsupervised visits with his mother three times a week. Jack's mother is the regular victim of domestic violence at the hands of a rotating cast of boyfriends living with her. Sometimes she is too strung out, sick, or anxious to see Jack. Nevertheless, the case plan for reuniting him and his mother has not changed.

When the visits with his mother do occur, the results are not good, according to Samantha. Jack, who is now three years old and has severe asthma, comes home coughing and smelling like weed. Often, he has not been given his asthma medication. And sometimes, he has unexplained bruises on his body. At one point, Samantha and Mitchell learned that Jack's mother had punched him in the face. They presented the court with a medical report showing a contusion on his face and damage to his eardrum.

But a few months ago, things grew worse. "Now that he can talk pretty clearly, he's telling me his mother 'kisses his peepee.'" At first, Samantha assumed she must be misunderstanding him, but she has found Jack trying to kiss the genitals of the six-month-old boy she and Mitchell are trying to adopt. And she says he makes comments that are sexual in nature to the baby—"things a three-year-old would not say."

Samantha has been told by her caseworker that the authorities "cannot take statements from someone his age." He has to be at least five years old. The only way that they will believe he is being sexually abused, Samantha was told, is if he contracts a sexually transmitted disease. Another worker assured her that the boy won't remember anything that happened before the age of three anyway.

In the meantime, Samantha has observed Jack's behavior worsening. "He rages in daycare, throws things, punches things." And when she and her husband observe court proceedings—Samantha is a corporate lawyer—she marvels at how judges "put family reunification above the interests of the child. They will put a child in danger of serious bodily harm in furtherance of family reunification."

A policy of "family preservation" seems like a no-brainer. Why take a child away from his or her parents and who, besides those parents, would want to raise a child anyway? To answer both of these questions, it is worth understanding the history of how authorities have treated the mistreated children in this country.

In the nineteenth century, a minister by the name of Charles Loring Brace came up with the idea for "orphan trains." With the mass influx of immigrants to large cities like New York, it seemed to Brace and his progressive allies that there was no one looking out for the welfare of children, many of whom were begging on the streets or working at menial jobs, shining shoes and the like. If they were caught committing crimes, children as young as five were thrown into adult prisons. In 1850, Brace created the Children's

Aid Society (now known as Children's Aid), which first sought to provide schooling and lodging for children who had no other alternative.

But a few years later, he hit upon what he believed was an even better idea—shipping these children out of the city entirely to Christian families in the Midwest. And so, despite the fact that many of these children had living parents, the Children's Aid Society began sending thousands upon thousands of them to work on farms in other parts of the country. It was seventy-five years and 200,000 children before the orphan trains ended, partly the result of a decreasing need for farm labor. The early twentieth century also saw a backlash against these forced separations. Child labor of any sort was banned, and the state and federal governments began to construct a safety net for children and families at risk, allowing them to stay together in most cases.

Today, any mention of separating children from their families provokes outrage, sometimes rightly so. The border policies of the Trump and Obama administrations, which kept migrant children away from the parents who had brought them to this country illegally, were inhumane. Whatever you think about the issue of immigration, these were largely parents who were trying to do right by their children, bringing them here from dangerous situations in their home countries. Punishing their children by keeping them away from their parents—even, infamously, in cages—was a horror unworthy of this country.

Not all parents have the same good intentions regarding their children, though. Some even wish them harm. And some parents with good intentions don't have the wherewithal to care for their children or to ask for help when they can't. Mental illness and substance abuse often play a role in that incapacity. It is those parents with whom our child-welfare system must be concerned, and it is those parents who must sometimes, hard as it is to fathom, be separated from their children.

But today, the world of child welfare is dominated almost completely by caseworkers, agency heads, academic researchers, family-court lawyers, judges, and policymakers who believe that separating kids from their parents creates more trauma than just about anything else children could experience. They believe that foster care, to the extent it should be used at all, is an endless holding pattern for a child while parents get their affairs in order. And they believe that just about every parent is capable of such improvement—given enough time.

To say that there is a "debate" over the policy of family preservation would be inaccurate. The system brooks almost no criticism. State child-welfare agencies are led and staffed by graduates of programs that believe in family preservation. These academic programs are led and funded by organizations like Casey Family Programs and the Annie E. Casey Foundation, which believe in family preservation at almost all costs. State agencies are funded by federal leaders who believe in it, with occasional help from private organizations like the "Caseys." There is a feedback loop that is almost impossible to interrupt. Over and over, it tells child-welfare workers and family-court judges that the trauma of removing a child is the most severe trauma a child can suffer and that foster care is the least desirable of all outcomes, not only for the child but for the family and even the community. Sadly, though, there are things worse than foster care.

Though it is common to measure our child-welfare problem by studying the number of kids in foster care and concluding that a higher number means a more severe problem and a lower number means things are getting better, this is not necessarily the case. Foster care is an artificial measure of child welfare, and authorities are perfectly capable of ignoring or minimizing child abuse and neglect to make those numbers go down. Substantiated maltreatment rates are considered by many a more reliable measure of what is going on in the lives of children, but foster care reentry may be even better because they tell us whether a family reunification failed so badly that a child had to be removed again.

Despite the popular perception, most child-welfare agencies are doing everything in their power to keep parents and children together. According to the Administration for Children's Services, the number of New York City children in foster care at the end of FY 2017 reached a historic low of fewer than 9,000, less than one-fifth of the number of children in care twenty-five years ago.[1] Much of this decrease, the agency claims, is the result of offering families more preventive services to keep them together. Though this sounds like a success story, it's important to acknowledge that these services are not technically preventive because some incident has brought these families to the attention of child-protective services in the first place. There has been an allegation of abuse or neglect, for which there has been at least some substantiation, and now, the authorities are intervening, albeit in a less severe way than removing the child. But these services are offered *after* a child has been harmed or placed in harm's way.

Samantha and Mitchell became foster parents because they want to adopt children eventually. Samantha had been through six rounds of IVF before they gave up. She initially wanted to try the route of a private adoption, in which a mother voluntarily decides to put her child (usually while she is pregnant) up for adoption. But Mitchell wanted to go through the foster-care system from the start.

Kids in foster care are typically harder to find adoptive homes for because they are older, have experienced trauma, and are likely still attached to their families in some way. Samantha and Mitchell have also been trying to adopt another child, Justin, out of the foster-care system after he was abandoned in Harlem in 2018. Even that process, though, has dragged on for years.

As for Jack, there is a legal time limit, Samantha correctly notes, on the number of months that a child can spend in foster care before

---

1 "Foster Care Strategic Blueprint." (NYC Administration for Children's Services, accessed August 9, 2020), https://www1.nyc.gov/assets/acs/pdf/about/2018/StandAloneReportFosterCareStrategicBlueprintFinalMay152018.pdf.

the state is supposed to move for a termination of parental rights (TPR). According to the Adoption and Safe Families Act, a federal law enacted in 1997, if a child has been in foster care for fifteen of the past twenty-two months, that process is supposed to begin.[2] But that is supposed to be the outside limit. Lawmakers did not intend to ensure that parents who severely harmed children in the past get multiple chances to reform their ways.

But regardless, the law is rarely enforced. Sarah Anne Font of Pennsylvania State University looked at children who entered the foster-care system in 2010 and whose parents had their rights terminated by 2016. In unpublished research, she found that for children who spend more than eighteen months in care, more than half of all TPRs occur after eighteen months. For children who entered the system between the ages of two and five and spent more than eighteen months in care, 35 percent of them had to wait more than two years for parental rights to be terminated, and 8 percent of them had to wait more than four years. "It's the biggest farce I've ever seen," Samantha says about the lack of compliance with AFSA. "I don't know how judges get away with it."

Currently, New York offers among the longest paths to permanency from foster care of any state in the country, with foster care lasting thirty months, on average.[3] The national average is twenty months. And as long as a family's official case plan is "reunification," the state does everything in its power to continue the connection between parents and children. The requirement of visits that clearly seem to be harming the child baffles Samantha. A friend, she tells me, is fostering a boy whose mother beat him so badly it put him in a wheelchair for six weeks. But he has to attend supervised visits with her. The child is terrified. Samantha asks: "Should you have the right to torture a child just because you gave birth to them?"

---

2 Pub. L. No. 105–89, www.congress.gov/105/plaws/publ89/PLAW-105publ89.pdf.

3 "Foster Care." (*Child Trends*, 2017), https://www.childtrends.org/wp-content/uploads/assets/child-welfare/pdf/state_profiles/foster/New_York.pdf.

This is a good question--one that anyone looking at our nation's child-welfare system should be forced to confront. The recent focus on preventive measures—the federal Family First Prevention Services Act of 2018, for instance, offered states more money for programs that would keep families together—has reinforced the idea that child welfare should be a kind of early-intervention program rather than one that involves removing children from their homes. In fact, Family First funds programs that help families after a report of abuse or neglect has already been made.[4] Usually, by the time the state gets involved, a child needs to be rescued, and an adult should be held responsible.

Some programs aim to completely avert a child's contact with the child-welfare system, as opposed to waiting until an allegation has been made and substantiated. But these are the exception. An organization called Safe Families, for instance, offers help when a parent in crisis—experiencing homelessness or a medical emergency, for example—needs someone to take in her child temporarily. Launched in 2003, Safe Families has arranged more than 35,000 hostings at its chapters in eighty cities across the United States.[5] It also has locations in the UK and Canada. Parents voluntarily place their children with background-checked volunteers (who are generally recruited through churches) for an average of forty-five days; they can ask for their children to be returned at any point and can see them whenever they want. The program, which has trained counselors assigned to each case, has prevented many children from having to enter the foster-care system. But Safe Families relies on parents to know that they are in trouble and to reach out for help. This is not typical of families who are in the child-welfare system.

In 2018, New York City's Department of Investigation reported that the Administration for Children's Services was fail-

4 Pub. L. No. 115-123, https://capacity.childwelfare.gov/states/about-states/cb/family-first-prevention/.
5 Dr. Dave Anderson, "History." Safe Families for Children, https://safe-families.org/about/history.

ing to ensure the safety of foster children.[6] While many may have assumed that it was foster parents who were mistreating their children, that was not the case. A majority of the maltreatment incidents while kids were in ACS custody (which include cases of both abuse and severe neglect) happened while foster kids were visiting their biological parents. Foster parents were the perpetrators in just 19 percent of maltreatment incidents in 2017.[7] That's terrible, but more disturbing is that children who have been removed from their parents' homes because of abuse or neglect are then brought back to visit or stay with those parents. And they are subject to physical or sexual abuse all over again.

In 2014, the median rate of reported maltreatment of children in foster care was 0.27 percent, which is much lower than the rate for the general population—around 1 percent.[8] On the other hand, according to Elizabeth Bartholet, the faculty director of Harvard Law School's Child Advocacy Program, roughly a third of children who are returned to biological parents who maltreat them will be maltreated again.[9] A court-appointed panel in New York found, in 1997, that 43 percent of children who entered the child-welfare system were again abused or neglected by their families.[10]

So why are we sending kids who are in danger on unsupervised visits home? The real reason is that ACS, like almost every other

6 Mark Peters and Jodi Franzese, "Review of ACS' Systemic Safety Accountability Mechanisms for Foster Care Providers." (The City of New York Department of Investigation, October 2018), https://www.google.com/url?q=https://www1.nyc.gov/assets/doi/reports/pdf/2018/Oct/ACS_Rpt_Release_Final_10122018.pdf&sa=D&ust=1597441601264000&usg=AFQjCNFDkd0q0p1Qy-IDjtC0c7oDpWM36A.

7 "Child Maltreatment 2017," U.S. Department of Health & Human Services, https://www.acf.hhs.gov/sites/default/files/documents/cb/cm2017.pdf.

8 [33]"Child Welfare Outcomes Report," *Administration for Children & Families* (U.S. Department of Health and Human Services, n.d.), https://www.acf.hhs.gov/sites/default/files/cb/cwo10_14.pdf; "Child Maltreatment." (*Child Trends*, 2019), https://www.childtrends.org/indicators/child-maltreatment.

9 Elizabeth Bartholet, "Differential Response: A Dangerous Experiment in Child Welfare." (*SSRN Electronic Journal*, 2014), https://doi.org/10.2139/ssrn.2477089.

10 Rachel L. Swarns, "Experts Denounce Children's Agency." (*The New York Times*, October 22, 1997), https://www.google.com/url?q=https://www.nytimes.com/1997/10/22/nyregion/experts-denounce-children-s-agency.html&sa=D&ust=1597441601263000&usg=AFQjCNEJ2WWWiVlzKRt2aW0gsMZLj9Xjxg.

child-welfare agency and family-court system in the country, pursues a goal of family reunification, even if it can mean risking a child's safety. Indeed, the Department of Investigation reported that in 2016, of the worst-performing private contractors that manage the foster children's cases for the agency, four listed as their main focus of improvement on a self-evaluation "permanency," while only two chose "safety."[11]

The commissioner of the ACS, David Hansell, said that the agency continues to "safely reunify families when appropriate" because "all of the research shows that children are most likely to thrive when they can be reunified with their parents." Since one in five children reenters foster care within five years of being reunified with parents, it is worth noting that reunifications are also placing many children in danger. And whether they "can be" reunified is obviously a subjective decision.[12] If the children who can be reunified are the ones who are safe with their families, then obviously these children are more likely to thrive. The logic is circular.

The agency has said that the investigation did not account for the most recent data, which shows improvement from these particular contractors. It's still hard to believe that safety wasn't the first priority of all of the agencies in 2016, especially given the city's recent history.

Indeed in 2016, Zymere Perkins, six years old, was beaten to death, and his mother's boyfriend was charged with the crime, after multiple investigations by caseworkers into the child's safety and welfare.[13] According to a report by New York City Comptroller Scott Stringer, at least ten children died in their family homes in

---

11 Peters and Franzese, "Review of ACS' Systemic Safety."

12 Sarah Font, PhD, Kierra Sattler, MA, and Elizabeth Gershoff, PhD, "When Home Is Still Unsafe: From Family Reunification to Foster Care Reentry." U.S. National Library of Medicine, National Institutes of Health, https://www.ncbi.nlm.nih.gov/pmc/articles/PMC6251317.

13 Laura Nahmias, "City and State Release Separate Reports on Death of Zymere Perkins." (*Politico*, 2016), https://www.politico.com/states/new-york/albany/story/2016/12/city-and-state-release-separate-reports-on-child-abuse-death-of-six-year-old-hAdam-boy-zymere-perkins-108061.

the twelve weeks leading up to that incident, despite each being the subject of at least four maltreatment complaints.[14]

Hansell's predecessor Gladys Carrion was forced to resign in disgrace in the wake of Perkins's death, and no doubt, Hansell has made some significant improvements, but like so many other child-welfare commissioners in the country, Hansell believes strongly in family reunification.

Imagine for a moment if we took the same approach to other sorts of domestic violence. If a woman reports that her husband has been beating her, police officers don't give her an ice pack and suggest they come up with a plan to work things out. Imagine if the same excuses we make for biological parents were made for men who beat their wives and girlfriends. Like any sympathetic observer of the system, Samantha understands why some people might be sympathetic to the biological parents—they themselves suffer from addiction, they have been beaten themselves, and many may have been raised in the foster system—but she says, "I don't really care about your childhood because you can't tell a two-year-old you threw him against a wall because someone threw you against a wall."

Family preservation and reunification, despite what should be clear warnings, is the driving policy not just in New York and not just in urban areas. Take Indiana, for instance, which in 2016 had the highest rate of fatalities from child maltreatment, according to the Department of Health and Human Services.[15]

It is true that Indiana has a higher rate of children in foster care than neighboring states, but the question is not just whether kids are removed from dangerous situations but also whether they

---

14 Rich Calder, "In Just 3 Months, 10 Kids Died on NYC Child Services' Watch." (*New York Post,* December 22, 2016), https://nypost.com/2016/12/22/acs-on-the-hook-for-deaths-of-10-at-risk-kids-in-3-months-probe/; Emma Whitford, "Comptroller: At Least 10 Children Died on City's Watch Ahead of Zymere Perkins Death." Gothamist (New York Public Radio, December 22, 2016), http://gothamist.com/2016/12/22/acs_child_abuse_stringer.php.

15 Brian Slodysko and David Crary, "New Data: Child Abuse Deaths Rise, Notably in Texas, Indiana." (*U.S. News & World Report,* February 2, 2018), https://www.usnews.com/news/best-states/indiana/articles/2018-02-02/new-data-child-abuse-deaths-rise-notably-in-texas-indiana.

are kept out of those situations in the long term. It is likely that in Indiana some children are simply being removed from parents for a short period and then returned to those same dangerous environments. We have two strong pieces of evidence for this.

The percentage of kids whose parental rights have been terminated in Indiana has dropped precipitously in recent years; indeed, according to calculations by Richard Gelles, former dean of the University of Pennsylvania's School of Social Policy and Practice, it is an outlier among surrounding states.[16] And Indiana lags well behind its neighbors in the percentage of kids who are adopted out of foster care. In fact, the percentage of kids adopted out of foster care in the state plummeted by 50 percent between 2006 and 2015.[17]

Many advocates will cheer all this as evidence that more children in Indiana are being kept with biological families—or are being removed only temporarily and then put back after their parents receive services. The problem, though, is that many of these parents are not capable of caring for their children. And that's the most likely reason maltreatment and fatality rates have skyrocketed there.

The trend is occurring elsewhere too. According to a report from Pennsylvania, between 2014 and 2016, fatalities and near fatalities resulting from child abuse increased by 44 percent. Significantly, the report found: "Of the 220 substantiated fatality and near-fatality incidents, nearly two-thirds (64 percent) of the children and/or families were involved with the county children and youth agency prior to or at the time of the incident," reports the Pennsylvania Department of Human Services. "Among the 140 children and/or families known to the agency, 58 [cases] were open at the time of the incident, and the remaining 82 cases had involvement prior to,

16 Richard Gelles, unpublished data.

17 Ibid.

but not at the time of, the incident."[18] Most of the children who died and who had been known to the agency had seen their cases closed in the year prior to their deaths.

Arizona reported that 56 percent of the seventy-nine children who died from maltreatment in 2017 came from families with prior involvement with a child-protective services agency.[19] New Jersey reported that same year that a third of its child-fatality cases involved kids already known to a child-welfare agency.[20]

Until I started writing about child welfare, I assumed that the real reason children were suffering from severe maltreatment at the hands of their parents was that we didn't know what was going on. How can we tell if a child is being beaten or deprived of food or whether an infant or toddler is left for long periods without supervision? It turns out, though, that we know a lot about families. Mandated reporters (including teachers, doctors, social workers, and law enforcement) are everywhere. And the penalties for not reporting suspected abuse or neglect, if you are among them, can be stiff. Neighbors are nosy. Schools have to report long absences. We don't know all the children who are in danger, but we know a lot of them, and we know a lot about the ones who are at the greatest risk.

So why are we keeping children with the adults who endanger them? The first reason offered by advocates is that, especially in the case of older children, reunification is what the children want. In a special investigation of foster care by the *Kansas City Star*, the reporters profile a young man who is now serving eight years in prison for aggravated battery with a deadly weapon, theft, and

---

18 "Pennsylvania Child Abuse Fatality/Near Fatality Trend Analysis Team Report," Pennsylvania Department of Human Services, https://www.dhs.pa.gov/docs/Publications/PublishingImages/Pages/Child-Fatality-Near-Fatality-Reports/2015-2016 percent20Child percent20Abuse percent20Fatality_Near percent20Fatality percent20Trend percent20Team percent20Report.pdf.

19 "Twenty-Fifth Annual Report." (Arizona Department of Health Services, November 15, 2018), https://www.azdhs.gov/documents/prevention/womens-childrens-health/reports-fact-sheets/child-fatality-review-annual-reports/cfr-annual-report-2018.pdf.

20 https://www.nj.gov/dcf/documents/about/commissions/fatality/CFNFRB.Report_2017.pdf.

eluding law-enforcement officers.[21] He had spent his childhood, from the age of three, bouncing around the foster-care system. The authors write that he was "moved between dozens of foster homes; struggled with school work; and only wanted to be back with his biological family."

When he was fourteen, he finally made contact on Facebook with his mother, who was living in Florida at the time. "She ended up selling her car and buying a bus ticket and moving down here to the Salvation Army in Wichita," he said. "She got a job and she was doing real good and she was trying to get me back." Unfortunately, she relapsed, turned back to crack cocaine and died a few years later. But still, he wonders, what if: "You'll never have a bond with anybody like you would with your own." There is understandably a tendency for these children to romanticize their biological parents, to think that things would have been better off if they had never been removed.

In a perfect world, every child would be raised in a loving home by the parents who are responsible for his or her existence. And every adult who wanted a child would be able to have one and be able to raise him or her with great care and love. But we live in an imperfect world where we are left to make choices about what happens to children whose parents cannot or will not care for them.

The second line of reasoning one often hears from family-preservation advocates is that it's better for the parents to have their children back. In a moving essay for the blog at the Institute for Family Studies, Amber Lapp writes about meeting an Ohio woman named Emily whose four children were removed from her home because of her heroin addiction.[22]

Emily told Lapp: "Well, I think a lot of people like me, they stay on [drugs] because they lose their kids.... And I think if Children's

---

21 Laura Bauer and Judy L. Thomas, "We Are Sending More Foster Kids to Prison than College." (*The Kansas City Star,* December 15, 2019), https://www.kansascity.com/news/special-reports/article238206754.html.

22 Amber Lapp, "When Drug Policy Separates Families." (Institute for Family Studies, October 22, 2019), https://ifstudies.org/blog/when-drug-policy-separates-families.

Services and the government could be a little bit more lenient and not just keep sending people to prison…" Even going to rehab, she says, is too severe because it also restricts how often you can see and talk to your children by phone.

Parents like Emily, as well as the vast majority of child-welfare caseworkers, family court judges, academic researchers, and policymakers, see the child-welfare system as needlessly punitive. Emily talks about how the removal of their kids puts them into a kind of funk where they don't bother to get clean.

But the evidence doesn't bear this out. A 2020 study from the University of Michigan's Youth Policy Lab found that removing children from a home actually had a significant impact on children's outcomes—which can be attributed at least in part to a change in parents' behavior.[23] Looking at cases that were "borderline," in which some Michigan caseworkers might have chosen to leave a child in the home with "services" and others would have removed the child, the authors found that "12% of foster children in our analysis sample were alleged to be the victim of abuse or neglect in the future (either during their time in the foster system or after exiting) compared with 26% of children in our sample who were not placed. This means that placement reduced the likelihood of being alleged as a maltreatment victim by 52%. Though not all allegations represent actual incidents of abuse or neglect, we find a similar 56% reduction in the likelihood of being confirmed as a victim of child maltreatment—4% relative to 9%."

Indeed, for all the talk about how removal to foster care causes trauma and worse outcomes for kids who should have just been left with their families, recent studies have suggested that the picture is more complicated. The Michigan study also found that children who were placed in foster care were more likely to attend school and have better academic outcomes.[24] These findings echo a 2019

23 Max Gross, "Foster Care and Children's Wellbeing." (*University of Michigan Youth Policy Lab*, June 2020), https://youthpolicylab.umich.edu/uploads/fostercare-final.pdf.

24 Gross, "Foster Care and Children's Wellbeing."

paper that looked at kids in Rhode Island and found that educational outcomes improved significantly for girls who were placed in foster care before the age of six, with the authors even likening the effects to those of placing children in a high-quality preschool.[25]

Max Gross, author of the Michigan study, tells me that it could be that the removal of the children from a home could provide an "incentive" for parents to finally clean up their acts or get the help they need. Alternatively, it could be that parents can't accomplish those things—including drug rehab, for instance—while they are caring for their children.

Whatever its effects, removing children from a home and placing them in foster care is not meant to punish parents. If that is going to be done, it is the job of the criminal-justice system (which rarely gets involved). Rather, child-protective services are supposed to protect children. Yet child-welfare agencies are charged with ensuring that parents get "services," trying to put them on a path to rehabilitation and then ultimately determining (with the imprimatur of the judicial system) whether parent and child should be brought back together.

It is hard not to feel sorry for parents like Emily. Lapp concludes that "We need a system that is by default integrative, acknowledging and nurturing the mother-child relationship and recognizing that, for many mothers, keeping the connection strong with their children may be the most powerful motivation to get better."[26] But this is a utilitarian approach to child welfare. Just as parents see the removal of children as the stick, now they want to see reunification as the carrot. The children in this scenario merely serve as tools to get parents to clean up their acts.

Making family reunification the goal of the child-welfare system instead of child safety or permanency expands significantly

---

25 Anthony Bald et al., "The Causal Impact of Removing Children from Abusive and Neglectful Homes." (*The National Bureau of Economic Research*, January 2019), https://www.nber.org/papers/w25419.pdf.

26 Lapp, "When Drug Policy Separates Families."

the role of the agency because now it is responsible not only for the well-being of the child but also for the good behavior of the adults. Given that the workers at these agencies are often underpaid, undertrained, and overworked, this mission creep won't end well. Indeed, there is a constant litany of complaints about how these workers don't visit children frequently enough, how they are not prepared for court cases, how they don't arrange for support services fast enough. If you make these workers responsible for the well-being of the entire family, it becomes impossible for them to keep up. Moreover, for those who worry about the intrusion of government into family life, turning child-welfare agencies into family-welfare agencies will give authorities much more of an excuse to meddle.

But legislation both at the state and federal level has cemented this dual role into place. The Families First Prevention Services Act, which passed with bipartisan support, ensures that the dollars flowing to states through Title IV-E to support foster-care programs can now be used by states instead for prevention programs including anger management support, parenting classes, and addiction programs.[27] At a speech to parents' rights advocates in New York in the spring of 2019, David Kelly, a civil servant who worked at the Children's Bureau in both the Obama and Trump administrations, explained: "If we're going to change what the country thinks about child welfare and what it's intended to do, if we're going to change the language, we need to stop mythologizing vulnerable families. We need to let go of the system that was designed to rescue children and construct a system that's designed to promote health and well-being for all families."[28]

Never mind that no programs have been shown to "promote health and well-being for all families." At a 2018 panel at

27 Pub. L. No. 115–123.

28 Daniel Heimpel, "In Era of Family Separation, a Top Federal Official Vows to Fight the Practice in Child Welfare." (*The Imprint,* April 17, 2019), https://imprintnews.org/politics/in-era-of-family-separation-a-top-administration-official-vows-to-fight-the-practice-in-child-welfare/34573.

the Brookings Institution, Ron Haskins noted that only 7 percent of the programs examined by the California Evidence-Based Clearinghouse for Child Welfare would meet the threshold for support by the federal government.[29] What evidence exists that the government could "promote health and well-being for all families," or that it should even try?

Jack's mother was offered drug counseling and a variety of other services, some of which she completed and some of which she didn't. But nothing seemed to help. Samantha and Mitchell kept trying to understand why the lawyer for ACS wouldn't change Jack's plan from reunification to adoption and why ACS wasn't asking a judge to remove Jack from his mother permanently.

One possibility is that as long as Jack's visits with his mother were supervised, a judge simply determined that he was in a safe place and that Samantha and Mitchell were caring for him well. So why rock the boat? The termination of parental rights can be an arduous process, involving the time and effort of multiple lawyers, caseworkers, doctors, and other experts. Family courts are already flooded with cases. Why add to the burden?

If a child seems to be in a safe and stable foster home, many caseworkers will also simply turn their attention elsewhere to more urgent cases rather than take the extra step of a TPR. Many judges may simply conclude that parents have not been given ample opportunity or resources to complete rehabilitation.

Dominique Elie, who did the home study for Samantha and Mitchell on behalf of one of the private agencies the city contracts with, explains: "There are judges known as being pro-parent no matter what. You could tell them a child came with a gash…and they're like, 'Return to parent.'" Elie, who recently left the agency, says, "They'll suspend the visits for a while then they'll instate it back. I don't know what drives them, I really don't…. Even if the

29 "Helping Children of Incarcerated Parents and Children in Foster Care." (The Brookings Institution, 2018), https://www.brookings.edu/wp-content/uploads/2018/05/es_20180509_children_justice_transcript.pdf.

parent's been missing for a year or sporadically…they will not change the goal." She recalls a case "that had not gone into fact-finding [the first stage of a termination hearing] after two years." In terms of the problem, she says: "Sometimes it's the judges, sometimes it's the ACS attorneys." Attorneys often won't bring up the case unless they know it will be a slam dunk. Unfortunately, in this case, a slam dunk means a child has been unquestionably (possibly severely and repeatedly) harmed. And if a judge finds that the agency has not made "reasonable efforts" to help biological parents reunify with their child, he may throw out the case and start the clock again.

In the short run, this means that Jack is probably being exposed to the kind of abuse and neglect the system is supposed to save him from. But it's not just that the unsupervised visits mean his mother can mistreat him again. It also means that if he is ultimately sent back to live with his mother, which caseworkers and judges still consider a distinct possibility, that he will be cut off from the only parents with whom he has formed a secure attachment. He will be ripped away from the only family he has known, in the service of keeping him with the woman who gave birth to him.

We know that children are hardwired—that is, biologically programmed—to seek out and form a strong bond with a primary caregiver. (Scientists theorize that this drive has evolved because babies are born entirely dependent on the adults around them for survival.) The quality of a child's bond with a primary caregiver in the first weeks and months of life has enormous influence on social and emotional development.

John Bowlby, who is considered the "father of attachment theory," introduced the idea in his book, *Attachment*, and another two volumes subsequently (published in 1969, 1973, and 1981). A great deal of research has been done—with both humans and animals—showing that a baby's early relationship with a reliably responsive and nurturing primary caregiver is foundational to learning, development, and well-being.[30] An absence of that relationship changes how the brain develops.

In the 1950s, American psychologist Harry Harlow conducted experiments on rhesus monkeys to understand better how babies attached to their mothers. In the experiments, Harlow put some baby monkeys with a real mother, some with a cloth "mother," and some with a wire "mother." The babies became emotionally dependent on *whichever* mother they had. But those with the cloth/wire mothers developed various degrees of social and emotional problems because those mothers were entirely nonresponsive.[31]

As early childhood researcher Katharine Stevens notes, these results have important implications for foster care. "Harlow's research underscores why leaving a baby with his biological mother who is *not* reliably responsive and nurturing or is frequently absent is unjustifiable." She notes that while "not all children will be equally damaged, for many children it's likely to lead to serious damage that's difficult or impossible to reverse." The solution is clear: "Infants with neglectful/abusive biological mothers should be placed elsewhere, at least for the first two or three years (if there's any decent place to put them, that is)—and finding those places should also be a top priority."

These days, Harlow's research on monkeys is widely considered unethical. If purposely keeping a baby monkey with a nonresponsive mother is considered abusive, what should that tell us about keeping young children with caregivers who serially neglect them? Instinctively, we know that it is deeply damaging to pull a young child away from the adults he has come to rely on to meet all of his basic needs. Advocates of reunification at all costs acknowledge these difficulties, but they say that the benefits of putting biological families back together outweigh these smaller tragedies.

---

30 Inge Bretherton, "The Origins of Attachment Theory: John Bowlby and Mary Ainsworth." (American Psychological Association, 1992), https://psycnet.apa.org/record/1993-01038-001.

31 "Harry Harlow: 1905–1981," People and Discoveries." (Public Broadcast Service), https://www.pbs.org/wgbh/aso/databank/entries/bhharl.html.

Unfortunately, the truth is that there are no large-scale studies demonstrating that children who are reunified have better outcomes than children who are adopted or placed in a guardianship situation. A 2007 article in the *British Journal of Social Work* notes that there is "limited evidence on the outcomes of reunification, including evidence on reentry, reabuse and psychosocial outcomes, arguing that such evidence as exists clearly indicates a need for caution when returning abused or neglected children to their families."[32]

The article goes on to note that "greater attention to assessment, planning and follow-up support is needed if children are to be successfully reunited with their families." Indeed, defenders of the current system would argue that to the extent reunification is not working, it is because we are not giving parents the proper services and support to make it work. But how many times can we go around in the same circle? We can always blame the system for failing these parents, for not giving them better housing, more money, job training. We can even blame the system—racism, poverty, a lack of adult role models, weakened churches, uncaring communities—for the fact that the children ended up in foster care to begin with. We can ask for more addiction-treatment programs, parenting classes, and anger-management lessons.

But what does that mean for the children suffering in this system right now? For one thing, it means that their reunification may not be successful. Between 20 percent and 40 percent of children who are reunified with their biological parents end up back in the foster-care system, meaning that there is another incident of maltreatment so severe that they have to be removed again.[33]

Moreover, even if the reunification becomes a permanent arrangement, it is still not clear that the kids are better off. According

---

32 Nina Biehal, "Reuniting Children with Their Families: Reconsidering the Evidence on Timing, Contact and Outcomes." (*The British Journal of Social Work* 37, no. 5, 2007), 807-23, accessed August 10, 2020, www.jstor.org/stable/2372253.

33 Heather N. Taussig, et al. "Children Who Return Home from Foster Care: A Six-Year Prospective Study of Behavioral Health Outcomes in Adolescence." (*Pediatrics* 108, no. 1, July 2001, doi:10.1542/peds.108.1.e10.

to a 2018 article in the *American Sociological Review* that looked at data on young adults in Wisconsin, "youth who aged out of care had significantly higher odds of graduating high school and enrolling in college than did reunified youth and youth who exited to guardianship, and they had similar odds as adopted youth."[34] Kids who were reunified with their biological parents actually had lower educational attainment and lower average earnings than kids who simply aged out of the system, without being adopted or taken back by any family at all.[35]

This sounds counterintuitive. How is it that a child who seems to have no strong connections to adults could possibly be outperforming on measures of education and income than kids who are returned to their parents? For one thing, the parents may care little about education or long-term earnings. They may not be sending their kids to school very much or providing them with the kind of environment that would encourage hard work. Even foster kids who end up in a group-home environment would be required to attend school. And many states offer college scholarships and vocational-training programs for teens in foster care.

It is possible to argue, of course, that living with one's family is more important than whether one obtains a high-school diploma, let alone a college degree, and that the benefits that accrue to a family that has been reunified are more important than the measures of economic success for kids. In that case, though, we should acknowledge that the reunification-first policy is not first and foremost a policy designed to meet the best interests of the child.

Even after three years of exposure to the system, Samantha is still shocked. "I think they get away with it because most people don't know." To the extent people pay attention, all they know is that child-welfare agencies remove children from dangerous situa-

34 Sarah A. Font, et al. "Permanency and the Educational and Economic Attainment of Former Foster Children in Early Adulthood." (*American Sociological Review* 83, no. 4, August 2018), 716–43, http://doi:10.1177/0003122418781791.

35 Ibid.

tions. They don't know what happens next. "They take the kid, but the kid is put back." This endless back and forth from foster home to biological home and back again is largely for the benefit of the adults. Especially when it comes to children as young as Jack, they need stability and consistent nurturing and love. No ideological commitment should trump that.

CHAPTER 3

BLOOD MAY BE THICKER, BUT IT'S NOT ALWAYS BETTER: THE PROBLEM WITH KINSHIP CARE

"It is God's miracle that they survived." That's what Jen Yearout says about her nieces, who were placed in her care more than a decade ago by West Virginia's CPS when they were eight and eighteen months old. Yearout's older sister was addicted to drugs and engaged in prostitution, sometimes living with her, sometimes in hotel rooms, and sometimes nowhere at all. At the age of nineteen, Yearout was in school and working and knew nothing about caring for babies. She is "horrified" to remember that she would put both of them to sleep in a king-sized bed with her, not knowing they might roll off. She would wake up to find the toddler eating toothpaste. "The caseworker never came to my apartment to see the conditions or whether I was qualified or whether I took them to the doctor." It was only once her sister was giving birth to her third child—exhibiting withdrawal symptoms while in labor—that Yearout alerted nurses at the hospital to her situation.

The children were eventually adopted by another family, and Yearout still sees them. She and her husband even got married in the family's backyard a few years ago. Looking at her nieces now, she has no regrets. They are thriving in a loving home. But she still wonders why a caseworker would have put the children with her in the first place.

The answer is kinship preference––the idea that if parents can't care for their children, extended family is always the next-best option. As of 2018, there were 2.7 million children living in kinship arrangements, meaning that they are not living with a biological parent but are living with a relative.[1] That number includes three different kinds of arrangements. The first is made privately—a mother, for instance, believes she can't care for a child because she is sick and gives custody of the child to an aunt. The second is a relative foster-care placement in which a child is removed from a parent's home because of abuse or neglect and then placed by the state with a relative. About a third of children in the foster-care system are living with a relative.[2] The last kind is a kinship diversion, in which a child-welfare worker has reason to think a child is at risk living with a biological parent, but—rather than go through the formal process of removal—he or she encourages the parent to send the child to live with a relative. Unlike in the second category, many states that engage in diversion do not keep track of the numbers of these diversions. Like classifying victims as "non-victims," kinship diversion is a way of pushing problems off the books.

How is it that the once-prevalent belief that only the most caring, stable families should be prioritized as placement options for foster children has been replaced with the assumption that relatives of foster children should always be looked to for assistance first?

---

1 "Report to the Special Committee on Aging, U.S. Senate." (United States Government Accountability Office, July 2020), https://www.gao.gov/assets/710/708020.pdf.

2 Catherine Williams and Kristin Sepulveda, "The Share of Children in Foster Care Living with Relatives is Growing." (*Child Trends*, May 21, 2019), https://www.childtrends.org/blog/the-share-of-children-in-foster-care-living-with-relatives-is-growing.

Like the policy of family preservation, kinship preference might appear sensible; for most of human history, the inclination to keep children with extended family need hardly have been articulated. Until about the middle of the twentieth century in America, kinship care had been considered the default solution for children whose parents were unable or unwilling to properly care for them. Relatives were expected to step up to help such children, and few others were willing to take them in. The state was rarely involved. Orphanages were relatively uncommon prior to the 1830s, and even when urbanization and immigration made such institutions common, the children who lived there (many were not technically orphans) were seldom placed with strangers except to serve as apprentices or indentured servants.

"The emergence of modern adoption," Barbara Melosh writes in her book, *Strangers and Kin*, "required a radically different understanding of family, one that overturned deeply held beliefs about blood and nurture, obligation and love, choice and chance."[3] The idea that families would not only willingly raise strangers' children, but that this practice could become commonplace, did not really take hold until after World War II. From around 1945 to 1973, a period sometimes referred to as the "Baby Scoop Era," there was a significant increase in the rate of premarital pregnancies.[4] Many single women were pressured into giving up their babies for adoption to protect their reputations, and the rate of newborn adoptions rose significantly during this time. In a way, the concept of adoption had been turned on its head: instead of being viewed primarily as a means for families to support their farms or businesses, it was now seen as an altruistic act. Soon, the number of strangers interested in adopting children exceeded the number of healthy babies available for adoption.

---

3 Barbara Melosh, *Strangers and Kin: The American Way of Adoption* (Cambridge, MA: Harvard University Press, 2002).

4 "What Was the 'Baby Scoop Era'?" (The Baby Scoop Era Research Initiative [1945–1972]), https://babyscoopera.com/home/what-was-the-baby-scoop-era.

But the past forty years have seen a reversal of this trend. Between 2006 and 2016, the percentage of foster children placed in kinship homes nationwide increased from 24 percent to 32 percent, according to the federal Department of Health and Human Services. The total number of children in foster kinship homes grew by nearly 15,000 during that time, even though the number of children in foster care declined overall.[5]

There has also been an increase in kinship-care arrangements outside the formal foster-care placement system. In West Virginia, for example, an estimated 28,000 children lived with a relative (with no parent present in the home) between 2013 and 2015, but fewer than 6,000 children were registered in the state's foster system during that time.[6] In Kentucky, approximately 81,000 children lived in kinship-care arrangements between 2015 and 2017, while fewer than 8,000 were listed in the foster system.[7]

Many states have decided to recruit more kin for such cases, due in part to federal guidance on the issue: "Relatives are the preferred resource for children who must be removed from their birth parents because it maintains the children's connections with their families. Kinship care is often considered a type of family preservation service."[8]

The impact of kinship preference on children's lives can be devastating. Like family preservation and reunification, kinship preference is regularly applied with little common sense and little interest in the well-being of the child. Often, such placements exacerbate the problems that foster care is meant to correct.

Consider the case of Mia, who came to live with Susan and her husband in a suburb of Maricopa County, Arizona, when she was

5 "Foster Care."

6 "Children in Kinship Care in West Virginia," The Annie E. Casey Foundation KIDS COUNT Data Center (The Annie E. Casey Foundation), accessed August 18, 2020, https://datacenter.kidscount.org/data/tables/10454-children-in-kinship-care?loc=19&loct=2#detailed/2/50/false/1687.

7 "Children in Kinship Care in Kentucky," The Annie E. Casey Foundation KIDS COUNT Data Center (The Annie E. Casey Foundation), accessed August 18, 2020.

8 "Kinship Care," Child Welfare Information Gateway (August 18, 2020), https://www.childwelfare.gov/topics/outofhome/kinship.

fourteen months old. She weighed only eleven pounds. Born prematurely to a drug-addicted mother, Mia was originally taken in by an aunt, but more than a year after leaving the hospital, she still needed supplemental oxygen and a gastrointestinal tube for feeding. She had a large cyst on her head with an opening directly to her brain. She needed eye surgery urgently. But the aunt could not keep up with her medical needs. Child-protective services removed the child from her aunt's care after doctors reported her condition to authorities.

Susan, a former social worker who has been fostering "medically involved" children for more than thirty years, understood what she was getting into. She has cared for dozens of children in fragile health and adopted seven of them. In the 500 days after she took Mia into her home, the girl made impressive strides. She didn't need an oxygen tube anymore, she could speak several words, and she had become part of Susan's family. The aunt who was caring for Mia's three older siblings visited once.

Imagine Susan's surprise when Mia's caseworker at Arizona's Department of Child Safety told her that she had located a distant cousin who wanted to adopt the child. The cousin, who had no previous contact with the girl and had expressed no interest in taking her in before, was preferable in the eyes of child-welfare workers because she was "kin." This is where the kin preference starts to go off the rails. Who would think that it's better to rip a medically fragile child from a stable home where she's been for two years to go live with someone she's never met?

Amelia Franck Meyer, the founder and CEO of the child-welfare nonprofit Alia, told me that family members have a biological impulse to care for one another, even if they've never met or are related only remotely. "We're driven from a sociological basis to protect and prolong our gene pool," Meyer says, expressing views that seem fairly representative of social workers I've spoken to.

She argues that the opposite is true of nonrelative caregivers. To Meyer, "there is little that is more unnatural than to give up your own survival needs to care for the young of another." She asserts that "living in a community where people look like you will only enhance your ability to thrive." Meyer also believes that kinship care is preferable because a disproportionate number of minority kids are removed from their homes due to societal bias. As she puts it, "The cultural norm is that people of color aren't capable of caring for their children." A continued emphasis on kinship preference could solve this problem, Meyer suggests.

Whatever evidence there is for Meyer's assertions about our evolutionary imperative, there is little evidence that such impulses extend to second cousins. And are we really supposed to believe that a relative who has never met the child before will have a greater investment in that child's well-being than a family that has cared for the child for years?

This story is sadly not uncommon. Since I started writing about this subject, I get phone calls and emails almost every week from foster parents around the country telling me their stories. In November 2015, Jill Barefoot and her husband took two foster children into their home near Athens, Georgia. The five-year-old girl had been severely traumatized. Her father was incarcerated—a minimum ten-year sentence—and her mother had been in and out of drug treatment. As Barefoot recalls, the girl "would have rages where she would kick, scream, hit, and bite between fifteen and twenty times a day." The Barefoots, who had fostered other children before, arranged for extensive therapy for the child. She started to form an attachment with her foster parents and brother and sister. She formed friendships in school and began to participate in gymnastics.

She had little contact with her mother after she was placed with the Barefoots. After regular visitation, her half-brother was reunited after twenty-two months with his (different) father. But the girl remained with the Barefoots. Suddenly, after two full years, the Barefoots were told by their caseworker that an aunt who had cared for the child on weekends when she was an infant was interested in taking the child permanently.

The aunt had been considered as a placement when the child was first removed from her mother's custody, but her home could not be approved because she had a previous child-protective services violation. The Barefoots were asked to start bringing the girl for short, supervised visits outside the aunt's home, which was still not approved. The girl started to regress at home, acting out after each visit, and her school noticed a change in her attitude there, suggesting that she be held back.

Despite these signs, a judge determined that because the aunt was a blood relative, the girl belonged with her. Georgia's Division of Family and Children Services gave the Barefoots ten days' notice, and after almost three years living with them, the girl was sent to live with her aunt in another county. The Barefoots can see her once a month for a couple of hours. She continues to refer to them as "Mama" and "Daddy."

The Barefoots do not know exactly the nature of the CPS violation leveled against the aunt, but it is certainly true that many of the problems that plague parents and lead to a child's removal can also affect the extended family. Margaret Nichols Honeycutt, a pediatrician who works in a town on the southern tip of West Virginia, notes that drugs "are a multigenerational problem" in that area. She explained that many of the children she has seen who were born drug-exposed "may have the grandparent listed on the guardian certificate but…are going to the same home." When that happens, she says, "the pathology is still right in their face."

Even if they are not residing in the same home, the children are often exposed to the same kind of dysfunction. What's more, these kinship caregivers often seem reluctant to step in at all. There was a survey done of foster parents in twelve counties in Georgia (which included about 450 foster families) last year.[9] Of the 102 surveys that were filled out, twenty-one said that no kin came forward. Of the remaining respondents, almost half said that a relative

9 "Broken Road Home in Georgia, 2021 Georgia Foster Care Legislation," unpublished data, www.brokenroadhome.com.

volunteered between nine and twenty-three months after the initial placement, and the remainder took more than two years.

Why did these relatives take so long, and why, if they knew the child in question, did they not intervene earlier? Why wait for the state to remove the child at all? Why not offer to care for a niece or a grandchild before the authorities are involved? The answer is complicated but surely involves money.

Today's kinship-care arrangements look very different from those of the eighteenth and nineteenth centuries. Federal and state legislation, rulings by the Supreme Court, and evolving practices among child-welfare agencies have all introduced new incentives into the kinship-care system. The 1979 Supreme Court case *Miller v. Youakim*, for example, highlighted tensions between new and old ways of viewing kinship care.[10] The case concerned four siblings who had been removed from their mother's home in Illinois and made wards of the state. Two of the siblings had been placed in the homes of nonrelatives, and the other two in the home of their older, married sister, Linda Youakim. Linda and her husband were deemed ineligible for certain federal foster-care payments distributed by Illinois because of their relation to the children. These payments *were*, however, granted to the nonrelative foster parents.

When the state requested that the Youakims also take in the other two siblings, they refused, citing the financial burden this would impose. In *Miller*, they argued that they should have received the same level of federal financial support as the nonrelative foster parents, in part because they had no legal obligation to care for Linda's siblings. The Court ruled that relative caregivers cannot be denied federal foster-care benefits if otherwise eligible.

The state of Illinois had arguably been operating on a more traditional understanding of kinship care: that it is desirable for children to remain with their families, that families would willingly take in their relatives' children, and that such arrangements cost the government less in time, energy, and actual funds than other

10 Miller v. Youakim (1979).

institutional placements. The *Miller* decision prompted Illinois and other states to view nonrelative foster care and kinship care in a new, more equivalent light. This led to a range of policy changes and legislative proposals across the country, including granting preference to kin when determining foster-care placements, expanding the definition of kin, and providing new sources of support to kinship-care families.

A widely publicized 1986 lawsuit against New York City had a similar effect. In *Eugene F. v. Gross*, the Legal Aid Society alleged that the city had not provided adequate support, information, and services to relative caregivers.[11] Compelling testimony by kinship caregivers demonstrated that they often lacked basic necessities for the children under their care, including beds, clothing, and school supplies. New York City subsequently expedited procedures for approving relative foster parents and began to provide them with the same level of reimbursement as nonrelatives.

As Nina Bernstein noted in *The Lost Children of Wilder*, by 1993, in part due to the influence of Malcolm X's brother Robert Little, 43 percent of all children placed by New York City were assigned to kinship-care homes.[12] In 1990, Little had been named head of the Child Welfare Administration in New York City, and he endorsed kinship care as an antidote to the type of struggle he and his siblings had undergone. Bernstein noted that although he had been raised in a home with family friends, it was still a foster home. Because of this, he had grown up "feeling that the social workers who trooped through the house twice a year were an extension of oppressive white authority, like the courts, the police and the prisons."

Many of these kinship placements were significantly subsidized by the city. In general, foster-care grants in New York City were considerably more generous than grants offered by the federal Aid to Families with Dependent Children program, which mostly sup-

---

11 "Report to the Congress on Kinship Foster Care," *ASPE*. (U.S. Department of Health and Human Services, June 2000), https://aspe.hhs.gov/system/files/pdf/73116/full.pdf.

12 Nina Bernstein, *The Lost Children of Wilder: The Epic Struggle to Change Foster Care* (New York: Vintage Books, 2002).

ported poor children living with their own mothers. Further, kinship-care payments from the city were often even larger than standard city foster-care payments, and up to seven times the amount of AFDC benefits. This presented a straightforward economic incentive for poor families to place their children in foster care and arrange for kinship-placements.

According to Bernstein, "Little heard critics complain that foster care was now being used as a form of economic development for the black community, a back-door method of income redistribution, but he saw nothing wrong with that. For years black children had been the raw material for a white-run foster-care industry that treated them to second-class service. Why shouldn't money for their care stay within the black community instead, and help their own kind?"[13] Little was not wrong that the foster-care system, to the extent that it existed, was fractured with individual agencies getting to decide which children it would take on.

Shirley Wilder, whose mother died when she was four and whose father threw her out when she was eleven, entered the foster-care system in 1972, when she was thirteen. She was a black Protestant; every religious agency in the city (mostly Catholic or Jewish) turned down the opportunity to place her with a family. The girl was sent to a residential facility upstate, where she was raped and beaten. (The ACLU filed a class-action suit against the city, and the 1986 settlement known as the Wilder Decree mandated reforms of the system, including professional evaluation of children when they arrive in foster care and placement of children with families on a first-come, first-served basis. The responsibility for ensuring that such children were treated well and had access to quality foster care would ultimately rest with family courts.) New York City was not alone in generously financing kinship care. For example, in 1996, two children living with relatives licensed by the Maryland foster-care system would have received up to $1,100 a

13 Bernstein, *The Lost Children of Wilder.*

month; if they had been living at home, they would have received $292 per month from the state's AFDC program.[14]

All of this helps to explain why kinship care seems to work for the kin. But why are social workers placing kids with kin even when it might not be the best fit and when it often costs the state just as much as nonrelative foster care? Fred Wulczyn, the founder and director of the University of Chicago's Center for State Child Welfare Data, has argued that the relative ease of placing children with kin may influence the decisions of caseworkers, who are generally not required to conduct extensive background checks and follow-up assessments for kinship caregivers. Therefore, overworked agents who can save time and resources by placing children with relatives may sometimes do so regardless of whether such placements are truly in a child's best interests.

James Dwyer, a professor at William and Mary Law School, also has raised the issue of liability, explaining that, generally, "Caseworkers prefer relative families [because] if something goes wrong, it's the families' fault." In addition, because a preference for kin has become standard, according to Wulczyn, states often devote fewer resources to recruiting nonkin foster families. This has created a chicken-and-egg problem. Nonrelative foster families may be in short supply because the political tide has turned toward seeking kinship-care families, who may in turn feel pressured to provide homes for children they cannot properly care for.

New Jersey stopped recruiting nonrelative foster parents altogether in 2020, telling applicants in an automated message that "the number of youth in foster care continues to be reduced each year because we are focusing first on kinship placements."[15] It's true that the state has reduced the number of kids in foster care by two-thirds since 2003, from 13,000 to 4,000. But there are only about 1,700

14 "Report to the Congress on Kinship Foster Care. Costs and Sources of Funds for Kinship Care." *ASPE.* (U.S. Department of Health and Human Services, June 2000), https://aspe.hhs.gov/report/report-congress-kinship-foster-care/costs-and-sources-funds-kinship-care.

15 "Foster & Adoption Services." State of New Jersey Department of Children and Families, https://www.nj.gov/njfosteradopt.

kids who are being officially removed from their homes and cared for by relatives now (compared with 2,000 in nonrelative homes).[16] In other words, according to the state's numbers, state-sanctioned kinship care hardly can be the real reason for this dramatic drop. What happened to the other 7,300 kids who would have been in foster care? If the state's account of things is correct, and kinship is the reason behind the drop, then kids who are at risk are being diverted into kinship care rather than being officially removed into the foster-care system. The state doesn't certify the homes where they are going or continue monitoring them in any way after the move.

This kind of kinship diversion seems to be part of a concerted effort on the part of the state to push some serious problems under the rug. The fact that New Jersey has been hit hard by the opioid epidemic—and has one of the highest rates of overdose deaths in the country—would normally be a sign that more kids need to be removed. But the state moved in the opposite direction, even at the height of the drug crisis. (From 2014 to 2019, the number of kids in foster care plummeted from about 7,500 to 4,500).[17]) The fact that the number of reports to the state child-abuse hotline rose from 75,000 to 80,000 between 2012 and 2019 suggests that child-safety problems are growing worse, not better.[18]

If you want to get a sense of what a kinship diversion looks like, you could do worse than read the bestselling memoir *Hillbilly Elegy*. After years of turmoil, living with a mother who abused drugs and put his life in danger, the author, J.D. Vance, describes how his grandmother "Mamaw" eventually took custody of him.[19] Not officially, of course, but this is exactly the kind of arrangement that states like New Jersey are increasingly counting on.

---

16 "Outcomes Report and Executive Summary--2017." State of New Jersey Department of Children and Families, https://www.state.nj.us/dcf/childdata/exitplan/Outcomes.Report.and.Executive.Summary-2017.pdf.

17 "Children in Placement--Point in Time," (Rutgers School of Social Work), https://njchilddata.rutgers.edu/portal/children-placement-reports.

18 Ibid., "Total Hotline Referrals." https://njchilddata.rutgers.edu/portal/total-hotline-referrals.

19 J.D. Vance, *Hillbilly Elegy: A Memoir of Family and Culture in Crisis* (New York: Harper, 2016).

The climactic moment in Vance's childhood story occurs when his mother takes him on a car trip where she gets increasingly agitated, starts driving over 100 mph and says, "I'm going to crash this car and kill us both. I'm going to crash this car and kill us both." When she eventually pulls over, she starts hitting him. He gets out of the car, and she starts chasing him. His mother is eventually arrested on domestic-violence charges, but to avoid being sent into foster care, Vance would not tell the authorities what happened. As he explained to NPR's Terry Gross, "The judge asked whether she had done anything to threaten me. And I lied. I told him no because I knew that if I kept on pushing the case, one, it would cause a lot of problems for the family. And, two, it might land me in a foster home."[20]

Instead, Vance lived for most of his adolescence with Mamaw. "Luckily," he recalls, "I had enough faith in my grandma. I knew that she wouldn't let anything too bad happen to me." Vance's story of remaining in the care of his extended family and not being put into the system turned out well—he eventually goes into the Marines, college, and Yale Law School—but it is easy to imagine how the situation might have gone south. Indeed, for other kids, it often does. Vance's mother's addiction problems stem at least in part from her own childhood. Her father was an alcoholic who beat his wife regularly. To teach him a lesson one night, Mamaw actually set him on fire. Advocates of kinship care often claim that we cannot assume that just because parents are not behaving well that there is widespread dysfunction in an extended family. But for Vance, that clearly was the case.

At the age of twelve, Vance says he knew that his grandmother would protect him, but there are plenty of kin who might not have. And what if Vance had been younger? Would we have wanted a seven-year-old to make such a decision, knowing that if things

---

20 "'Hillbilly Elegy,' Recalls a Childhood Where Poverty Was 'The Family Tradition.'" (*Fresh Air,* August 17,2016), https://www.npr.org/2016/08/17/490328484/hillbilly-elegy-recalls-a-childhood-where-poverty-was-the-family-tradition.

turned out badly, he would have no way of fending for himself or of independently going to the authorities. Kids will almost always choose kinship care because they want to remain with the people they know—it is traumatizing to place a child with strangers. But if we are worried enough about a child's welfare to remove them from the home of their parents, we should also be concerned enough to see that they are placed into a safe environment after that.

It is true, as the defenders of kinship care point out, that children in kinship care tend to be moved around less frequently than those in nonrelative care. In New York, for instance, between 1990 and 2000, 8 percent of children in relative's homes had four or more placements compared with 13 percent of children placed in nonkinship homes.[21]

Obviously, it is important for children to experience as much stability as possible, and it is reasonable to assume that relatives might be more likely than nonrelatives to hold on to a difficult child out of a sense of familial obligation. But the difference actually seems relatively small. Moreover, the data also suggest that children spend much more time in kinship foster care than they spend in nonrelative care. During this same period, children in New York State spent a median number of 492 days in care if they were living with nonrelatives and 1,358 if they were living with kin.[22] Supporters of kinship care would say that the current disparity is not as much of a problem as it seems because the kids are not experiencing the trauma associated with living among strangers. Indeed, they probably have more contact with their biological parents when they are living with kin.

On the other hand, the fact that they are having this contact may mean that biological parents do not have the same kind of incentive to change their behaviors in order to get their children

21 Fred Wulczyn, Emily Zimmerman, and Ada Skyles, "Relative Caregivers, Kinship Foster Care, and Subsidized Guardianship: Policy and Programmatic Options." (Chapin Hall Center for Children, 2002).

22 Naomi Schafer Riley, "Reconsidering Kinship Care." (*National Affairs*, no. 47, Summer 2018), https://www.nationalaffairs.com/publications/detail/reconsidering-kinship-care.

back. And relative foster parents are less willing to adopt the children permanently because they don't want to be seen as responsible for separating the child from his parents. And the temporary nature of the arrangement means it is harder for anyone to help make decisions about the child's future.

A few years ago, Jen Yearout married, and she and her husband Caleb decided to try to become foster parents themselves. They purchased beds, toys, and linens, and generally made their home secure for children. They also underwent extensive background checks and hours of training, which Yearout said she had never been asked to do prior to being granted state-sanctioned responsibility for her nieces. After meeting with a caseworker, however, their application was denied. As Yearout explained, the caseworker had accused her husband of being an alcoholic because his hands shook—he has a nervous-system disorder—and of leering at women. She concluded that they were not fit to be foster parents.

Shortly afterward, the Yearouts moved to Virginia and decided to try again. This time, their application succeeded, and they ultimately took in four foster children. The last child they fostered, whom they have since adopted, was born drug dependent in 2014 and spent several months in the NICU before coming home. He had to wear a helmet for a time because he kept hitting himself in the head, and he has a number of neurological and pulmonary issues. Yearout quit her job to care for the child full time, but caseworkers continually sought to send him back to live with his father and aunt. After two years of shuttling him back and forth, the state determined that the aunt's record of problems with child-protective services was reason enough to end her bid for placement and sever the father's parental rights.

It is nothing short of outrageous that twelve years after the child-welfare system pushed two babies into the young and inexperienced care of a girl without any kind of reasonable home visit or supervision, the same system is giving her a hard time about adopting children even though she is married, living in her own home, with a good income, and now has experience raising children.

In 2018, Georgia's governor Brian Kemp signed a groundbreaking piece of foster-care legislation that puts some limits on kinship preference.[23] It states that "If a relative entitled to notice…fails, within six months from the date he or she receives the required notice, to demonstrate an interest in and willingness to provide a permanent home for a child, the court may excuse DFCS (the Division of Family and Children Services) from considering such relative as a placement."[24]

Arizona passed similar legislation in 2017 to end the effects of this policy on infants, asking courts to consider the best interests of the child over other considerations, like kin connection, if an infant has been with a foster family for nine months.[25] Darcy Olsen, the founder of Generation Justice, which advocated for the law in Arizona explains: These laws say that "if biological relatives fail to step up early, a child in foster care can stay where they are bonded and loved. It's that simple, and it's literally life-saving."[26]

While it is possible to sympathize with the sentiments underlying the kinship-care movement, it is important to reevaluate it in light of our decades-long national experience with its consequences. It is not at all clear that the principles on which it was founded are just nor that the results have served children well. As well intentioned and sensible as the kinship-care movement may appear, the assumption that children will be well cared for by those close to their abusers—in many cases, the people who raised their abusers—is shortsighted and often destructive.

23 "2019–2020 Regular Session––SB 167," Georgia General Assembly (2019), http://www.legis.ga.gov/legislation/en-US/Display/20192020/SB/167.

24 Ibid.

25 Mary Jo Pitzl, "Ducey Signs Bill to Cut Off Parents' Rights to Drug-Exposed Babies After One Year," (*Azcentral*, n.d.), https://www.azcentral.com/story/news/local/arizona-child-welfare/2018/04/05/legislature-oks-bill-cut-off-parents-rights-drug-exposed-babies-after-one-year/487842002.

26 "About Us," Gen Justice, accessed August 18, 2020, www.genjustice.org/about-us.

CHAPTER 4

SEPARATE AND UNEQUAL: HOW A RACIALIZED IDEOLOGY IS PUTTING KIDS IN DANGER

Five-year-old old Brandajah Smith grabbed the loaded .38-caliber revolver after her mother left her alone in their New Orleans apartment. It's still not clear why she pulled the trigger, whether it was an accident or related to the suicidal thoughts the child had expressed. But when her mother returned from the store, Brandajah was dead from a single gunshot to the head.

Brandajah's death in 2013 was shocking, but few people who knew her were surprised. For almost a year, her teachers had repeatedly reported suspicions that she was being sexually abused. They also told authorities that she talked about her own death, what it would be like in heaven, and the gun in her home.

Following Brandajah's death, officials from Louisiana's Department of Children & Family Services (DCFS) told the *Times-Picayune* that the agency "thoroughly investigated each of the complaints received." But they also said that Brandajah's mother, Laderika Smith, was not complying with the "safety plan" that the agency had set up. In November 2012—after months of leaving the child in a home with her mother and the mother's boyfriend--who owned the gun (both are felons)—DCFS asked the local court to either order compliance or give the agency the authority to take the child away. By the time of the kindergartner's death, the court had done neither.[1]

Child-welfare case files are not public, so it is not clear why the court did not act in Brandajah's case. But that inaction came amid a growing push by liberal advocacy groups, child-welfare agencies, and some judges to leave children in troubled homes instead of placing them in foster care, particularly if they are members of a racial minority group.

A prime mover of this effort is Judge Ernestine Steward Gray, who has served in the Orleans Parish Juvenile Court since 1984. It is not publicly known whether she was directly involved in Brandajah's case. But she is the judge primarily responsible for the vast majority of child-in-need-of-care cases. She has long argued that the child-welfare system unfairly targets minority children for removal from their homes (because she sees minority children being removed at disparate rates) and is widely acknowledged to have almost singlehandedly shifted the parish's policies on foster care.

She also has a powerful ally in the effort: Casey Family Programs. The organization, which has a $2.2 billion endowment, gave Judge Gray a leadership award honoring those who have "had a significant impact in improving outcomes for children and families and building Communities of Hope."[2] The money for Casey Family Programs, originally an offshoot of the Annie E. Casey Foundation, came from James Casey, the founder of the shipping company UPS.

---

1 Helen Freund, "Still in Jail Months After Charges Dropped, Mother of Dead Five-Year-Old Waits for Court Action, https://www.nola.com/news/crime_police/article_d5a3cbfe-70f7-5274-bbb7-057d5875ddc9.html.

2 "2019 Awards Announced for Individuals and Communities Dedicated to Improving the Lives of Children and Families." (Cision PR Newswire, 2019), https://www.prnewswire.com/news-releases/2019-awards-announced-for-individuals-and-communities-dedicated-to-improving-the-lives-of-children-and-families-300779720.html.

Casey Family Programs, whose mission is eliminating the need for foster care, has given grants to state child-welfare programs across the country and funds much research on child welfare at universities as well. It is impossible to write about child welfare without citing research from Casey philanthropies—they have contracts with federal and state governments to conduct surveys, analyze data, and publish research on the effectiveness of various policies. Because not many foundations are interested in this area and because child welfare is often squeezed for resources, Casey has an outsized effect on child-welfare policy.

JooYeun Chang, the managing director of public policy at Casey Family Programs, argued in 2018 that the foster-care system "traumatize[s] kids by removing them from the only communities they have known" only to place them in living situations that "are no better than jails."[3] The reason so many kids, particularly minority kids, are removed from their homes, she said, is that "our system has been built on centuries of racism, classism and xenophobia."

Across the country, advocates influenced and sometimes even trained by Casey Family Programs, espouse the view that the child-welfare system is racially biased and structured to break up minority families rather than protect children. In response, they say, the system should try to keep kids in their homes, reunify them more quickly if they have been removed, or keep them with extended family because they share the same racial background. Almost anything, they argue, would be better than placing them with a family of another race. Despite all the evidence to the contrary, the idea that the child-welfare system is racist has taken hold, and legislators are now trying to act on it.

There's no doubt that black families make up a disproportionate number of those who end up encountering child-welfare agencies. According to the 2018 federal data, black children made up 23 percent of the kids in foster care, though they only make up about 14

---

3 "Helping Children of Incarcerated Parents and Children in Foster Care," *Brookings.*

percent of the population of children in the country. White children, on the other hand, make up 51 percent of the child population in the US, but they are only 44 percent of the kids in foster care. Hispanic children are also underrepresented, interestingly, making up 25 percent of the child population but only 21 percent of the population in foster care. Asians account for approximately 0 percent of kids in foster care though they make up 5 percent of kids in the US. And finally, though only 1 percent of the population is American Indian or Native Alaskan, they make up 2 percent of the kids in foster care.[4]

In New York City, the numbers are even more stark and have remained unchanged for decades. African American children made up 31.5 percent of the population of kids in the city in 1987 but accounted for 63.1 percent of children in foster care. In 2012, they made up 25.9 percent of the population and accounted for 59.8 percent of those in foster care.[5]

As with all claims about the "disparate impact" a system may have on a particular population, it's important to note that not all populations of people behave the same way, and so it would be strange if they had the same outcomes. It would be hard to explain these outcomes with racial bias anyway. According to recent data in New York, 65 percent of ACS employees are black.[6] Is it really true that these workers are unfairly targeting their own communities? Are we to believe that social workers are prejudiced against African Americans but not against Hispanics? Do they believe Asians are better parents than whites?

In fact, in 2018, 67 percent of abuse and neglect reports were made by professionals (often legally mandated reporters), includ-

---

4 "Black Children Continue to Be Disproportionately Represented in Foster Care," The Annie E. Casey Foundation KIDS COUNT Data Center. (The Annie E. Casey Foundation, April 13, 2020), https://datacenter.kidscount.org/updates/show/264-us-foster-care-population-by-race-and-ethnicity.

5 Ronald E. Richter, "Disproportionate Minority Representation in the NYC Child Welfare System, Past and Present." (Presentation, April 20, 2013).

6 "New York City Government Workforce Profile Report FY 2016." (New York City Department of Citywide Administrative Services,2016), http://www.nyc.gov/html/dcas/downloads/pdf/misc/workforce_profile_report_fy_2016.pdf.

ing teachers, social workers, and doctors, who are also disproportionately members of minority communities.[7] The highest percentage are from teachers, and racial minorities make up a large share of the teacher population, especially in urban areas. In Washington, DC, for instance, 56 percent of teachers are black.[8] In other words, it's unlikely to be nosy white women who are calling the authorities when they suspect there is abuse or neglect going on in a black child's home.

Bill Baccaglini, the president and CEO of the New York Foundling, the oldest foster agency in New York City, suggests that the argument that child welfare is racist misses the point. "You couldn't even consider race a variable," Baccaglini tells me dejectedly. "It's a constant. All the kids who come into this system, unfortunately, are nonwhite. The racially disparate aspects of the system happened well before with our opportunity structure—the 'tale of two cities,'" as Mayor Bill de Blasio has called it.[9] "The fact that the mom in the South Bronx cannot get decent medical care; the fact that the mom in the South Bronx cannot get a good job; the fact that the mom was put into an [individualized educational program] and never got a degree and then had a child." The fact that these phenomena happen at a higher rate in certain communities is also not necessarily a sign of racism, but it does help us understand what happens to children downstream of these problems.

When I ask Sharonda Wade, an African American woman who works as a supervisor in the Department of Children and Family Services in Los Angeles, what she makes of the claim that racial bias is responsible for the disproportionate rate of child removal

7 "Child Maltreatment 2018," *Administration for Children and Families.* (U.S. Department of Health & Human Services, Administration for Children and Families, Administration on Children, Youth and Families, Children's Bureau, 2018), https://www.acf.hhs.gov/sites/default/files/documents/cb/cm2018.pdf.

8 "District of Columbia Teacher Workforce Report" (Office of the State Superintendent of Education, October 2019), https://osse.dc.gov/sites/default/files/dc/sites/osse/publication/attachments/DC%20Educator%20Workforce%20Report%2010.2019.pdf.

9 Hunter Walker, "Bill DeBlasio Tells a Tale of Two Cities at His Mayoral Kickoff." (*The Observer,* January 27, 2013), https://observer.com/2013/01/bill-de-blasio-tells-a-tale-of-two-cities-at-his-mayoral-campaign-kickoff.

among black families in Los Angeles, she tells me, "Racism exists inside our system—in healthcare, mental health, and criminal justice." Wade says that "because black parents have had not-so-good relationships with other agencies, when our agencies come knocking, they witness us as someone they can't trust." And the reaction to investigations can often exacerbate the situation.

Indeed, Wade tells me that a black person working for CPS may actually make the situation worse from the perspective of black families. "Some people—even black people—feel like a black social worker won't do a good enough job, that they're not as educated, not as professional." Even worse, "They see me as being a traitor." During the four years she was an emergency response worker, clients would call her supervisor to complain. "They wanted a white social worker." Others attacked her for working for CPS at all. "Some of the moms would be screaming: 'How dare you work for CPS? You're going to get your ass whupped for working for the man.'"

But if the bias of investigators is not the reason, what is behind the disparities? Abuse and neglect happen in higher rates in certain families. According to the 2019 Child Maltreatment report, white children were victimized at a rate of 7.8 per 1,000 compared with 13.8 per 1,000 for black children. And lest people assume that these findings of substantiated abuse are also simply the result of bias, it is worth keeping in mind that *fatalities* from child maltreatment are also more than twice as high among black children (5.1 per 100,000) than among white children (2.18 per 100,000). The fact that black children are more than twice as likely to die as a result of abuse or neglect should give pause to anyone who thinks the judgments of child-welfare officials are behind the disparities in removals.[10]

These disparities exist for a variety of reasons. Poverty, for instance, is correlated with abuse. *That is not the same as saying that we are just removing kids because their families are impover-*

10 "Child Maltreatment 2019," *Administration for Children and Families*. (U.S. Department of Health & Human Services, Administration for Children and Families, Administration on Children, Youth and Families, Children's Bureau, 2019), https://www.acf.hhs.gov/sites/default/files/documents/cb/cm2019.pdf.

ished. Poverty causes stress in marriages and other relationships, and sometimes that stress is taken out on kids. And impoverished families are also disproportionately minority families.

Another commonly correlated factor in child abuse is domestic violence between partners. As an article in *Time* pointed out in the wake of the video of football player Ray Rice beating his wife, "Black women are almost three times as likely to experience death as a result of [domestic violence/intimate-partner violence] than White women. And while Black women only make up 8 percent of the population, 22 percent of homicides that result from DV/IPV [domestic violence/intimate partner violence] happen to Black women and 29 percent of all victimized women, making it one of the leading causes of death for Black women ages fifteen to thirty-five."[11] Why are we willing to believe that black women are disproportionately more likely to be abused but not black children?

Family structure is another major predictor of child abuse--perhaps the most important one. Single parenthood, and especially the presence in the home of a man who is not the biological father, is a common theme in a significant percentage of abuse cases. Someone steeped in evolutionary biology might speculate that a man would be less inclined to treat well the offspring of another man (with his own sexual partner) living in his home.

According to data from the US Department of Health and Human Services, the incidence of physical abuse for a child living with a single parent and a "partner" who is not the child's father is 19.5 per 1,000.[12] That's almost twice as high as for children living with unmarried biological parents or a parent married to a nonbiological parent, and almost 10 times as high as for married biological parents. The data are similar for sexual abuse. And the data for child deaths are similarly stark. According to a 2005 paper in the journal *Pediatrics*, "children residing in households with unrelated

---

11 Feminista Jones, "Why Black Women Struggle More with Domestic Violence." (*TIME*, September 10, 2014), https://time.com/3313343/ray-rice-black-women-domestic-violence.

12 "Child Welfare Outcomes 2000: Annual Report." (*Administration for Children and Families*, 2000), https://www.acf.hhs.gov/sites/default/files/cb/cwo00.pdf.

adults were nearly 50 times as likely to die of inflicted injuries than children residing with 2 biological parents." And "in households with unrelated adults, most perpetrators (83.9%) were the unrelated adult household member and only...6.5% of perpetrators were the biological parent of the child."[13]

According to data from *Child Trends*, in 2014 70 percent of all births to black women occurred outside of marriage compared with only 29 percent of all births to white women.[14] For Hispanics, the rate is 54 percent, and Hispanic couples are more likely to remain together even if they don't marry (which could explain some of the difference between black and Hispanic families with regard to interactions with CPS). Family structure is a deeply important factor in determining the likelihood of interaction with child-welfare officials, and it is one that disproportionately affects black children. Child-welfare officials almost never mention these statistics, but they are vital in explaining why there are racial disparities in child maltreatment and the child-welfare system and why, unless we have a different standard for tolerating the abuse of black children, they are not going away.

The accusations of racism in child welfare began long before our current obsession with racial disparities. Between 1968 and 1972, approximately 50,000 black and biracial children were adopted by white parents.[15] American couples also began to adopt internationally as well as across domestic racial lines. But as Barbara Melosh noted in *Strangers and Kin*, "adoptions across national and racial lines...claimed a public visibility disproportionate to their actual numbers, a measure of the ways in which such families remain provocative—evoking utopian possibility, for some; and for others, providing a galling instance of white privilege at home and

---

13 "Child Deaths Resulting from Inflicted Injuries: Household Risk Factors and Perpetrator Characteristics." (*Pediatrics*, November 2005).

14 "Births to Unmarried Women: Indicators of Child and Youth Well-Being." (*Child Trends*, October 2016), https://www.childtrends.org/wp-content/uploads/2015/12/75_Births_to_Unmarried_Women.pdf.

15 Deann Borshay Liem, "Adoption History." POV (Deann Borshay Liem & NAATA, 2000), http://archive.pov.org/firstpersonplural/history/#:~:text=Between percent201968 percent20and percent201972 percent2C percent20approximately.

abroad."[16] Eventually, prominent African American and Native American leaders began to protest this trend.

In 1972, the National Association of Black Social Workers issued a statement that took "a vehement stand against the placements of Black children in white homes for any reason."[17] The statement read, in part:

> *We affirm the inviolable position of black children in black families where they belong physically, psychologically and culturally in order that they receive the total sense of themselves and develop a sound projection of their future.*
>
> *Ethnicity is a way of life in these United States, and the world at large; a viable, sensitive, meaningful and legitimate societal construct. This is no less true nor legitimate for black people than for other ethnic groups....*
>
> *We fully recognize the phenomenon of transracial adoption as an expedient for white folk, not as an altruistic humane concern for black children.*[18]

The NABSW's president at the time, Cenie Williams, argued that temporary foster or even institutional placements for black children were preferable to their adoption by white families.[19] This position resulted in a swift decline in transracial foster arrangements and adoptions. In 1973, the Child Welfare League of America revised its adoption standards (which had been rewritten in 1968 to reflect a friendlier stance toward transracial adoption) to clarify that same-race placements were always preferred.[20]

The fact that these social workers actually preferred placement in institutions for black children over foster care or adoption with

---

16 Melosh, *Strangers and Kin*.

17 Ellen Herman, "National Association of Black Social Workers 'Position Statement on Trans-Racial Adoption' September 1972." (The Adoption History Project, 2012), https://pages.uoregon.edu/adoption/archive/NabswTRA.htm.

18 Ibid.

19 Judy Klemesrud, "Furor Over Whites Adopting Blacks." (*The New York Times*, April 12, 1972, sec. Archives), https://www.nytimes.com/1972/04/12/archives/furor-over-whites-adopting-blacks.html.

20 Ellen Herman, "Transracial Adoptions."

a white family is the tell. It was not that transracial adoption was an "expedient" for white folk—anyone who has ever adopted a child can tell you there is nothing expedient about the experience—but rather that opposition to transracial adoption was a way of pushing a particular political message about black power and black solidarity. These social workers were willing to throw individual black children just like Shirley Wilder—whose horrific abuse, remember, was suffered during institutional placements—under the bus in order to further their political aims.

Even today, NABSW's statement is cited as evidence of the problems with transracial adoption. A 2020 article in the Catholic magazine, *America*, noted that "when white parents adopt a child of another race or ethnicity, they are depriving that child of a profoundly valuable resource: a mother and/or father who can guide that child in navigating U.S. culture as a minority and can also connect that child to the rich cultural heritage that is their birthright." And the author went on to provide a link to the 1972 statement.[21]

Activists for Native American rights viewed white adoption of Native American children with the same sort of suspicion and antipathy. In the late-nineteenth and early-twentieth centuries, Native American children often had been placed in boarding schools, in the hope that education would speed their cultural assimilation. (Though the boarding schools are almost universally decried today as abusive, many children were sent voluntarily by parents who wanted better opportunities for their children, and many of the children reported positive experiences at them.) In the 1950s and 1960s, the Indian Adoption Project, a program administered by the Child Welfare League of America and funded by a federal contract from the Children's Bureau and the Bureau of Indian Affairs, placed hundreds of Native American children with white

21 Holly Taylor Coolman, "White Parents Adopting Black Kids Raises Hard Questions. We Can All Learn from Them," *America The Jesuit Review*. (America Press Inc., July 8, 2020), https://www.americamagazine.org/politics-society/2020/07/08/white-parents-Black-kids-transracial-adoption.

adoptive parents.[22] At the time, this was considered by many to be a triumph for civil rights, made possible by a decrease in racial prejudice. Soon, however, tribal advocates denounced the project as only the most recent in a long line of policies meant to weaken or destroy Native American communities.

The tribes' objections were not that children were being torn away from loving parents or even that it was in the child's best interests to remain in his or her community. Rather, it was that the *tribes* would be better off if the child stayed. In their book, *Saving International Adoption*, Mark Montgomery and Irene Powell describe how leaders of certain war-torn countries whose orphans were adopted overseas talk about children as a kind of "natural resource" who should be kept home—not because it is better for them but because it is better for their country.[23] It is easy to see this kind of attitude among opponents of domestic transracial adoption as well.

These advocates believed that resisting such policies would entail recruiting more families from the same racial background to take in Native American children, or else finding ways to keep children with their immediate or extended families. The Indian Child Welfare Act (ICWA), passed in 1978, gave tribes jurisdiction over children living on and off reservations who were wards of the state and made it extremely difficult for nonnative people to adopt Native American children.[24]

Despite the growing support for race-based placements, however, there were attempts to push back against their acceptance. In 1994, for example, Congress passed the Multiethnic Placement Act (MEPA), which, among other things, "prohibited State agencies and other entities that receive Federal funding…from delaying, denying, or otherwise discriminating when making a foster-care

22 Karen Balcom, "The Logic of Exchange: The Child Welfare League of America, The Adoption Resource Exchange Movement and the Indian Adoption Project, 1958–1967." (*Adoption & Culture* 1, no. 1, 2007), 5–67, https://www.jstor.org/stable/44755459?seq=1.

23 Mark Montomery and Irene Powell, "Saving International Adoption: An Argument from Economics and Personal Experience." (Vanderbilt University Press, January 30, 2018).

24 "Topic 18. Adoption," National Indian Law Library, accessed August 20, 2020, https://narf.org/nill/documents/icwa/faq/adoption.html.

or adoption-placement decision on the basis of the parent or child's race, color, or national origin."[25]

MEPA was enacted, as law professor Joan Heifetz Hollinger stated in a 1998 report for the American Bar Association, "amid spirited and sometimes contentious debate about transracial adoption and same-race placement policies."[26] The bill was sponsored in the Senate by a bipartisan coalition, including Republicans Dan Coats of Indiana and Nancy Kassebaum of Kansas as well as Democrats Carol Mosely-Braun and Paul Simon of Illinois, Daniel Inouye of Hawaii and Dianne Feinstein of California. According to Hollinger, Congress had found not only that African American and other minority children were, on average, forced to wait in limbo in child-protective systems for far longer than white children, but also that "racial and ethnic matching policies" had significantly contributed to these delays.

The law, which was amended in 1996, included--among its specific goals--decreasing the length of time that children wait to be adopted and "facilitat[ing] the recruitment and retention of foster and adoptive parents who can meet the distinctive needs of children awaiting placement."[27] The idea was that perhaps if agencies did enough outreach through community groups and churches serving racial-minority populations it could start to make a dent in the problem. In 1997 and 1998, the Department of Health and Human Services issued guidance documents based on the law that, according to Hollinger, suggested that "a child's race, color, or national origin cannot be routinely considered as a relevant factor in assessing the child's best interests."[28]

---

25 "Major Federal Legislation Index and Search," Child Welfare Information Gateway, accessed August 21, 2020, https://www.childwelfare.gov/topics/systemwide/laws-policies/federal/search/?CWIGFunctionsaction=federallegislation:main.getFedLedgDetail&id=173.

26 "Chapter 11 Relevant Federal Laws and North Carolina Statutes Codifying Federal Laws," *North Carolina Judicial Branch*. (Administrative Office of the Courts, State of North Carolina, 2007), https://www.nccourts.gov/assets/documents/publications/chapter11.pdf?JeyYoCq0bBxkF7dXwlkab9iKHXoy8Tn1.

27 "Multi-Ethnic Placement Act of 1994," Oklahoma Fosters Bridge Resource Family Handbook, accessed August 24, 2020, https://okfostershandbook.org/section-11-juvenile-court/multi-ethnic-placement-act-of-1994.

28 Idaho Admin. Code r. 16.06.01.050.

Since MEPA and the Adoption and Safe Families Act (which reduced the allowable time for kids to remain in care) were passed in the mid-90s, adoptions "have increased from about thirty thousand to fifty thousand per year," according to a 2020 article by the Brookings Institution's Ron Haskins. "Moreover, the average time states took to complete adoption of children from foster care was reduced by about one year." What this means in practice is clear, writes Haskins: "More kids adopted; faster adoptions. A double victory."[29]

But now a growing chorus of voices is looking to undo that victory. In 2021, Bethany Christian Services, one of the largest adoption agencies in the country, released a report arguing for "overhauling" the Multi-Ethnic Placement Act.[30] As part of its "long journey toward becoming an anti-racist organization," Bethany's leaders now believe a child's race should be considered "as part of the best interest determination for child placement." The report was written by the Annie E. Casey Foundation.

The continued growth of kinship care, however, served as a workaround for those who favor race-matching in foster care and adoption but suddenly found the explicit consideration of race to be illegal. But they needn't have worried. For decades, MEPA has been regularly ignored by child-welfare agencies and family courts. I have spoken to numerous foster and adoptive parents, not to mention lawyers and CASA workers, who tell me they often hear race mentioned in open court as a reason to resist placing children with a particular family.

These days, it seems that the law of the land will be consigned to the dustbin of history thanks to agencies, activists, and media outlets determined to show that the system itself is discriminatory. In 2017, the *New York Times* published a story called "Foster Care as Punishment: The New Reality of Jane Crow."[31] The reporter

29 http://us.sagepub.com/en-us/nam/the-annals-of-the-american-academy-of-political-and-social-science/book277892.

30 https://bethany.org/resources/what-the-pandemic-taught-us-innovative-practice-report.

31 Stephanie Clifford and Jessica Silver-Greenberg, "Foster Care as Punishment: The New Reality of 'Jane Crow.'" (*The New York Times*, July 21, 2017, sec. New York), https://www.nytimes.com/2017/07/21/nyregion/foster-care-nyc-jane-crow.html.

chronicled the stories of black mothers who have had their children removed for what seemed trivial reasons. The story claimed that when it comes to black parents, ACS is engaged in a "criminalization of their parenting choices." In a story for *The New Yorker* that appeared around the same time, Larissa MacFarquhar quoted an attorney from the Bronx Defenders, a group that represents, in family court, parents who have been charged with abuse or neglect by child services, saying: "We are members of this system which we all strongly believe is racist and classist and doing harm to the families it claims to serve."[32]

It is not that racial bias doesn't exist or could never be an explanation for a particular removal. Take, for instance, a black mother in South Carolina, who, unable to pay for childcare, left her nine-year-old daughter at a park to play while she worked her shift at a nearby McDonalds.[33] The girl was subsequently removed from her custody. Or the case in 2015 of the black Houston woman who was arrested for child abandonment after bringing her kids, ages six and two, to a food court and leaving them there—where she could see them—while she interviewed for a job thirty feet away.[34]

Hardly a week goes by that I don't have a conversation with a friend or a reporter who has read one of these stories and is outraged. These are decisions that any one of us could have made, but because we live in predominantly white neighborhoods in the suburbs, the narrative goes, no one notices. On the occasion when middle-class white parents make perfectly reasonable decisions about their children's safety and leave them in a car while they run into the dry cleaner's and a nosy neighbor does call CPS, there are

32 Larissa MacFarquhar, "When Should a Child Be Taken from His Parents?" (*The New Yorker*, August 7, 2017), https://www.newyorker.com/magazine/2017/08/07/when-should-a-child-be-taken-from-his-parents.

33 "S.C. Mom's Arrest over Daughter Alone in Park Sparks Debate," CBS News. (CBS Interactive Inc., July 28, 2014), https://www.cbsnews.com/news/south-carolina-moms-arrest-over-daughter-alone-in-park-sparks-debate.

34 "Mom Accused of Leaving Kids at Food Court During Job Interview," CBS News. (CBS Interactive Inc., July 20, 2015), https://www.cbsnews.com/news/texas-mom-accused-of-leaving-kids-at-food-court-during-job-interview/#:~:text=HOUSTON percent20 percent2D percent2DA percent20mother percent20claims.

weeks of uproar about the government's overinvolvement in our lives and the interference with reasonable parenting.

The most famous instance of this was in 2015 when Alexander and Danielle Meitiv got into trouble with Maryland's CPS after deciding to let their children, ages ten and six, walk to neighborhood parks by themselves.[35] When they refused to sign a document saying that the children would be supervised at all times, the agency threatened to take away their children permanently. Self-described "free-range parents," the Meitivs helped to publicize the nascent movement and spark outrage among the public.

Writing in *The Nation*, Michelle Goldberg noted that the case was "highly unusual, but not because of the arbitrariness or overreaction of CPS. It was unusual because the Meitivs are white, affluent, and highly educated: He's a theoretical physicist, and she's a science writer and consultant." Goldberg observes that "advocates for families caught up in the child-welfare system hope that the national debate sparked by the free-range parenting movement will draw attention to the threats and intrusions that poor and minority parents endure all the time."[36]

As Martin Guggenheim, a New York University law professor and codirector of the school's Family Defense Clinic, told Goldberg, these are "communities that are already highly regulated and overseen by low-level bureaucrats like the police."[37] And the larger presence of such local officials may serve to magnify or bring to the attention of authorities activities that would go unnoticed in other areas.

---

35 Candace Smith and Lauren Effron, "'Free Range' Parents Found Responsible for Child Neglect After Allowing Kids to Walk Home Alone." (*ABC News*, March 3, 2015), https://abcnews.go.com/Lifestyle/free-range-parents-found-responsible-child-neglect-allowing/story?id=29363859.

36 Michelle Goldberg, "Has Child Protective Services Gone Too Far?" (*The Nation*, September 30, 2015), https://www.thenation.com/article/archive/has-child-protective-services-gone-too-far/?utm_source=facebook&utm_medium=socialflow.

37 Radley Balko, "Child Protective Services and the Criminalization of Parenthood." (*The Washington Post*, October 2, 2015), https://www.washingtonpost.com/news/the-watch/wp/2015/10/02/child-protective-services-and-the-criminalization-of-parenthood.

But that, in and of itself, does not suggest we are unfairly targeting racial minorities. (Maybe there are more kids in the lily-white suburbs who could use some intervention.) The truth is that while these cases of black parents (and white parents) being punished for reasonable decisions or mistakes than anyone could have made often get a lot of headlines, they are a fairly small percentage of the cases that result in the removal of a child to foster care.

Jill Duerr Berrick, a professor at UC Berkeley's School of Social Welfare, agrees that the crackdown on parents letting older children play or walk somewhere independently is not statistically significant. "These are outlier stories that easily make it to the press and to social media because they are outliers." The author, most recently of "The Impossible Imperative: Navigating the Competing Principles of Child Protection," adds that "the vast majority of child neglect cases involve very young children and parents who are struggling with substance abuse."[38]

The prevalence of substance abuse as a factor in child welfare is a subject we will return to in the next chapter, but for now it is enough to say that the parents who are investigated after leaving children in the car while they go into the supermarket or letting their kids walk to the park alone usually are not drunk or high or mentally unbalanced when they are making these decisions.

Moreover, before we become outraged over cases that seem trivial, a word of caution is in order. These accounts are often one-sided, and it is not uncommon for important details to be left out. Even the most diligent journalist often will find him or herself stymied in reporting about such removals because child-welfare agencies are barred by law from discussing the details of a case with reporters, even if the case has already been closed. This is not to say that there are never cases of overreach by CPS, but parents who feel wronged may not reveal that they were the subject of previous investigations or release other pertinent information. Just like it is hard to judge

38 Jill Duerr Berrick, *The Impossible Imperative: Navigating the Competing Principles of Child Protection*. (Oxford University Press; 1st edition, November 6, 2017).

individual cases on a small scale with incomplete information, so it is hard to make sense of the charge that our child-welfare system is racist without all the relevant facts.

But we are now barreling toward legislation to combat this problem. The African American Family Preservation and Child Welfare Disproportionality Act, which was approved by the Minnesota House Health and Human Services Policy Committee, attempts to "minimize out-of-home placements and promote the reunification of families and children belonging to groups disproportionately represented in the state's child welfare system."[39] The problem, according to the bill's sponsor, Rep. Rena Moran, is that "in many cases, children are not taken from their homes because of any actual abuse or neglect, but because of the subjective impressions of child protection workers. Usually, inadequate food, clothing, or shelter are just the result of poverty, and families need to be connected to services, not separated."[40] This is quite a broad claim, and Moran doesn't offer any evidence for it.

But never mind that. If passed, her bill would require (only for African American children):

- sixty-day in-home safety plans to be completed before a removal could be allowed;
- the right to appeal the termination of parental rights within 120 days of receiving the order;
- the addition of six specialists to the Department of Human Services to monitor outcomes and assist counties in the elimination of disparities;
- cultural competency training for individuals working in the child protection system;
- increasing the minimum visitation requirements for the parents and siblings in out-of-home placements

39 Victoria Cooney, "Expanded Bill Aims to Address Racial Disparities in State's Child Protection System through Sweeping Change." (Minnesota Legislature, March 5, 2019), https://www.house.leg.state.mn.us/SessionDaily/Story/13704.

40 Cooney, "Expanded Bill Aims."

The bill would still protect children who are the victims of physical abuse, sexual abuse, or "egregious harm" (which includes allegations of physical assault or hiring out a child as a prostitute, for instance). But it would not be egregious harm if, for example, a mother is addicted to drugs and repeatedly leaves a toddler at home all night by himself so she can get her fix. And she would be allowed sixty days with the child in her care before the child could be removed.

The right to appeal termination of parental rights within 120 days will end up causing more problems than it solves. TPRs are typically multiyear-long processes in which the state has to present significant evidence that a parent has been offered a number of chances at rehabilitation and access to services that can help in that regard. Only once all of these avenues have been exhausted—on average about twenty months but typically longer for older children—will a state issue a TPR. The idea that, after all that time, a parent should be able to go back and re-litigate the entire matter will not only be a strain on the court system but will likely result in an even longer delay in finding a stable permanent home for a child. New York's legislature actually passed a similar bill in 2019—which would have allowed parents whose rights have been terminated to petition the court for visitation—but the governor rightly vetoed it.[41]

Once legislators and child-welfare agency heads start demanding racial parity in removals to foster care, there will be widespread unintended consequences. In Diane Redleaf's book, *They Took the Kids Last Night*, the lawyer and family advocate writes about a white, upper-class couple whose children were removed despite clear evidence of their innocence of the charges leveled against them.[42] She writes: "Making middle-class white parents like Ben and Lynn out to be child abusers would establish the State's evenhandedness." In

41 Latoya Joyner, Pub. L. No. A02199A (2019).

42 Diane L. Redleaf, *They Took the Kids Last Night: How the Child Protection System Puts Families at Risk.* (Santa Barbara, CA: Praeger, 2018).

other words, in an effort to escape the charge that the system is racist, child-welfare workers may be going out of their way to find innocent white families to investigate and charge. It is hard to separate out the different larger trends that go into these decisions. But it's likely that a growing number of cases of obviously competent parents being persecuted by child-welfare agencies is a result of these demands for racial parity. Here is a startling side effect of crying "racism" at every sign of unequal outcomes.

Once we take into account that abuse and neglect are occurring at different rates in different racial communities, there are a limited number of ways to "establish the state's evenhandedness" when it comes to child-welfare outcomes. One way is to simply have different standards for when we remove black children from their homes and when we remove white children. The Minnesota legislation all but demands this course of action in mandating "cultural competency training for individuals working in the child protection system."[43] What does this mean? In practice, applying different "cultural standards" means that we expect parents of different races to subject their children to different levels of abuse or other danger.

When she was responsible for approving foster placements for kids who had been removed from their homes, Wade says, parents would often become frustrated that a child couldn't be placed immediately with a member of the extended family. But extended family members have to pass background checks and meet other requirements in order to foster children. One of her black colleagues questioned the need to jump through so many hoops: "So Grandma has got domestic violence on her record. What's wrong with that? I've had a little domestic violence too." Says Wade, "That's not the kind of sensitivity I'm looking for."

These kinds of double standards can also be applied in court. In a 2018 article for the *Louisiana Bar Journal* titled "The Color of Justice for Children," Judge Gray wrote, "Nationally, youth of

---

43 Cooney, "Racial Disparities."

color are disproportionately represented at every decision point in the child-welfare system. Their families are disproportionately referred to the system by institutions such as hospitals, schools and law enforcement."[44] Even the phrasing here should be offensive. Children are not "representative" of a racial group; they are individuals whose cases need to be examined individually.

When I asked Judge Gray how she could support such double standards, she told me she tries to make decisions on a case-by-case basis, but she said she knows that "African Americans don't make up 100 percent of the poor people in New Orleans. I have to wonder why poor white parents and poor Vietnamese parents aren't being brought in." And so, she has decided to do something about it. Since she can't mandate that child-welfare workers bring more Vietnamese kids into her courtroom, she will leave more black children with the parents who abused or neglected them.

Judge Gray (and scores of other judges across the country who are less open about it) are conducting a high-stakes experiment—applying a new standard for what constitutes abuse and neglect for minority children and where at-risk children should be placed if they are removed. She is doing it with the full knowledge of state officials, but without any public announcement or scrutiny. Gray says that she decides cases on an individual basis, but the people in her courtroom say that the issue of race is regularly invoked there, and state officials say it is absolutely impacting her decisions. I spoke with a local pediatrician specializing in abuse cases, a lawyer who has appeared in Gray's court, foster families, and others who have worked in local foster care and child welfare. None of them were willing to speak on the record because they continue to appear in the judge's courtroom, but they all told a similar story about an abuse of power that Gray proudly acknowledges. Trying to report on Judge Gray is like trying to report on the mob. Everyone worries about getting on her bad side because she has so much power over

44 Judge Ernstine S. Gray, "The Color of Justice for Children." (*Louisiana Bar Journal* 66, no. 2, 2018), https://www.lsba.org/documents/ChildrensLaw/BJFeature6.pdf.

children's lives, and they worry about the backlash if they dare to speak out.

Gray told me that "there is not a lot of clarity about the standards" for when to remove children from their homes. She says she will only remove a child "when it is absolutely necessary to ensure the health, safety, and well-being of that child." But she also knows that her standard differs significantly from that of other judges. "I do believe I have a higher standard in terms of proof. I believe it is the appropriate one."

Gray even notes that when she is the duty judge—the one who gets called if a DCFS worker wants to remove a child during the night—"the calls are substantially down." In other words, some caseworkers who have determined a child is in an emergency situation evidently presume Gray likely will turn down the request, so they don't ask. Can you imagine bragging about this?

Gray's views seem to have become the law of the land in her city. Between 2010 and 2018, the number of children in foster care in Orleans Parish fell almost 75 percent, from 126 to 36.[45] During the same period, neighboring parishes have seen significant increases. East Baton Rouge, for instance, has gone from 126 to 208 during the same period.[46] A map of Louisiana suggests that Orleans is a startling outlier with a rate of 1.7 children in foster care per 1,000 compared with neighboring St. Tammany and St. Bernard with rates of 4.9 and 6.8, respectively.[47] The national average is 6 per 1,000 children.[48]

Nationwide, there is evidence that as substance abuse rises, so do the number of kids being taken into foster care. And Louisiana's

45 Louisiana Department of Children and Family Services, unpublished data.
46 Louisiana Department of Children and Family Services, unpublished data.
47 "Children in Foster Care," The Annie E. Casey Foundation KIDS COUNT Data Center. (The Annie E. Casey Foundation, accessed August 25, 2020), https://datacenter.kidscount.org/data/tables/10087-children-in-foster-care?loc=20&loct=5#detailed/5/3236.
48 "Children 0 to 17 in Foster Care," The Annie E. Casey Foundation KIDS COUNT Data Center. (The Annie E. Casey Foundation, accessed August 25, 2020), https://datacenter.kidscount.org/data/tables/6242-children-0-to-17-in-foster-care?loc=47&loct=2#ranking/2/any/true/870/any/12986.

drug problem (among families of all races) has certainly been getting worse. Its rate of overdose deaths has increased to 24.5 per 1,000, compared with the national average of 21.7.[49] In the past decade, reports of child abuse and neglect in Orleans Parish have almost doubled from 2,556 to 5,589, and the number that merit an investigation has risen from 1,044 to 1,777.[50] All of this suggests that, if anything, Orleans should be seeing a rise in the number of kids needing to be removed from their homes. But the parish is moving in the opposite direction.

All of the people who spoke to me said they are deeply concerned about efforts to leave children in troubled homes. And they all report that Gray's reputation for denying state's petitions for removal matters for both investigations and prosecutions. But Rhenda Hodnett, Louisiana's assistant secretary of child welfare, said there's another way of interpreting the relatively low number of Orleans Parish children in foster care, though she admitted that it is "hard to wrap your head around." She said that "different communities have different ideas and thoughts around what is abuse and what isn't." Though she says the state "does a lot of training on how to recognize abuse and neglect," she adds that "community norms are a little different."

This seems an odd explanation, because the number of reports of abuse and neglect in Orleans Parish doubled between 2010 and 2018.[51] Most abuse and neglect calls are not made by bureaucrats who swoop in from the outside but by doctors, teachers, and social workers, many of whom are from the same racial background as

49 "Louisiana's Opioid Response Plan." (*Louisiana Department of Health*, accessed September 4, 2020), https://www.ldh.la.gov/assets/opioid/LaOpioidResponsePlan2019.pdf.

50 "Child Protection Investigations by Finding in Orleans," The Annie E. Casey Foundation KIDS COUNT Data Center. (The Annie E. Casey Foundation, accessed August 25, 2020), https://datacenter.kidscount.org/data/tables/10026-child-protection-investigations-by-finding?loc=20&loct=5#detailed/5/3255/false/37,871,870,573,869,36,868,867/2838,2839,2837,2840/19413,19414.

51 Naomi Schaefer Riley, "The Race Theory That Keeps Imperiled Black Kids Right Where They Are." (*Real Clear Investigations*, September 27, 2019), https://www.realclearinvestigations.com/articles/2019/09/27/disparate_impact_and_the_danger_to_kids_who_should_be_in_foster_care_120404.html.

the children being reported. So, the "community" doesn't seem to have lowered its standards for reporting abuse and neglect. Why should anyone else?

Gray "is truly an eminent judge and respected across the nation on issues of disproportionality," Hodnett said. "Her antenna is high. She watches that closely. Race is absolutely something that impacts her decision-making. She makes no bones about that."

Assistant Secretary Hodnett claims the child maltreatment situation is under control. She said that the repeat maltreatment rates for Orleans Parish have not changed since the foster care rates started falling. The state, however, does not seem to have the numbers to back up that claim. A representative of Louisiana's Department of Children & Family Services says repeat maltreatment claims are tracked only as a regional total for three parishes, and data for Orleans cannot be broken out (even though almost all other child-welfare indicators are tracked by parish). And the numbers they do have are only available for six months despite the fact that repeat maltreatment often takes longer to manifest.

Gray said, "I'm not doing research. I don't know if a family comes back to the attention of the department unless it results in another court case" and she happens to be the one hearing it. She says that "we are trying to figure out how we can gather those numbers," but right now, "it's all kind of speculation."

It's not just that race seems to play a role in Gray's decisions about removals, but also about where children should be placed if they do have to be removed. In the interview, she said she is committed to ensuring that those children can be placed with their extended family (who likely share their skin color). She worries that "restrictions on placing kids with relatives who have criminal records" have created a problem for these families because "who are the people who have more relatives in the criminal justice system? It's minorities." In other words, Gray is suggesting that the standards for which homes may legally take in minority children should be lowered.

Gray has also recommended that judges should "consider race as a factor when placing children for adoption (e.g., by applying provisions similar to those in the Indian Child Welfare Act to African American children)...[and] vigorously recruit families whose background reflects that of children waiting to be adopted and who will adopt older children."[52]

If you want to know what will happen to black children whose parents are held to a lower standard, Native children are the canaries in the coal mine. The goal of foster care and adoption out of foster care is to place children in stable, loving homes. But Congress passed the Indian Child Welfare Act in 1978 as a kind of remedy to prevent social workers from removing Indian children from their parents and placing them with white families simply because of poverty or bigotry. Over time, though, ICWA has called into creation a separate and unequal child-welfare system, the kind that some activists want to create for black children next.

One of the first questions a social worker must answer when determining whether to remove a child from a home is whether that child is Indian, because every decision may be different as a result. There will be different standards to determine whether to remove a child, how long a child may remain in foster care and where a child should be placed if they are removed. Indian foster children—regardless of whether they live on a reservation, regardless of how much or how little of their DNA is Native American, and even regardless of their biological parents' wishes—may be adopted only by other Indians. Preference for adoptions goes first to family, which is the same for non-Indian adoptions. But once family ties are exhausted, children must be placed next with members of their tribes. Or even members of other tribes.

The results of this legislation have been devastating for Indian children. When Chad and Jennifer Brackeen of Texas received a call in June 2016 from a child-welfare worker asking if they would

52 "Judicial Viewpoints on ASFA." (*ABA Child Law Practice* 29, no. 4, 2009), https://isc.idaho.gov/cp/docs/Judicial percent20Viewpoints percent20on percent20ASFA.pdf.

be willing to take in a ten-month-old foster child, they did not hesitate. They had two biological sons and had already had one foster placement that lasted about five months. But this baby was different. "We were told that because he was an Indian child, he would only be with us for a couple of months and then would be moved to an Indian family," she recalls.

The Brackeens' child, referred to in court documents as Baby A.L.M., had been born with drugs in his system and removed from his parents because of neglect. In May 2017, almost a year after the Brackeens began fostering Baby A.L.M., his mother relinquished her parental rights. His father didn't show up at the hearing, so his rights were severed.

During those eleven months, child-welfare officials failed to come up with another family who wanted him, let alone someone from the Navajo or Cherokee tribes whose ancestry he shares. But officials continued to tell the Brackeens they couldn't adopt Baby A.L.M., although by then the Brackeens were the only parents he knew.

A couple of months later, the Brackeens received word that a Navajo couple in Albuquerque was interested in adopting Baby A.L.M. After the child spent just two hours with the couple, officials announced it was a done deal, the two-year-old would shortly be put on a plane to New Mexico. Despite the fact that everyone who knew the boy supported his adoption by the Brackeens—his biological parents, his paternal grandmother who had raised him until he was ten months old, the government's guardian ad litem for the child, and a court-appointed special advocate—a family-court judge ruled against them based on ICWA.

Lawyers for the Brackeens and the other families, as well as attorneys general from Texas, Louisiana, and Indiana who joined the suit, argued primarily that the law discriminates on the basis of race. The defendants, including the Cherokee Nation and other tribes as well as the federal government, responded by claiming, as they have in the past, that Indian tribes are individual political entities—analogous to nations, not racial groups.

The plaintiffs successfully countered that if each tribe is a single political entity, and that entity should have precedence over adoptive parents from other groups, why does ICWA allow Indian kids to be adopted by any native family from any tribe? If the goal is to preserve a child's heritage, how is that accomplished by sending him to live with members of another tribe or putting hundreds of miles between a child and his biological relatives?

Baby A.L.M. is thriving with his adoptive family. But until the Supreme Court strikes it down, ICWA is still the law of the land. Jennifer Brackeen says that until that changes, if her family has the choice of whether to take in a native child again, they would "almost certainly say no." In her view, the Indian Child Welfare Act creates a system that she doesn't want to be a part of. It leaves Indian children in foster care for long periods (longer than is allowed for children of any other race) while officials seek native families to take them in. And when it can't find them, the law ignores the family bonds that have formed in foster care.

Frankly, though, Baby A.L.M. is one of the lucky ones.

In late 2019, five-year-old Alexander "Tony" Renova was beaten to death by his biological parents and a guest in their apartment after having been transferred out of a stable, loving, albeit white, foster family.[53] The Crow Tribal Court had decided to remove Tony from what was, by all accounts, the happy and safe Montana home of Jeff and Christy Foster—the couple who had cared for him since he was three days old—and put him with his biological parents, Crow Tribe members Emilio Emmanuel Renova Sr. and Stephanie Grace Byington, who were in jail when the child was born, having both been charged with violent felonies (including child endangerment).

No other family or tribe members apparently stepped up to take care of Tony in his parents' absence, so the tribe placed him with the Fosters. Hundreds showed up for a vigil where neighbors,

53 David Murray, "Foster Family Who Raised Slain Five-Year-Old Explains How System Repeatedly Failed Him." (*Great Falls Tribune*, November 22, 2019), https://www.greatfallstribune.com/story/news/2019/11/22/foster-family-who-raised-slain-child-explains-how-system-failed-him/4275866002.

families from his school and fellow church members remembered him as a happy child.[54] Christy's father told the *Great Falls Tribune*, "Tony was a little boy who loved to play in the mud, throw pebbles in the water and watch cartoons about Mickey Mouse."

The Fosters were told early on it was unlikely they would be able to adopt Tony, because he was a member of the Crow Tribe. The best they could do was to try to show the tribe that they were exposing him to the Crow culture. So, they took the boy to pow-wows and other cultural events, sometimes traveling long distances to get there.

But that was not enough. Because the Fosters were not members of the tribe, they could not appear before the court and could only find out about the case from the Crow social worker who was assigned to supervise Tony. In 2018, they were instructed to have Tony meet with Renova and Byington. There were a few supervised visits, and then in March of 2019, the Fosters were instructed to turn Tony over to his parents.

The parents did not want the Fosters to bring a bed or any of his toys, and any communication with the only people he had known as his mother and father were cut off. The Fosters were not informed when Tony was brought to a local emergency room for bruising on his face in June.[55] And they were not informed about his death by authorities.

The circumstances of that death are gruesome.[56] When police found Tony, he was unresponsive and bleeding from the nose and mouth, with bruises on his knees, torso, ribs, and face. His leg appeared to be broken. He had a gash on his head, and there

54 Karl Puckett, "'We Have to Do Something,' Residents Say at Vigil for Five-Year-Old Tony." (*Great Falls Tribune*, November 24, 2019), https://www.greatfallstribune.com/story/news/2019/11/24/residents-come-far-and-wide-remember-5-year-old-tony/4293515002.

55 David Sherman, "Three People Charged in Great Falls for Child's Death." (*3KRTV Great Falls*, November 21, 2019), https://www.krtv.com/news/crime-and-courts/3-people-charged-in-great-falls-for-childs-death.

56 Meridith Depping, "Several Agencies Investigating the Death of a Child, Three People Charged in Connection." (*KULR-8*, November 21, 2019), https://www.kulr8.com/regional/three-people-charged-in-connection-with-the-death-of-a/article_7434d733-232a-5484-b877-027ec8c67652.html.

appeared to be "brain matter" on the carpet. Another person who spent time at the house said they had shared several cases of beer and that the boy had been held under a cold shower as punishment for being awake at night.[57] There was blood in the bathtub as well. And Byington told police they had beaten the boy before with electrical cords.

The safeguards we have for other children in this country were not in place for Tony Renova. While it is not unheard of for adults with criminal records to regain custody of a child, state courts impose a high bar for violent felons to demonstrate their rehabilitation. It's hard to imagine that any non-Indian family would have met the threshold. As scandals like the regular placement of foster children with known sex offenders on North Dakota's Spirit Lake Reservation have shown, there is little oversight of tribal courts and child-welfare services.[58]

And the effects on Native children have been devastating. The rate of substantiated maltreatment for Indian or Alaska Native children is 15.2 per 1000, almost twice as high as for white or Hispanic children.[59] Rates of sexual abuse are also grossly disproportionate—a 2001 report found that, among Indian children, one in four girls and one in six boys is molested by the age of eighteen.[60] It's not surprising, then, that Indian kids are overrepresented in foster care at a rate 2.7 times greater than their proportion in the general population."[61]

The Adoption and Safe Families Act has exceptions if the state can show that a termination of parental rights is not in the child's

57 Traci Rosenbaum, "Three Arrested in Death of Five-Year-Old Child in Great Falls." (*Great Falls Tribune*, November 21, 2019), https://www.greatfallstribune.com/story/news/2019/11/21/three-arrested-death-5-year-old-child/4260198002.

58 Timothy Williams, "Officials See Child Welfare Dangers on a North Dakota Indian Reservation." (*The New York Times*, July 7, 2012, sec. U.S.), https://www.nytimes.com/2012/07/08/us/child-welfare-dangers-seen-on-spirit-lake-reservation.html.

59 "Child Maltreatment 2018," 31.

60 Judy L. Postmus, *Sexual Violence and Abuse: An Encyclopedia of Prevention, Impacts, and Recovery*. (Santa Barbara, CA: ABC-CLIO, 2013).

61 "Report on Disproportionality of Placements of Indian Children," *NICWA*. (National Indian Child Welfare Association, 2017), www.nicwa.org.

best interests, but ICWA has defined a child's best interests to be placement with an Indian family; so if one is not available, then a termination of parental rights is frequently not ordered.[62] The Multi-Ethnic Placement Act also does not apply to Indian children, for whom race is deemed more important than other factors.[63]

ICWA's provisions have superseded all of the other laws and regulations we have in place to ensure the safety of America's most vulnerable children. Judge Gray and far too many other judges, social workers, and activists are trying to make ICWA the template for how we treat black children. Having seen what has happened under this law, it strains the imagination to think that we would want to place any other group of children in this situation.

But these days, racial considerations seem to take precedence over everything else. It is doubtful whether the Multi-Ethnic Placement Act could pass Congress were it voted on today. The cultural forces seem to be aligning to make race-matching paramount rather than finding a safe, loving family for a child in need. A 2020 article in the *Guardian* described an organization called Race 2 Dinner, which organizes events at which women pay large sums to be berated for their white privilege by women who are racial minorities.[64]

Here was one scene:

> *Morgan Richards admits she recently did nothing when someone patronizingly commended her for adopting her two Black children, as though she had saved them. "What I went through to be a mother, I didn't care if they were black," she says, opening a window for [one of the nonwhite women] to challenge her: "So, you admit it is stooping low to adopt a Black child?" And Richards accepts that the undertone of her statement*

62 "Topic 19. Application of Other Federal Laws." (National Indian Law Library, accessed August 31, 2020), https://www.nicwa.org/wp-content/uploads/2017/09/Disproportionality-Table.pdf.

63 "Topic 19. Application of Other Federal Laws." (National Indian Law Library, accessed August 31, 2020), https://narf.org/nill/documents/icwa/faq/application2.html#Q11.

64 Poppy Noor, "Why Liberal White Women Pay a Lot of Money to Learn over Dinner How They're Racist." (*The Guardian*, February 3, 2020, sec. World news), https://www.theguardian.com/world/2020/feb/03/race-to-dinner-party-racism-women.

> *is racist.... "Well done for recognizing that," [another Black woman] says...."We are all part of the problem. We have to get comfortable with that to become part of the solution."*

And the solution, when it comes to taking care of children, presumably, is to stick to our own. This kind of sentiment is appalling, and the idea that otherwise educated women who claim to be enlightened and tolerant are indulging in this nonsense is infuriating and will only result in greater racial tension and fewer children growing up in loving homes. These are the changes happening at the 30,000-foot level of our culture, but the effects are trickling down.

After five-year-old Brandajah Smith shot herself, her father, Brandon Pierre, who did not have custody of the child, spoke to the *Times-Picayune*. Finally allowed access to records from his daughter's school, including all the times signs of abuse were reported to the authorities, he said: "To read all of that now, to hear all of those things, I choked up all over again. I can't believe this was going on, and I had no idea."

While state officials and advocates such as Casey Family Programs are talking up Judge Gray and her innovative jurisprudence inside of elite circles in Washington and academia, the people of Orleans Parish who vote for their family-court judges have received no notice of these changes. And because court records are kept sealed, it's impossible to evaluate the plan to leave more and more children in homes where parents are putting their children in danger. It is time to shed light on these policies and let the American people know that the child-welfare system has an agenda entirely unrelated to child welfare.

CHAPTER 5

THE PROBLEM IS NOT POVERTY, IT'S DRUGS

Headlines like "'Poor' Parenting—When Poverty Is Confused with Neglect"; "Live in a Poor Neighborhood? Better Be a Perfect Parent"; and "Poverty Isn't Neglect, But the State Took My Children Anyway" have become ubiquitous in the past couple of years.[1] Neglect is cited as a factor in most of the cases in which children are removed from their homes into foster care nationally. But advocates suggest that neglect is just a code word for poverty. And poverty is no reason to remove a child from his or her home. Instead of taking children into foster care, they ask, why don't we just give a family more money (or a housing voucher, food stamps, or free childcare) instead? If 63 percent of the cases of children being removed to foster care are because of neglect, as was

1 Sharkkarah Harrison, "'Poor Parenting—When Poverty Is Confused with Neglect." (*Rise*, November 15, 2017), http://www.risemagazine.org/2017/11/poor-parenting-when-poverty-is-confused-with-neglect/.; Emma S. Ketteringham, "Live in a Poor Neighborhood? Better Be a Perfect Parent." (*The New York Times*, August 22, 2017, sec. Opinion), https://www.nytimes.com/2017/08/22/opinion/poor-neighborhoods-black-parents-child-services.html.; and Elizabeth Brico, "Poverty Isn't Neglect, But the State Took My Children Anyway," Talk Poverty. (Center for American Progress, November 16, 2018), https://talkpoverty.org/2018/11/16/poverty-neglect-state-took-children.

the case in 2019, we could easily cut our foster-care numbers in half by just subsidizing poor families, right?

Some states like New York are even citing this argument in efforts to change the standards for investigating child maltreatment or determining whether adults should be placed on the state registry for child abusers.[2] As one state senator recently explained, "We are starting to talk seriously about how we can provide some level of support to families in crisis and actually respond to their needs as opposed to punishing them for being poor."

But the idea that poverty is the reason for children being taken into foster care is misguided and dangerous. A serious look at the data shows that the real driving force in child removals is not a lack of financial resources but rather our raging national drug crisis.

Sara Baker Pendleton used to wonder if poverty was the thing driving foster care. Sara, a stay-at-home mom, and her husband Nick, who works as a nurse practitioner in family medicine, have five kids (one biological, three adopted, and one foster). They have cared for twenty-nine foster children in their home in the suburbs of Biloxi over the past decade. There's a sign on the door informing visitors that there's a medically fragile child inside and not to come in if you've recently been sick. Inspirational quotations like "Be Brave" and "Move Mountains" line the walls. There are biblical verses too: "Be strong and courageous, do not be afraid or discouraged for the Lord your God will be with you wherever you go."

Sara remembers the first time she took in a foster child. It turned out to be one of the few cases where poverty—and a resulting lack of education about what to do with a child—brought the attention of a family to CPS. The family "lived out in the country in a trailer. They're the kind of people that will put Kool-Aid in a bottle [for a baby] and do not have the proper car seat." The baby was delivered to Sara in a light receiving blanket on a twenty-degree

---

2 Mitchell Fitzgerald, "Child Welfare Reforms Delivered to Cuomo in New York." (*The Imprint*, June 24, 2019), https://chronicleofsocialchange.org/news-2/child-welfare-historic-policy-new-york/35857.

December day at a gas station. The diaper bag, she recalls, smelled of smoke and was covered with roaches. Before she became a foster parent, Pendleton admits, "I would have been like, 'Those people don't need to have kids.'"

But the boy was reunified with his family a few months later. The mother and father took some parenting classes, and Sara and her husband have maintained contact with the family, helping where they can. "We see this child is thriving and growing and loved and cared for, even though, financially, he would have been better off with us. He would have had everything afforded to him, but he is where he belongs. He is a happy, healthy, thriving boy who makes straight As and plays football. He doesn't go to Disney World. He doesn't have camp and horseback riding and all these things. But he is just as happy as every single child in this house," she says, "because his parents' best is enough." And, she says, "he'll never have *that* question. He will never wonder why he wasn't good enough for somebody, why he wasn't fought for, why he couldn't be with the parents" who gave birth to him. "I've always said my kids would all be better off with Bill Gates, but that doesn't mean that he should be their parent," Sara says.

Unfortunately, it is Sara's adopted son, Jude, who is much more representative of the children who are taken into the foster-care system because of neglect. Having tested positive at birth for methamphetamines, cocaine, and opioids, Jude was taken in briefly by his grandmother, but she had serious medical needs and could not care for him in the long term. His mother was bipolar and did some time in jail. His father was off drugs briefly but relapsed. After two years, his parents relinquished their parental rights, in part so that CPS would close their case and allow them to bring Jude's newborn brother home from the hospital. (That child was subsequently removed and was being cared for by other elderly grandparents and an older half-sister. He has severe behavioral and emotional problems now.) Jude is seven, and recently, he came to Sara and asked, "Why didn't my mom quit doing drugs?" Sara says, "No matter how good his life is and how much he loves us—he's happy to be here, and I believe it. And I don't think he would want a different life than what he has—but that question is still there: Why didn't she just stop?"

Of the children that Sara and her husband Nick have cared for, almost every single one has had parents affected by chronic substance abuse, and their cases were classified as neglect. These are not children who were removed from their homes because their parents lived in trailers or fed their babies sugary drinks or didn't use car seats properly. They weren't removed because their parents couldn't afford warm clothes or heating or pest control. They were children who were born with multiple drugs in their system to parents who were incapable of caring for them. In the case of one, the child was simply abandoned at the hospital for several days. In another, the mother actually gave birth to the child while in prison. Judges offered the parents a variety of services to get their addiction under control. But more often than not, the parents failed to follow their case plan. Even if they got clean, they didn't stay clean. In addition to the children that Sara and Nick bring into their home, Sara regularly spends time in the NICU, holding and rocking a steady stream of babies who were born substance-exposed.

"The number one, predominant problem in all these cases we have had has been drugs. It's the number one thing," says Nick. And while he says that "there are some good caseworkers who shoot for shifting some of these people into drug court and therapies and in-patient stays…that system is limited in how many people they can take." Even the ones who do get into the programs that are appropriate, Nick says, "they're gonna be right back in that same situation again, most of them, just by statistics." He says, "I've got family members who are alcoholics and drug addicts, and they don't clean up after one stint in rehab."

While it is true that poverty is often correlated with allegations of child neglect—as well as *substantiated* allegations of child neglect—there is little evidence that poverty itself is actually the reason that children are investigated, let alone removed from their parents' homes. In her 2014 paper "The Effect of Material Hardship on Child Protective Service Involvement," Mi-Youn Yang of Louisiana State University notes that "even though [there is] a considerable body of research [that] shows a relationship between poverty and maltreatment, it is still unclear whether this relationship is causal and how poverty is associated with maltreatment."[3]

Similarly, in their 2015 paper, "Housing Insecurity, Maternal Stress and Child Maltreatment: An Application of the Family Stress Model," authors Emily J. Warren and Sarah A. Font note that while the "presence of housing insecurity as a risk factor for maltreatment is further evidence of the need for increased government investments in affordable housing," their "analytic strategy does not allow us to make any causal estimates regarding the association between housing insecurity, stress and maltreatment rates."[4]

In other words, while it may be true that poverty and homelessness happen in the same families as child neglect, there does not appear to be proof that the former precipitates the latter.

Indeed, there is clear evidence that child neglect is something entirely different and much worse than poverty. In an article called "'Just Poverty': Educational, social, and economic functioning among young adults exposed to childhood neglect, abuse, and poverty," in the 2020 *Journal of Child Abuse and Neglect*, Sarah A. Font and Kathryn Maguire-Jack of the University of Michigan looked at outcomes for almost 30,000 individuals born between 1993 and 1996 in Milwaukee County, Wisconsin. They compared "individuals with CPS-investigated neglect, abuse, or both abuse and neglect in early childhood or adolescence to those who experienced poverty but not CPS involvement" and then "calculated cumulative

3 Mi-Youn Yang, "The Effect of Material Hardship on Child Protective Service Involvement." (*Child Abuse & Neglect* 41, March 2015), 113–25, https://doi.org/10.1016/j.chiabu.2014.05.009.

4 Emily J. Warren and Sarah A. Font, "Housing Insecurity, Maternal Stress, and Child Maltreatment: An Application of the Family Stress Model." (*Social Service Review* 89, no. 1, March 2015): 9–39, https://doi.org/10.1086/680043.

measures of poverty duration and poverty depth between ages 0 and 16 for the full sample using public benefit records."[5]

They found that "outcomes among children with alleged or confirmed neglect were statistically significantly worse in all domains than impoverished children without maltreatment allegations, and similar to children with alleged or confirmed abuse. The authors looked at the likelihood of incarceration, teen parenthood, high-school graduation, employment, and the use of public assistance and found that "CPS allegations of neglect are distinct from poverty and an important risk factor for adverse outcomes in adulthood."

Take, for instance, the percentage of these kids who graduate high school by age twenty. Of kids with parents who received food assistance, 77.53 percent graduated compared with 63.59 percent whose parents were alleged to have neglected them, or 59.10 percent of those who have been alleged to have abused and neglected them.[6]

Or what about the percentage of these kids who ended up in state prison by the age of twenty? Only 1.81 percent of kids who were on food stamps did time in state prison before the age of twenty compared with 2.92 percent (or more than half again as many) of those whose parents were investigated for abuse, 3.92 percent (or more than twice as many) of those whose parents were investigated for neglect, and 4.85 percent (or more than two-and-a-half times as many) of those who were investigated for abuse and neglect.[7]

Finally, 12.85 percent of those who grew up with poverty experienced teen pregnancy. That number jumped to 18.10 percent for those who experienced alleged neglect, 23.49 percent for those who experienced alleged neglect and abuse, and 15.99 percent for those who experienced alleged abuse alone.[8] There

---

5 Sarah A. Font and Kathryn Maguire-Jack, "It's Not 'Just Poverty': Educational, Social, and Economic Functioning among Young Adults Exposed to Childhood Neglect, Abuse, and Poverty." (*Child Abuse & Neglect* 101, March 2020), 104356, https://doi.org/10.1086/680043.

6 Font and Maguire-Jack, "It's Not 'Just Poverty.'"

7 Font and Maguire-Jack, "It's Not 'Just Poverty.'"

8 Font and Maguire-Jack, "It's Not 'Just Poverty.'"

were also statistically significant differences in employment and average earnings.

Moreover, the authors also report that their findings "challenge the perception that neglect is less harmful than abuse. Prior researchers have speculated that this perception may be due to the consequences of abuse being more immediately observable than the consequences of neglect.[9] Nevertheless, the divergence in outcomes for neglected youth and impoverished nonneglected youth is significant, at least by early adulthood. Given the prevalence of neglect and the increased risk of adverse outcomes associated with neglect, targeted efforts to prevent and treat the effects of neglect warrant greater priority."[10]

Advocates argue that if we only offered parents more services in the form of housing, food, and childcare subsidies—programs that supposedly alleviate poverty—these parents might never be investigated by CPS in the first place, let alone suffer the trauma of family separation. We can dispute the size of the safety net in this country, but there is no doubt that families living in poverty have access to food stamps, housing vouchers, programs to heat their homes, and medical care. Indeed, as economist Angela Rashidi notes, the U.S. "spends more on children per capita than many other developed countries and falls in the middle when it comes to spending as a percent of gross domestic product (GDP) when considering three major categories of spending, including cash support/tax breaks for families, education, and health."[11] Moreover, there has been a "seven-fold increase in federal spending on children broadly from 1960–2018, and a 17-fold increase in spending on poor children through programs like Medicaid, refundable tax credits, and the

9 Howard Dubowitz, "Understanding and Addressing the 'Neglect of Neglect:' Digging into the Molehill." (APA PsycNet, 2007), https://psycnet.apa.org/record/2007-11600-002.

10 Font and Maguire-Jack, "It's Not 'Just Poverty.'"

11 Angela Rachidi, "American Exceptionalism Five Ways Government Spending on Low Income Children and Child Poverty Is Misunderstood." (American Enterprise Institute, November 2019), https://www.aei.org/wp-content/uploads/2019/11/American-Exceptionalism-Five-Ways-Government-Spending-on-Low-Income-Children-and-Child-Poverty-Is-Misunderstood-1.pdf.

Supplemental Nutrition Assistance Program (SNAP)" even as the number of children in foster care has risen and fallen by more than 100,000. The problem is not that services to help children who are poor do not exist; rather, it's that parents are not sober enough to access them. Substance abuse is at the heart of a large portion of neglect cases.

Substance abuse was listed in 36 percent of the removals to foster care nationwide.[12] Another 5 percent listed alcohol abuse. And 14 percent cited a caretaker's "inability to cope," which is often a sign of substance abuse and/or mental-health issues. These numbers likely still undercount substance abuse, since children often are removed for multiple reasons, and caseworkers who remove them for reasons of, say, physical abuse but then later find evidence of substance abuse in the home do not go back and amend their reports accordingly.

Even when children are removed to live with a relative—a stable grandparent—the results of parental substance abuse can still be emotionally devastating. A recent paper by three economists at Notre Dame concluded that "if drug abuse had remained at 1996 levels, 1.5 million fewer children aged 0–16 would have lived away from a parent in 2015."[13]

At a meeting in the fall of 2019, sponsored by the Department of Health and Human Services and the Institute for Research on Poverty at the University of Wisconsin, experts gathered to discuss the opioid crisis and its effect on child welfare. Researchers presented this chart.[14] It probably is one of the most absurdly uninformative and inaccurate charts ever produced.

---

12 Kristin Sepulveda and Sarah Catherine Williams, "One in Three Children Entered Foster Care in 2017 Because of Parental Drug Abuse." (*Child Trends*, February 25, 2019), https://www.childtrends.org/blog/one-in-three-children-entered-foster-care-in-fy-2017-because-of-parental-drug-abuse.

13 Kasey Buckles et al., "The Drug Crisis and the Living Arrangements of Children," *The National Bureau of Economic Research*. (National Bureau of Economic Research, July 2020), https://www.nber.org/papers/w27633.pdf.

14 Ken DeCerchio, "Human Services and the Opioid Crisis." (Presentation, Annual Poverty Research and Policy Forum, Washington, DC, September 17, 2019).

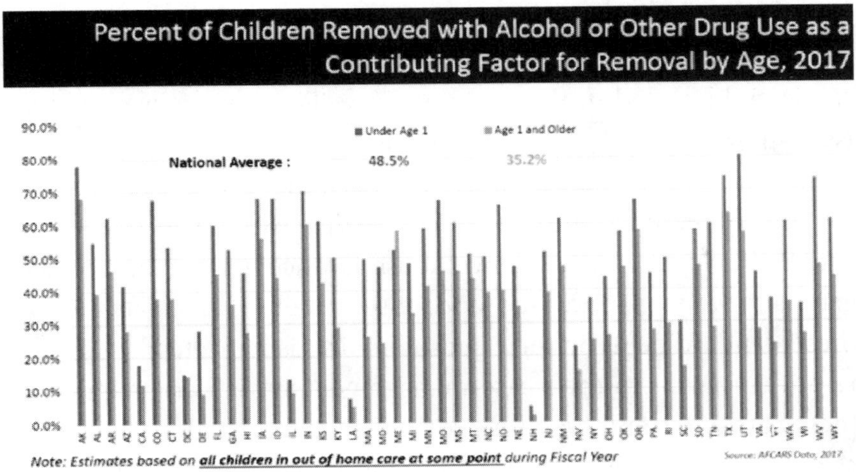

The federal government asks states to hand over data on the number of removals that involve substance abuse. But as this chart suggests, the feds are not providing much guidance on how those numbers are calculated. Look at New Hampshire, for example. It has one of lowest rates of removal as a result of substance abuse, but its overdose rate at 37 per 100,000 is almost twice the national average of 21.7.[15] Or what about Washington, DC, whose percentage of children removed with drug or alcohol use as a factor is around 15 percent, but whose overdose rate is 44 per 100,000.[16] The researchers at the conference conceded that this chart (and these numbers) is next to useless. In states across the country, they acknowledged that the number of cases of removal that involve substance abuse is well over 80 percent.

Unfortunately, we don't have very good data on the extent to which substance abuse is a factor in both allegations of and substantiated instances of child maltreatment. We do know that since 2000, the percentage of cases nationally in which a child has been removed to foster care and cases in which substance abuse was a

15 Associated Press, "Editorials from Around New York." *US News & World Report* (October 23, 2019), https://www.usnews.com/news/best-states/new-york/articles/2019-10-23/editorials-from-around-new-york.

16 Associated Press, "Editorials."

factor has been growing almost every year.[17] In interviews I've conducted with foster parents across the country, few can think of a single child placed in their home where illegal drugs were *not* an issue in the removal.

But in many instances, unless the substance abuse is apparent at the time of removal (the worker sees evidence in the home), it's not listed. If evidence of substance abuse is uncovered later, workers generally won't go back and update the record. How states utilize these standard fields on their questionnaires is impacted by how the removal reasons in their case-management system are mapped to these categories and how caseworkers are instructed to determine removal reasons for a child. Policy and practice vary significantly by state and even among jurisdictions within states. And when state child-welfare leadership changes, the policies about how to count substance abuse can change too.

To understand just how arbitrary this data becomes, let's take a deeper dive into Arizona, where state workers list "neglect" as the reason for child removal in 84 percent of cases, significantly higher than the 62 percent national rate.[18] But they list "caretaker inability to cope" in less than 1 percent of the cases compared with 14 percent nationwide. One might speculate that Arizona investigators are using neglect as a catch-all that includes a parent's inability to cope.

It is also noteworthy that Arizona's investigators list parental substance abuse as a factor in only 30 percent of the cases compared with 39 percent nationally.[19] Given that the state has a rate of 22.2 overdose deaths per thousand people, which is higher than the national average, it seems strange that the state's foster care cases seem significantly less likely to involve drug use than the national average.

---

17 Angélica Meinhofer and Yohanis Angleró-Díaz, "Trends in Foster Care Entry Among Children Removed from Their Homes Because of Parental Drug Use, 2000 to 2017." (*JAMA Pediatrics* 173, no. 9, July 15, 2019), https://doi.org/10.1001/jamapediatrics.2019.1738.

18 Data Advocacy. "Why Do Children Enter Out-of-Home Care?" (Presentation, Casey Family Programs, July 19, 2019).

19 Ibid.

Looking at the patterns over time, Arizona's reports have been all over the place. In 2000, drug abuse was a factor in 19 percent of the cases and alcohol abuse in 1 percent of the cases.[20] In 2005 and 2006, it was listed in almost none of the cases. In 2010, drug abuse was listed in 34 percent of the cases, and alcohol abuse was listed in 4 percent of the cases. And then it was back to 6 percent for parent drug abuse in 2013 and 0 percent for alcohol abuse. It seems unlikely that these reflect how often substance abuse was a problem in these families. Rather, these numbers suggest an agency that has significantly altered the way it tells workers to report substance abuse in child-welfare cases. In the past three years of reporting, there has been some consistency, but with another turnover in the leadership of Arizona's child-welfare agency, it hardly would be surprising if it changed again.

A finding of neglect against a parent is not something to be taken lightly. When the general public thinks about neglect, they assume it is something clearly less dangerous than physical or sexual abuse. But when parents' judgment is impaired, things can go drastically wrong, especially for young children. Neglect can include leaving children in the care of known abusers, giving children illegal drugs, subjecting them to harsh corporal punishment, and failing to provide them with medical care. Neglect is often be more dangerous than physical abuse. It can mean that the home doesn't have heat or running water, for instance, and that a parent lacks the wherewithal to report the problem or ask for help. Richard Gelles told me that he and most other experts and child-welfare workers had long assumed that there would be "a progression of physical violence up to a fatal incident. That isn't the case. There are dysfunctions in the family that come to public attention," but they sometimes stop short of abuse.

Once they started to look at the data, Gelles says, "what you find is there are a series of neglect reports—four, five, six neglect reports—that predate a fatality." Indeed, if you look at child-mal-

---

20 Ibid.

treatment fatalities—kids who die because the adults in their lives did something to them or failed to do something for them—most occur because of neglect. In 2017, more than three-quarters of them resulted from neglect or neglect in combination with other factors.[21] Only 42 percent occurred as a result of abuse or abuse in combination with another factor. Most tragically, 78 percent involved children three or younger.

Especially when it comes to small children, we know that consistent supervision is required. It is exhausting for even a perfectly sober parent to make sure a toddler does not put small objects in his mouth, run out the front door into traffic, touch a hot stove, go under water in the bathtub, or hit her head on the corner of a sharp coffee table. Imagine how much harder it is to accomplish all this while using any kind of mind-altering substance.

If we want the public to have a better understanding of why children are being taken out of a parent's home, it actually might be useful to eliminate the category of neglect altogether and force caseworkers to choose a clearer reason or several—substance abuse, mental illness, lack of running water, etc.—for removing a child. Then we might be less likely to downplay the seriousness of the problems behind neglect and start to grapple with the ways in which substance abuse is destroying vulnerable families.

But once we understand just how prevalent the drug crisis is in child welfare, that still leaves the question of how to handle it. Generally, our doctors, politicians, policymakers, and even the general public recognize that we don't have any fool-proof ways of combating addiction. As the website of the National Institute of Drug Abuse, a division of the National Institutes of Health, notes, "Addiction is a complex but treatable disease that affects brain function and behavior. Drugs of abuse alter the brain's structure and function, resulting in changes that persist long after drug use has

---

21 "Child Abuse and Neglect Fatalities 2017: Statistics and Interventions." (*Child Welfare Information Gateway*, U.S. Department of Health and Human Services, Children's Bureau, March 2019), https://www.childwelfare.gov/pubpdfs/fatality.pdf.

ceased. This may explain why drug abusers are at risk for relapse even after long periods of abstinence and despite the potentially devastating consequences."[22]

It's not simply that it often takes many tries for a person to get clean. It's also that what works for one person may not work for another. And drug addiction often co-occurs with mental illness, making treatment more complicated. Despite advances that have been made in medically assisted treatment in recent years, addiction remains distressingly hard to solve. Somewhere between 40 and 60 percent of patients who complete an addiction treatment program end up relapsing.[23]

Two reports from the Department of Health and Human Services shed light on the problem.[24] It may seem obvious, but research finds definitively that rates of overdose deaths and drug-related hospitalizations have increased child-welfare caseloads. The authors find that a 10 percent increase in drug-related hospitalizations in a particular geographic area is correlated with a 3.3 percent increase in foster-care entry rates. While most middle- and upper-class Americans likely would be able to find a family member or friend to take in a child in case they were hospitalized, those most affected by drug abuse often lack social networks, and their kids are much more likely to end up being cared for by a stranger.

In the context of child welfare, the statistics on drug addiction and recovery are often ignored. Family-court judges regularly order parents to enter some kind of treatment program—anything from a meeting a couple of times a week to a month-long residential program. And the assumption is that once that program is completed,

---

22 "Principles of Effective Treatment," National Institute on Drug Abuse, accessed August 31, 2020, https://www.drugabuse.gov/publications/principles-drug-addiction-treatment-research-based-guide-third-edition/principles-effective-treatment.

23 "How Effective Is Drug Addiction Treatment?" National Institute on Drug Abuse, accessed August 31, 2020, https://www.drugabuse.gov/publications/principles-drug-addiction-treatment-research-based-guide-third-edition/frequently-asked-questions/how-effective-drug-addiction-treatment.

24 "Child Welfare and Substance Use," ASPE. (U.S. Department of Health and Human Services, n.d.), https://aspe.hhs.gov/child-welfare-and-substance-use.

children will be reunified with their parents. The number of times they have relapsed in the past or the likelihood of relapse in the future often goes unconsidered.

How many chances do parents get? Let's take the case of Kara, whom I met at the Village Church in South Lebanon, Ohio, outside of Cincinnati. Her story is difficult to hear and frustrating even in retrospect. Kara started smoking pot and drinking before she was sixteen. Her father died when she was ten, and she recalled a line of strange men coming in and out of her house. She was a "social user" of cocaine and acid into her twenties. But when her oldest son, Marcus, was born in 2007, she was prescribed Vicodin and Percocet. When those ran out, she became addicted to heroin. When her oldest was a year-and-a-half old, she was found guilty of theft and forgery. She spent 180 days at the Monday Program, a rehab program run by the Ohio Department of Corrections. She stayed clean for almost two years and then moved back home. "And then," she reports, "it just spiraled out of control."

She went back to rehab, and then during a brief stint where Marcus's father was home from prison, Kara got pregnant again. She went off of drugs when she was pregnant with Jade and for a year after that. At that point, she started buying Suboxone off the street. "At least I wasn't doing heroin," she told me. A year later, she was pregnant with Will. But unlike with the other two, she didn't get off drugs and didn't go in for any prenatal care. "I lied to everybody. I made people think I was just taking Subutex [a drug used to wean people off of opioids], but I was getting high. You could go to any street corner in Dayton or Cincinnati and get drugs." Someone called CPS. She acknowledges lying to CPS about her drug use, about having a job, about her car breaking down. "They were not good lies at all."

By the time she went into labor with Will, CPS would not let her take the baby home. Her mother now had custody of her three children, but Kara was living with her mother, so it was not really much different. There was a protection order against her boyfriend, but he wasn't complying with it. She took a garbage bag and left home when Will was two months old. She has no recollection of him as a baby. "I don't know when he started crawling. I don't know when he started walking. I didn't know any of that about my third child because I was an addict."

Will was six months old when she got pregnant with Max. Kara's fourth child was the one she says she never talked about. She and her boyfriend were living on the street in a town outside of Cincinnati, shooting heroin daily. "We never felt my belly. We didn't talk about what he would look like or what we would name him," Kara recalls. "It's not that it wasn't there, but we just knew that this baby was not going to be ours."

When she went into labor, a friend came and picked her up and took her to the hospital. Her boyfriend was in prison by that point. There was cocaine and heroin in her system when Max was born. And he was born addicted too.

In a tragic coincidence, a couple who was waiting to adopt another infant found out that the mother had committed suicide, killing herself and the baby. Kara's friend contacted her pastor about Kara's situation, and the pastor contacted other pastors, who eventually told Kara about this couple. They agreed to adopt Max.

After leaving the hospital, Kara started using again immediately. "They discharged me, and I went out and got high." For the next two months, she says, "I went harder than ever." Max's father, Richard, got out of prison, and while he was at work, she would steal or do anything she could to get drugs. She was in a store with her mother and three kids when she stole someone's purse. On the run from the police, she and Richard both had warrants out for their arrest. He went to prison for seventy days and got out and then proceeded five weeks later to die of a heroin overdose. Kara got a furlough to go to his funeral and then went to rehab for 152 days.

The judge let her move back in with her mother and her children again, this time wearing an ankle monitor, and two years later she got custody back. She finally realized: "I can't let my mom raise my kids. I can't let her bury me." She has gotten her mother to trust her again. Max is being raised by his adopted parents, but as long as Kara stays sober, she can continue to see him. She goes to a Celebrate Recovery program at the Village Church, and her kids attend a program there at the same time. She has a good support system and has had custody of her other three children for the past two years. She doesn't like to tell people that she had her kids taken away from her or that one was adopted. "I wouldn't even say that's the cards that were dealt to me. That's just how I play them."

Getting clean is something she says she had to do. "Grandma is getting old. Richard is in the grave. David [the father of her oldest child] is in a county jail.... Who else do the kids have?"

The end of Kara's story might seem like a happy one. And one can only hope that she stays on this path. But for almost a decade, she was incapable of caring for her kids, going in and out of their lives, exposing them to men who were in and out of prison, leaving them with her mother, who was not well and had difficulty caring for them, and even engaging in criminal activities while they were with her. Her older three children have never known from one year to the next, or even one day to the next, whether there will be a safe place for them to live, whether their mother will be around, and if she is around, whether she will be sober enough to understand what's going on in their lives. She has been gone or effectively gone during the formative years of brain development and attachment. Kara presents her story as one of success, but frankly, it seems more like the failure of a child-protection system. Her children represent years of caseworkers and judges making decisions to give Kara one chance after another, with little regard for the effect it will have on them.

One reason for this public-policy cognitive dissonance is that we fear a repeat of child-welfare officials' response to the crack epidemic of the '80s and '90s, as reflected in the numbers of kids in foster care. That total reached 567,000 in 1990, during the crack scourge.[25] And while it has climbed significantly during the opioid

25 "Foster Care." (*Child Trends,* May 24, 2018), https://www.childtrends.org/indicators/foster-care.

crisis, it still is only more than 100,000 below that high (even as the population of children under eighteen rose by 15 percent between 1990 and 2018).[26]

Martha Grace, retired chief justice of the Massachusetts Trial Court's Juvenile Department, remembers that during the '90s, "there was supposed to be a nexus between crack cocaine babies and 'super-predators.'" The implication was that social workers should remove these children from their homes before they could become part of a growing wave of violent crime. Some crack-addicted mothers did indeed give birth to babies with severe neurological and organ damage. Such examples were sensationalized in the press, but by the 1990s, researchers became aware of the difficulties in interpreting the effects of crack on fetal development. Multiple factors affected the fetuses and young children of women who used crack, including consumption of alcohol and cigarettes, poor prenatal care, and inadequate nutrition. Isolating these effects from the influence of cocaine was impossible among the relatively small groups of women examined, who self-reported their drug usage, offering low confidence in their accuracy.

Almost all reports were retrospective, meaning that only the worst cases came to attention; many "crack babies" were developmentally normal, though they were born in withdrawal from the drug. Ideally, researchers would have data on a group of pregnant women followed over several months. In a now-classic 1992 article in the *Journal of the American Medical Association*, Yale child psychiatrist Linda Mayes outlined a larger array of interpretive complexities and concluded that there was "an apparent rush to judgment about the extent and permanency of specific effects of intrauterine cocaine exposure on newborns."[27] All of these factors have influenced the way that social workers today approach families with substance-abuse issues.

26 "Foster Care," The Annie E. Casey Foundation. (The Annie E. Casey Foundation, n.d.), https://www.aecf.org/topics/foster-care?start=440.

27 Linda C. Mayes, "The Problem of Prenatal Cocaine Exposure." (*JAMA* 267, no. 3, January 15, 1992), 406, https://doi.org/10.1001/jama.1992.03480030084043.

But there is reason to worry that our child-welfare investigators have swung too far in the other direction. Melinda Gushwa of the Simmons College School of Social Work is often asked to analyze the reports of social workers who were involved in child-fatality cases. Her research shows that child-welfare workers are not paying enough attention to parental substance abuse. "The number one reason kids die is because of neglect. It's because the parents are impaired and not providing adequate supervision." Looking at the case notes after a fatality, Gushwa says, she always sees some variation of "child was happy, healthy and well cared for." But the caseworker is not asking questions about the parents' drug use or when they last met with a counselor or went to a meeting. And the agencies that are supposed to be providing treatment do little follow-up. "My research has shown most CPS workers say a death wasn't preventable," explains Gushwa. "But when you go back, you can see all these red flags."

Many investigators are overlooking those red flags, either intentionally or not. It's helpful to remember that even if they emerged from the womb without severe problems, many children of crack-addicted parents did experience abuse at the hands of their parents. Douglas Besharov, the first director of the U.S. National Center on Child Abuse and Neglect, says that "there was a consensus that crack made many users more violent." Besharov, who also served on the child-fatality review board in New York City during the epidemic, adds that the drug "created really violent nasty behavior" among many parents. "In hindsight," Besharov says, "it's easy to say it wasn't that bad. There's a lot of reinventing history."

Gushwa notes that the long-term prospects for children in homes where their primary caretaker is abusing drugs or has a history of doing so should make caseworkers pause more often. "What the research shows on substance use is that [addiction treatment] often doesn't take the first, second, or third time. It takes a lot of time to remain sober. And it's impossible for many to retain sobriety." While drug use may not be "prima facie evidence of child neglect," says Besharov, "it's not neutral information." Even if babies born exposed to drugs in utero do not have physical birth defects, they are still being sent home with parents who may not be capable of caring for them. These children are not getting the kind of nurturing love essential to proper social and intellectual development. Even worse, their parents may not be paying attention to their safety and well-being. In our quest to make up for past mistakes, we can't ignore these facts.

It is also worth noting that our attitudes toward drug use and drug legalization may be influencing how we (the public, caseworkers, and even judges) see drug use by parents. According to a 2019 survey sponsored by the Cato Institute and conducted by Gallup, "A majority (55 percent) of Americans favor recategorizing drug offenses from felonies to civil offenses so that the offenses would be treated as minor traffic violations rather than crimes."[28] How are these attitudes trickling down into the world of child welfare? First, it may be that folks in our child-welfare system increasingly see addiction as a "disease," that is, that substance abuse is to some extent outside the control of the user.

But that is not entirely true. As my AEI colleague Sally Satel has written, "Addiction is behavior: the persistent seeking and using of drugs despite negative consequences."[29] While she acknowledges that "changes in the brains of addicts make it difficult to resist using…a large majority quit voluntarily and permanently without treatment when they fully recognize the alternatives and the negative consequences of using drugs. By contrast, Alzheimer's disease progresses no matter what."

Unfortunately, though, the parents in the child-welfare system are among those least likely to quit voluntarily. As Satel has written,

---

28 Emily Ekins, "Poll: 55 percent of Americans Favor Decriminalizing Drugs," Cato Institute. (Cato Institute, October 2, 2019), https://www.cato.org/blog/55-americans-favor-decriminalizing-drugs.

29 Stephen J. Morse and Sally Satel, "Addiction Shouldn't Excuse Criminal Acts." (*Wall Street Journal*. October 1, 2017, sec. Opinion), https://www.wsj.com/articles/addiction-shouldnt-excuse-criminal-acts-1506889104.

"While anyone can theoretically become an addict, it is more likely the fate of some, among them women sexually abused as children; truant and aggressive young men; children of addicts; people with diagnosed depression and bipolar illness; and groups including American Indians and poor people."[30] These are exactly the parents who are caught up in the child-welfare system.

The other reason that people might want to recategorize drug offenses is that they are increasingly seen as "victimless" crimes. During one of the Democratic primary debates, then-candidate Joe Biden said that "nobody should be in jail for a drug problem" and that drug abusers should instead be in rehabilitation centers.[31] Whether or not this is true, parental drug abuse is not victimless.

It is incredible to hear, as I have, caseworkers talk about how parents with substance-abuse problems might simply drop off a child with another relative or caregiver while they get high for a few hours and then come back to pick him up afterward. In reality, mothers with addiction problems are leaving their children in the middle of the night to score drugs or are allowing dangerous men to live in their homes in order to get access to drugs.

There are obvious reasons to be patient with the parents of these children. Many drug abusers are poor, undereducated, and socially isolated. Many of them have spent time in the foster-care system themselves. And ideally, society would want children to be able to stay with their biological parents rather than placing them with strangers. But in designing a new national strategy for combating drug abuse, our compassion for parents cannot come at the expense of children. Child-welfare agencies and family courts will have to reorient themselves in order to serve the children's needs first.

30 Sally Satel, "Addiction Doesn't Discriminate? Wrong." (*The New York Times*, September 1, 2008, sec. Health), https://www.nytimes.com/2008/09/02/health/26essa.html.

31 Caitlin Oprysko, "Biden: 'Nobody Should Be in Jail for a Nonviolent Crime.'" (*MSN*, September 13, 2019), https://www.msn.com/en-us/news/politics/biden-nobody-should-be-in-jail-for-a-nonviolent-crime/ar-AAHdk3i.

CHAPTER 6

SEARCHING FOR JUSTICE IN FAMILY COURT

Justin started dating Adam shortly after he moved to Phoenix in 2004. Justin's mother actually dropped by her son's house unannounced during their second date and asked Adam to join the whole family on a planned trip to the lake the following day. Other suitors might have been scared off by the presumptiveness, but Adam was gung-ho. By 2005, the men had bought a house together and, in 2006, tied the knot—right after gay marriage was legalized in the state. And though it was many years before they were ready to have children of their own, this tendency to embrace family for all its intrusions has always been at the core of their relationship.

Justin knew from the age of six or seven that he wanted to be a dad someday. He has a gentle, patient manner—which helps in his work as a high-school counselor. At one point, he took a job on a reservation in Arizona. Witnessing the life-dictating setbacks children inherit from their parents, he thought about how much difference a person of good will can make. And it made him want to be a foster parent. The couple completed their training in July 2016 and made clear to the agency that they were interested in fostering to adopt. They had no idea the kind of ordeal they were signing up for. Like so many foster parents, it has made them wonder how the hell we ended up with the family court system we have and why no one can or will fix it.

In September of that year, Justin was contacted by DCS about two brothers, Alexander (age two) and Leo (age one). The call came at 6:30 p.m., and the couple ran to Target and frantically started looking for clothes, diapers, formula, pacifiers, and anything else they could think of. (They called their respective mothers for help.) By 7:30 p.m., they were in the checkout line, and the caseworker called to say he was at the house with the boys.

Their daycare had reported bruises and burns on Alexander, particularly around his crotch. From what Justin and Adam could tell, the boys were being abused by their mother's boyfriend, Timothy. The mother, Francine, told DCS the burns were from a cigarette lighter. Francine "is not the one that causes the harm," says Adam. "She just allows other people to harm her and her children."

Alexander and Leo have two different fathers, neither of whom is Timothy. A suspected gang member, Timothy is currently in prison. The man whom Francine is living with now is under a court order that prevents him from seeing his own child without supervision. That child's mother accused him of beating her to the point where she lost a child she was pregnant with.

Amazingly, though, after almost three years of living with Justin and Adam, Alexander and his sister Ruby (who was born in December 2016 and whose father is someone else entirely) are living with Francine and this man, thanks to the decisions of the local family court. Francine has shown no signs of changing her ways—a confidential psychologist evaluation given to them by a caseworker even concluded that she would never be fit to be a parent. But a judge came to a different conclusion. After an unimaginable odyssey through the family-court system, Alexander has wound up in a home that has been proven unsafe; he has been permanently separated from his brother and best friend; and Justin and Adam, the only stable parents he has ever known, are heartbroken and filled with worry.

Sadly, their situation is not uncommon. Family courts are stretched thin, it's true, but they are also making irrational decisions with the information and resources they have. They let cases with young children drag on for years at a time. They treat foster parents—even those who care for children for long periods—as glorified babysitters. They keep these caretakers in the dark about children's needs and what's going on with their biological parents and rarely ask for foster parents' input when it comes to determining the best interests of a child. If we want to fix the child-welfare system, family court has to change.

The boys took to Justin and Adam right away, even "clinging" to them and throwing tantrums when they had to leave. Over time, they began to flourish. By the time he left, Adam describes how Alexander "would have met you at the front door and he would have said 'Hi,' and been like, 'Let me show you my room.' He would have taken you by the hand and showed you to his room and gave you a tour of the whole house." Adam remembers, "He was just this little man. He wanted everyone to feel welcome. He'd be like, 'Poppy, do you want my last piece of candy?'"

And as soon as Justin and Adam found out that Francine was pregnant, the men offered to foster Ruby, with the intention of adopting her as well, even officially changing the number of kids they were licensed for from two to three. For reasons they still don't understand, though, Ruby was sent to a different foster home, one not interested in a permanent placement. The caseworker said she had forgotten that they had volunteered, and the court approved a placement with a different foster mother. Ten months later, she was placed in a different foster home, again despite the fact that Justin and Adam had offered to care for her.

When the children were first removed from Francine's home, a caseworker reached out to Leo's father, Yolando, to ask him if he wanted to take custody. He was worried because he works for a moving company and is out of state a lot and not financially secure. But he had been sending Francine money to support Leo. In January 2017, the court changed Leo's case plan to reunification. Yolando began visits with the boy and took custody of him in July 2017. But, at Leo's request, Adam and Justin have been acting as co-parents since then, taking the boy on weekends.

Yolando had no experience caring for children and says, "I definitely think Justin and Adam bring a lot more than what I can provide or do for him." And it's not just a financial consideration. "I know they care for him and love him. I just want him to have the best.... They always have him around a lot of people, kids, and adults." Yolando is particularly happy that Justin and Adam's extended families have become family for Leo too. Justin's mother and sister would see the boys about once a week, taking them for pizza or on special trips sometimes to the aquarium or the train park in Scottsdale.

While Leo was headed toward reunification, the court had identified Adam and Justin as Alexander's "adoption placement" as early as April 2017. Francine was assigned a new caseworker who wanted to give her another chance, but she failed to meet any benchmarks for success. Indeed, in July 2017, the court seemed to have lost track of Francine altogether, with a court notice being "returned to sender."

During the remainder of 2017 and all of 2018, supervised visits during school hours continued, but they were not consistent, and the frequent cancellations changed Alexander's behavior for the worse, according to his preschool teacher. Francine also told Justin and Adam that they had to take Leo somewhere else when she dropped off Alexander at their house because she didn't want to have to see her other son. Caseworkers from the Department of Children's Services supported this request.

Ruby, meanwhile, was moved from one foster home to another in October 2017. Torrie, a foster mother who has older children, had begun noticing developmental delays right away and made appointments with doctors and specialists to find out what was wrong. At ten months, she couldn't sit upright or roll over on her own. "Nobody thought it was weird that she had no self-soothing skills," says Torrie. If she wasn't in Torrie's arms, she would scream until someone held her. The doctors asked her to time how long—most babies peter out after a few minutes. After fifty-one minutes of letting Ruby cry, Torrie couldn't take it anymore.

Francine did not seem interested in the problems. A neurologist told Torrie that they needed to do an MRI to determine why Ruby's face was sagging on the left side and why her tongue seemed to be hanging out, but Francine refused to give permission. She said there was nothing wrong, despite pleas from doctors and therapists. Finally, the day a caseworker was scheduled to go before a judge to force her hand, Francine relented. Ruby was diagnosed with cerebral palsy, caused by brain hemorrhaging either during pregnancy or childbirth.

One aspect of Francine's case plan was to acknowledge and understand her daughter's medical problems. (For those who continue to believe that neglect is just about poverty, these kinds of case plans should be a wake-up call. Parents who are simply poor do not deny their children's health problems or stand in the way when doctors want to treat them.) Torrie reported that Francine did start showing up to some of the medical appointments, but when she did, she was distracted, talking on the phone to her boyfriend. Meanwhile, Francine continued to post on Facebook—she is very active with an anti-CPS group—about how she didn't think there was anything medically wrong with her daughter.

For most of 2017 and all of 2018, things remained unchanged: Alexander was thriving, and Ruby was finally getting the medical care she needed; Francine was in and out of the picture. According to the person in charge of Alexander's developmental day-care center, Alexander went from a nonverbal child prone to outbursts for no discernable reason to one who mastered expression and who made friends in class. During those months, according to Justin, there were five different severance hearings scheduled, and each one was postponed. At one point, the court couldn't make contact with Francine's psychiatrist. On another occasion, a different witness was sick. They went more than eight months between seeing the judge.

In December 2018, there was another hearing, after which the case plan read: "Permanency goal: Adoption by foster parent" for both Alexander and Ruby. Francine, the court found, "is highly resistant combative, which is concerning as [she] may not understand the safety concerns that brought Alexander and Ruby into DCS care."

By 2019, there had been eight different case managers for Alexander, and in March 2019, there was a new judge assigned to the case who was not familiar with any of the details. During that hearing Justin and Adam were told that Ruby's and Alexander's case plan was going to change to reunification.

The couple was blindsided. So was Torrie. So was Alexander's guardian ad litem, who, before leaving for another job, advised Justin and Adam to get a lawyer. They filed a petition to intervene in the case, which meant that their lawyer could call witnesses and present evidence, something that foster parents in many states cannot do. After having cared for Alexander for almost three years by this point and having watched Francine's behavior, they couldn't imagine why the court was going to pull him away now.

To be reunified with her children, Francine was required, among other things, to show she was "able to identify appropriate adults to have around Alexander and Ruby" and that she had learned to "put her children's interests above her own." But how was living with a man who was not allowed to see his own child evidence that she had learned this? And what should we make of the fact that Francine completely cut Leo out of her life and told DCS she didn't want to have to see him? Justin and Adam were told that the way a parent treats one child has nothing to do with how they treat another one.

The judge told Justin and Adam that they are "just foster parents." The lawyer for the state "painted us as these crazy foster parents that just can't let go, that we're just too attached, and that we were causing more trauma" for the kids, according to Adam. But Justin and Adam's goal wasn't to keep kids away from parents who could care for them. They wanted to have Yolando testify about how the men had supported Leo's reunification and how helpful they have been to him, but the judge determined that wasn't relevant.

Over the years, different caseworkers had shared information about what was going on at Francine's house. One of the caseworkers found evidence of drug abuse, but that was never investigated. Another described how she failed to show up for psychiatric evaluations and therapy, but when Justin and Adam asked about these matters, they were simply told that DCS had given them "too much information."

But what exactly is "too much information" when you've been caring for a toddler for almost three years? And what does it mean to be "just a foster parent" when you have been acting as a parent for the vast majority of a child's life? On August 17, 2019, thirty-five months after Alexander went to live with Justin and Adam and twenty-two months after Ruby went to live with Torrie, both children were returned to Francine. Neither the foster parents nor their half-brother Leo have seen or heard anything from them since. Justin and Adam have talked about repainting their house, particularly a yellow door, but they worry that if Alexander ever comes looking for them, he won't recognize the house. So, they leave the door alone. They hope that they will see Alexander again, but they also dread it, because they know that if they do, it will only be because something terrible has happened to the boy.

Justin and Adam have plenty of complaints about the parade of caseworkers and lawyers who were in and out of the lives of Alexander and Ruby, but DCS does not have the final authority over these matters. Family-court judges are supposed to be the ones ensuring that children are safe and secure (with their families, if possible, but with foster families, if not), and that they are traumatized by this process as little as possible. Unfortunately, family courts across the country rarely live up to this standard.

At the state level, every family-court system is slightly different, but there are some problems common to all of them. One is that states have too few judges. In California dependency court, for instance, judges handle between 500 and 1,000 cases per year; in Los Angeles County, the average is 1,200 cases.[1] One reporter saw a judge address twenty-three cases involving thirty-eight children in a single day. A report on the New York Family Court system from The Fund for Modern Courts, a nonprofit, noted: "The disparity between the number of cases assigned to Family Court judges and other judges in New York State (e.g., Supreme Court, County Court, and Court of Claims) is unconscionable. The clear message to the public is that family matters are not as important as other legal matters."[2]

One of the reasons for this backlog, though, is that while new cases are opened every day, none ever seems to end. According to a 2013 report by the New York State Bar Association, more than 715,000 cases were filed in state family courts in 2011, and more than a quarter were still pending in 2012. New York has taken some incremental steps. In 2015, the state legislature added nine new judges to family court in New York City to deal with delays. The pending caseload per judge went from 525 cases in early 2015 to about 470 in 2018.[3] That remains an enormous number, and the system still seems painfully slow.

To understand how we came to this situation, I spent some time at Queens County Family Court in New York City. The New

---

1 Sarah Tiano, "California Ponders Cap on Caseloads for Dependency Court Judges." (*The Imprint*, March 26, 2019), https://chronicleofsocialchange.org/child-welfare-2/california-ponders-cap-on-caseloads-for-dependency-court-judges/34328.

2 "A Call to Action: The Crisis in Family Court: Recommendations for Leadership and Reform." (*The Fund for Modern Courts*, 2009), http://moderncourts.org/wp-content/uploads/2013/10/a_call_to_action.pdf.

3 Nicole Javorsky, "New Judges Help to Speed New York's Family Courts, But Holdups Remain," CityLimits, November 23, 2016, https://citylimits.org/2016/11/23/new-judges-help-to-speed-new-yorks-family-courts-but-holdups-remain/.

York Family Court system was established in 1962 to oversee cases involving neglect, support, paternity, adoption, juvenile and family offenses, and child custody. From its beginnings, according to a report by New York Law School's Diane Abbey Law Center for Children and Families, the court was "notoriously overworked."[4] In the early 1960s, though, no one imagined the family catastrophe that was about to ensue, with the rise in divorce and nonmarital births as well as the scourge of drug use. The child-welfare system went from overworked to overwhelmed.

In recent decades, the system has been inundated with cases, and not just those concerning children in foster care. Joint-custody cases, in which parents (whether married or not) have split up, have proliferated dramatically, in part because more fathers want to play a significant role in their kids' lives. Judges find themselves involved in the minutiae of family dynamics: Should the child go to public school? Should the mother be able to move to another town or county, making it harder for the father to see the child? Should a child stay in the same house with a mother's new boyfriend? Some of these decisions get foisted off on "parenting coordinators," both to relieve the courts and to show parents how to work together. Sometimes it helps, but often it leads only to another endless round of bickering over details, and the cases often wind up back in court.

Judges now take into consideration everything from how parents practice their religion to which parent feeds a child healthier meals. They consider whether parents smoke or help with homework or fail to get their child to a scheduled dental appointment. And no decision is ever truly final. Previously, a parent had to demonstrate that a child's best interest was seriously compromised to bring a custody case back to court. Now, they can just come back in six months to start the argument over again. The result: the most urgent cases, involving real allegations of neglect or abuse, compete for time and resources with less severe—even trivial—matters.

---

4 "The Evolution of New York State's Family Court System." (Diane Abbey Law Center for Children and Families at New York Law School, July 2013).

Some states try to separate abuse cases and custody disputes into two different court systems, but even then, they are competing for resources.

One morning, I walked into a small meeting room that stretches barely eight feet in either direction. Over the course of a few minutes, ten people crowded in to discuss a custody dispute. A divorcing mother and father were arguing over the placement of their eleven-year-old son. The mother, perhaps violating the terms of their temporary arrangement, had allegedly taken the boy to live with her in Connecticut. The mother said that she had not. But in the father's telling, she was pretending to live with relatives in the Bronx and forcing their son to sleep on a foldout couch in the living room. The mother, meanwhile, had accused the father and his sister of abusing the child. The boy tried to hit his father's sister, and when the sister held him back, she left a bruise on his arm. This allegation (no one disputed the facts) led to the involvement of the Administration for Children's Services, which recommended that both the father and the aunt attend parenting and anger-management classes.

For fifteen minutes or so, the father, the sister, their respective lawyers, the ACS caseworker, the lawyer representing ACS, the child's lawyer, and the support magistrate waited for the mother to show up. When she finally arrived, with her court-appointed lawyer, he announced that she had decided to hire her own counsel—but the new attorney would be on vacation for the next two weeks. The court's lawyer presented a letter to this effect and then excused himself. So, ten parties had assembled, consuming a half-hour of the lawyers' time and the support magistrate's time and the ACS worker's time (on the public dime) and most of a day's pay for the father (a construction worker), only for the support magistrate to look at her calendar and the judge's calendar and ask if everyone could come back—in two months.

I watched eight hearings and meetings during that visit, and all but one ended in an adjournment. Perhaps even more surprising than the inconclusive nature of many of these hearings is the way that they were postponed. I watched three judges turn to their computer screens, pull up their calendars, and offer a series of dates for the next meeting. It's astonishing to watch judges take on the role of administrative assistants, especially in a system in which most agree that more judges are needed to deal with the crush of cases.

And the inefficiency has real effects—not just in slowing things down but, more important, on children's well-being. "Children have a very different sense of time than adults," the National Council of Juvenile and Family Court Judges declared in guidelines published in 2016.[5] "Short periods of time for adults seem interminable for children, and extended periods of uncertainty exacerbate childhood anxiety. When litigation proceeds at what attorneys and judges regard as a normal pace, children often perceive the proceedings as extending for vast and infinite periods." Despite recent insights about children's neurological development and the impact of living in traumatic or unstable family environments, even for short periods, family court luxuriates in deferral and delay.

It's not only the children who are put out. Working-class parents often have to travel for hours on public transportation for these hearings, forcing them to give up wages for the day and find alternative child-care arrangements. And the system has other unseen consequences, including making it harder to recruit foster parents, who may not have the time or patience for the endless back-and-forth.

When I told Ronald Richter (CEO of the Jewish Child Care Association of New York and former Queens family-court judge) about my visit, he said that what I saw was "entirely representative of family court and has been that way since at least 1991, when I started practicing." He is especially frustrated by the calendaring process. During his three terms as a family-court judge, he would

---

5 "Enhanced Resource Guidelines," *National Council of Juvenile and Family Court Judges.* (National Council of Juvenile and Family Court Judges, 2016), https://www.ncjfcj.org/wp-content/uploads/2016/05/NCJFCJ-Enhanced-Resource-Guidelines-05-2016.pdf.

say to his clerk: "I have to see this case in a week" or "I really don't care when I see it next." But he notes that, for some reason, "judges want to have control over their calendar." This might seem like a minor issue, but Richter estimates that as much as 30 percent of a judge's time can be spent negotiating such administrative matters. One solution would be for judges to move to a trial more quickly. If criminals have the right to a speedy trial, then victims of abuse and neglect should too.

Critics argue that family court will need more financial resources to move more quickly. Judge Barbara Salinitro, a judge in the Queens Family Court and former president of the New York City Family Court Judges Association, says that "if you're going to give judges in the whole state six months to complete factfinding and a trial," then the legislature "would have to give us 100 more judges to allow us the resources to do that." She notes: "We would need more clerks, more courtrooms, more technology, and an extra layer of resources and additional attorneys for children and parents. It becomes an explosive proposition financially."

Putting more resources into family court is essential, but more money will only buy so much. Family courts are widely believed to be staffed with the least competent judges and lawyers in the system. Family law is a notoriously low-prestige field. In New York Family Court, a public advocate can make as little as $75 a day. And one lawyer told me the story of a judge who was punished by his colleagues for misbehavior by being made to spend a year on the family-court bench.

State legislatures, it's true, are notoriously stingy with these funds. Still, that doesn't mean that the system can't change. A 2016 report by the National Council of Juvenile and Family Court Judges noted that ASFA "clearly established juvenile and family court judges' role as the gatekeepers of our nation's foster care system."[6] It's true, the report continued, that "combating delays in juvenile

6 "Enhanced Resource Guidelines."

court, where there are many stages to the litigation and many participants in the process, can be more difficult than in other courts." But "efforts to speed litigation in child welfare can be successful. There are great variances in court delays from jurisdiction to jurisdiction, and while differences in caseloads can be the cause, docketing practices and case flow management can be factors in delayed proceedings. Some courts have very successfully used case flow management to reduce delays in child welfare litigation."

The simplest reforms should be pursued first. First, scheduling and other administrative matters should be done by clerks or—even better—with technology. As Richard Gelles has observed, "it would take your average high-school junior 15 minutes to develop such a program."[7] This technology could save not only valuable court time and give priority to more urgent cases; it also could allow for transparency, preventing lawyers and judges from double-booking cases for the same slots and then ruining everyone's schedule when they can't be in two places at once.

Maura Corrigan, a former Michigan Supreme Court judge who served on the Pew Commission on Children in Foster Care, says that judges often resort to scheduling during court time because they worry that otherwise lawyers will "run roughshod" over their clerks and delay matters even further. But this, too, is a sign of the dysfunction of family court: as in any business or organization, when senior officials have to make every minor administrative decision, the system breaks down. There need to be clear consequences for lawyers who fail to show up with proper paperwork or clients who fail to show up at all.

Second, judges should exercise their authority more vigorously. Lawyers get paid more, the longer a case goes on—this is true in all courts—but family court puts fewer brakes on such behavior. Other parties also have incentive to delay the legal process. In cases involving accusations of abuse or neglect, witnesses disappear and

7 Gelles, *Out of Harm's Way.*

forget. Their credibility wanes as the case gets older. One particular problem in family court is that child-welfare workers leave the agency, and the details of the case and the understanding of the family dynamic can be lost. Lawyers know this and take advantage of it. According to a 2016 report, one-quarter of ACS workers have been at the agency for less than a year—all the more reason that judges should force cases to move more quickly.[8]

Third, family-court judges should be better educated about what is at stake. They should be required to take courses in child development and adult behavior. "It's as if family court judges think a child's brain development is suspended and not taking place" while these decisions are being made, says Gelles. He recalls being asked to testify in a case involving a child of six months. With a golf tournament to attend, the judge postponed a hearing for six months. "That's 50 percent of the child's life." Family-court judges need to understand that lengthy postponements could have deleterious effects that will last a lifetime.

Judges are also too lenient with the adults. Those adults who want more time to change their ways—usually in promising to stop using drugs—are often granted years of second chances. Judges simply don't understand the likelihood of those adults following through on promises. If an adult hasn't started on a case plan in the first ninety days, what's the likelihood they will start it in the next ninety?

In Alexander's case, the court went for as many as eight months at a time without a hearing. It needlessly placed Ruby into a temporary home when a permanent one was available for her—with her brothers, no less. It left a child in a foster home for almost three years without severing the parent's rights when the federal standard (according to the Adoption and Safe Families Act) is supposed to be to terminate those rights if the child has been in care for fifteen

8 Rich Calder, "Some City Child-Welfare Workers Juggle More than 15 Cases." (*New York Post*, 2016), https://nypost.com/2016/10/27/some-city-child-welfare-workers-juggle-at-least-15-cases.

of the previous twenty-two months. And the court dismissed the concerns of the adults who knew Alexander best and had spent the most time caring for him.

In October 2019, Justin and Adam welcomed two more brothers into their home—Jerrick, age eight, and Jackson, age six—whom they are planning to adopt. Both boys' parental rights have already been terminated—their mother died, and their father surrendered his rights. Adam says that he is having a harder time bonding with them than he did with Alexander and Leo. "I still play with them. I do all those things. But I can just feel that I'm not giving everything. And I don't know if that's just more because I'm protecting myself. Because what if it happens again? What if all of the sudden an uncle comes out of the woodwork to take these two?"

Thinking about his experience with caseworkers and family-court judges, Adam says, "Their processes don't work. They can't keep anything straight. Nobody knows and there's not one consistent person that knows anything about these kids completely." And then the courts and DCS try to limit the involvement of foster parents. Says Adam: "They don't understand why foster parents love these children or are attached to these children. And I don't understand how they don't understand that."

There are some courts that seem to adjudicate family matters better and faster. In 2018, I visited Judge Alan Lemons's family drug court in Scioto County, Ohio. A screen next to his bench shows a set of slides, each with a picture of a young mother and a brief description of why she will be appearing this morning. Two numbers on each slide tell the real story: the ages of her children and the number of days she has been sober. Sometimes the numbers are quite low. "Child age: 3 months; days sober: 81." Several of these women were using drugs while pregnant and lost custody after giving birth.

The rate of opioid overdoses here is among the nation's highest. Lemons is hoping that this unconventional model of justice will help parents kick their habit, allowing them to reunite sooner with their children. Family drug courts have been around for more than twenty years, but they have attracted new interest amid the opioid epidemic and rising rates of foster care. More than 15,500 children were in Ohio foster homes in 2017, up from 12,600 four years earlier.[9]

The rules in states vary, but usually after a child has been removed there is a hearing, generally the next day, to determine if the removal was appropriate, who should care for the children now, and what steps the parent needs to take to remedy the situation. After that, a judge may not see the parent for more than three months. Usually little would have changed. Judge Lemons tells me he got tired of seeing parents after twelve months who hadn't even gone for their drug assessments. "They're not even beginning the case plan," he says. Meanwhile, the children may languish, moving between different foster homes, staying with relatives who may or may not be capable of or interested in caring for them.

Family drug court, on the other hand, meets every week. Participants, who opt into the program, are drug-tested at least once a week. At each hearing, the parent is expected to give the judge a progress report. It can seem like a support group at times. The judge then gives very specific instructions for what the parent needs to do. This eliminates the disconnect that sometimes occurs in regular family court between what a caseworker tells a parent to do and what a judge expects.

A hearing in family drug court typically includes representatives from several public and private agencies: rehab centers, transitional housing authorities, CPS, law enforcement, appointed guardians for the children. They are supposed to ensure that the parents have enough resources and support to carry out the judge's instructions immediately. If the judge says the parent is ready to move from an inpatient treatment facility to transitional housing, the agencies in

9 Andrew Welsh-Huggins, "Ohio Child Advocates: Opioid Crisis Straining Foster Care." (*Associated Press*, December 21, 2017), https://apnews.com/5de575b824a54127a41790098be82e50.

the courtroom know what to do. If he orders more counseling, they can set that up.

Parents who fail to follow instructions face real consequences. They are not subject to criminal charges, but a judge can put them in jail for a couple days for falling off the wagon. One woman I saw thanked Judge Lemons for "the wake-up call" he had delivered the previous week. Others are required to do community service or check in with a local sheriff's office every day. Psychiatrist and researcher Sally Satel says, "These immediate, certain but not severe kinds of judicial responses are very effective in helping drug-addicted people change their behavior."

The first family drug court was launched in Reno, Nevada, in 1995, and there are now hundreds across the country from Maine to Oregon. A 2012 research compilation by the National Association of Drug Court Professionals suggests that people in family drug court complete their treatments at a rate 20 to 30 percentage points higher than in the traditional court system.[10] Family reunification rates are 20 to 40 percentage points higher. Critics worry that these statistics suffer from selection bias, since only motivated parents will opt into the program. On the other hand, if we have motivated parents, this may be a good way to get them on the right path. Critics also wonder whether family reunification is the best measure, since judges who get to know young women by hearing their stories every week may return their children before it's appropriate.

Indeed, children whose parents are in family drug court reenter foster care at lower rates but not dramatically so. That isn't necessarily surprising: Treating addiction takes time, and even people who take the right treatment steps can relapse. But Judge Lemons thinks family drug court is better than the alternative. "The thought used to be that you can't force them into recovery," he says. "You can lead a horse to water, but you can't force him to drink." But with family

---

10 Douglas B. Marlowe and Shannon M. Carey, "Research Update on Family Drug Courts," *NADCP.* (NADCP, May 2012), https://www.nadcp.org/wp-content/uploads/Reseach%20Update%20on%20Family%20Drug%20Courts%20-%20NADCP.pdf.

drug court, the threat of a few days in jail can be strong motivation to stay clean.

Even for cases where drugs are not the main issue, the speed and efficiency of family drug courts should be applied. Some more legislation may be in order (though the fact that federal timelines are ignored hardly gives one hope for additional state regulations). Still, one law that was passed in Arizona and Georgia requires judges to sever parental rights within one year when babies are born to substance abusers and the parents have not quit their drug habit in the meantime. Other states have "right to a speedy trial" statutes for family court that would ensure such cases are decided in a timely manner.

Ultimately, caseworkers and judges also need guidance from medical and psychiatric professionals. How many chances should a parent get before the state says that a child needs to be placed elsewhere permanently? This guidance will vary depending on the age of a child. Parents of children between the ages of 0 and 3 should have a much shorter timeline because those years are so vital to a child's development.

Just as with any misdeed, there needs to be transparency in the law about the consequences. If, after six months, an offender returns to a judge without even having enrolled in a treatment program, should he or she retain custody for another six months until the next hearing, as frequently occurs? If a parent has enrolled multiple times in treatment but keeps relapsing, should a child be put up for adoption? Many parents argue that the state didn't provide enough services to help them kick their addiction. Should a judge rule that caring for a child is their responsibility, no matter how few treatment options are available? These are hard decisions but postponing them for years is not going to make them any easier, and it certainly won't help the children.

CHAPTER 7

THE CHILD-WELFARE CARTEL: WHY CPS INVESTIGATORS ARE UNDERQUALIFIED AND UNDERTRAINED

In June 2020, when the protests and rioting over the death of George Floyd at the hands of Minneapolis police officer Derek Chauvin were at their peak, activists and politicians called for "abolishing the police." What that meant precisely was unclear at first. But at least one answer began to emerge: get social workers to do some of the jobs police currently do.

People trained in social work will not carry weapons or seem threatening like members of law enforcement, the thinking goes. Social workers will be culturally sensitive and trained in the kind of social-justice theories that will make them more sympathetic to people involved in conflict. And they will, of course, see that even the perpetrators are really victims in their own right.

New York Mayor Bill de Blasio tweeted that he would move some of the money currently going to the New York Police Department toward "social services" because "our young people need to be reached not policed."[1] In Minneapolis, a city councilman called for replacing police officers with more mental-health professionals and social workers.[2] The idea caught on with Twitter celebrities, with thousands retweeting "Almost every role in our community a police officer fills would be better handled by a social worker."[3]

But those who are advocating sending more social workers to intervene in conflicts, to determine who is at fault, or to decide who needs to be removed from a situation, really have not spent much time studying the world of child welfare. This is the one area where we currently send people trained in the field of social work to perform a law-enforcement function. And it has not gone well.

Frontline workers in CPS have had their minds filled with useless theories about racial disparities and how poverty and racism prevent people from making good choices and how children are always better off with the family they are being raised in. In the meantime, they are undertrained in the skills they actually need to understand when children are in danger.

CPS is not a profession that attracts many high-quality applicants to begin with. Indeed, far too often, it attracts people who do not have any other options, who fail to understand what the job is about, and who lack the skills to carry out their responsibilities successfully. Agencies then compound the problem by offering investigators little training, little reason—financial or otherwise—to remain in the profession, and no career ladder for those who show promise.

The problems plaguing the profession are evident in the turnover rates for investigators, which are extraordinary: A report from

---

1 Bill de Blasio (@NYCMayor). "This morning we committed to move resources from the NYPD to youth and social services as part of our City's budget. Our young people need to be reached, not policed. We can do this AND keep our city safe." Twitter, June 7, 2020, https://twitter.com/nycmayor/status/1269650502284972032?s=11.

2 Steve Fletcher, "I'm a Minneapolis City Council Member. We Must Disband the Police—Here's What Could Come Next." (*TIME*, June 5, 2020), https://time.com/5848705/disband-and-replace-minneapolis-police.

3 Ellory Smith (@ellorysmith). "Almost every role in our community a police officer fills would be better handled by a social worker." Twitter, June 2, 2020, https://twitter.com/ellorysmith/status/1267878027645444096?s=21.

Casey Family Programs estimates that the average turnover rate at child-welfare agencies in the United States is approximately 30 percent, with individual agency rates reaching up to 65 percent.[4] As Sarah Font of Pennsylvania State University notes, these turnovers cost agencies "both financially, through recruitment and training costs, and qualitatively, through having an inexperienced workforce, staff shortages and discontinuity in the relationship between caseworkers and families."[5]

And frankly, in some situations, an employee leaving may be the best-case scenario. "For those workers who remain on the job," Font writes, "burnout manifests in the workplace as work avoidance, apathy toward the well-being of clients, and feelings of cynicism and futility." One study she cites found that, relative to their peers, "workers with high levels of burnout are more likely and quicker to conclude that children in hypothetical cases are at no risk of harm."

Regardless of whether you believe too many or too few children are being taken away from their parents, CPS investigators have an important job. These people will touch the lives of millions of families, especially families in crisis. In these respects, the recruitment and training of CPS investigators poses a challenge similar to the recruitment and training of police officers, firefighters, and other frontline responders.

The analogy grates on many people in the field who don't want to be grouped in with law enforcement and don't like to think of child welfare as a form of "rescue," but it also gestures toward smarter practices that could dramatically improve the capacity of child-welfare agencies to find better people and to train those people more effectively.

---

4 "How Does Turnover Affect Outcomes and What Can Be Done to Address Retention?" (Casey Family Programs, December 29, 2017), https://www.casey.org/turnover-costs-and-retention-strategies/#:~:text=The percent20available percent20data percent20currently percent20reflect.

5 Sarah Font, "Burnout in Child Welfare: The Role of Employment Characteristics and Workplace Opportunities." (*Social Service Review* 86, no. 4, December 2012): 636–59, https://doi.org/10.1086/668817.

Part of the problem with recruiting CPS investigators is that the goals of the child-welfare system seem to be ever-expanding. It's a particular irony that while increasing numbers of Americans think too many children are being taken from their homes due to overzealous child-welfare workers, leaders at both the state and national levels are committed to increasing the number of families the system touches. By providing more families with so-called "prevention services," of the kind funded in the 2018 Family First legislation, we are actually bringing more families into the web of child welfare.

One reason to focus on the narrower question of the people who pursue CPS careers, then, is that the mission of these workers is relatively clear. Some children are always going to be in need of rescuing. As such, the education, recruitment, and training of CPS workers—and of investigators in particular—is important to identifying and handling the most severe cases of child abuse and neglect in the system.

It is difficult to gauge the qualifications of the people who go into this field, in part because the requirements to work as a CPS investigator vary by state and locality. In some states, like Michigan, applicants are required to have a bachelor's degree in a subject related to child welfare. In other states, a college degree is not required. Texas, for example, allows applicants to present evidence that they have completed sixty credit hours of college work and have gained two years of relevant work experience, which can include "paid or volunteer work within social service agencies or communities providing services to families or other at-risk populations."[6]

When agencies are given a choice, they exhibit a strong preference for hiring applicants who have a social-work background. But this preference is a problem, given the state of social-work education programs in America today. In a paper for the journal *Research on Social Work Practice*, David Stoesz of the University of

6 "What is a CPS Investigator Specialist?" (Texas Department of Family and Protective Services, n.d.), https://www.dfps.state.tx.us/Jobs/CPS/cps_investigator.asp.

Illinois at Springfield pulls no punches.[7] "For decades," he writes, "the expectations of social work students as well as their abilities have been suspect." In terms of undergraduate programs, Stoesz cites the work of Richard Arum and Josipia Roksa, which indicates that undergraduates who major in social work perform worse on the Collegiate Learning Assessment than undergraduates in almost every other field of study.

As for Master of Social Work (MSW) candidates, their GRE scores "ranked second to last" among the scores of all graduate disciplines in combined verbal and math scores, behind even those of students pursuing degrees in physical education.[8] And on quantitative scores alone, the MSW candidates ranked dead last. He adds that the accrediting authority for schools of social work "has failed to even require that a research thesis be an option for [MSW] students," something that sets social-work programs apart from, say, nursing and public-health programs.

Of course, these numbers describe students enrolled in social-work programs; they do not represent all CPS investigators or even all people who go into child-welfare professions more broadly. But since CPS agencies tend to prefer to hire applicants with social-work backgrounds, it is likely that this assessment is representative of many, if not most, of those who go into the child-welfare field. More troublingly, because working for a public child-welfare agency is considered one of the less-desirable paths for people who have undergraduate or graduate degrees in social work, focusing on MSW students may paint an overly optimistic picture of the average CPS investigator's competence.

These schools do not improve much on the raw material. The Columbia School of Social Work—ranked third in *U.S. News & World Report*'s 2019 "Best Schools for Social Work"—requires students to take a course that extends their "understanding of distrib-

---

7 David Stoesz, "The Child Welfare Cartel." (*Research on Social Work Practice* 26, no. 5, August 3, 2016): 477–83, https://doi.org/10.1177/1049731515594236.

8 Stoesz, "The Child Welfare Cartel."

utive justice, human and civil rights and the dynamics of oppression."[9] Another foundational course emphasizes "issues of power, privilege, oppression, identity, and social justice" and an elective teaches students "to challenge bias, prejudice and forms of discrimination that operate in the lives of social workers and [their] clients." Hunter College's social-work program, ranked 25th by *U.S. News*, offers a series of foundational courses with a "specific focus of attention on issues of diversity (culture, class, ethnicity, race, age, sexual orientation, spirituality, ability, and gender)" and one that explores "poverty in the context of oppression, diversity and social justice."[10]

As Stoesz notes, this "[i]nfatuation with postmodern philosophy" not only sidesteps the development of real skills necessary to succeed in social work, it "compromises social work's epistemology."[11] He goes on to explain that postmodernism "repudiate[s] empiricism as an artifact of patriarchal, Western science" and instead "embrace[s] European, mostly French, philosophers who contended that reality should be depicted by narratives constructed by diverse 'voices,' none of which [are] more privileged than others."

The capture of schools of social work and child welfare generally by a social-justice ideology has produced the kind of sloppy thinking that guides child-welfare policy. If you don't understand statistics or have never been taught about the role of culture in educational and economic outcomes for children, it is easy to assume that every disparity is just the result of racism. If you don't understand the difference between correlation and causation, you will assume that every child in foster care who fails to graduate high school or ends up in prison is suffering because of foster care (as

9 "Social Work T7103 Advocacy in Social Work Practice: Changing Organizations and Communities, Influencing Social Policies and Political Processes," Columbia University, accessed August 28, 2020, https://www1.columbia.edu/sec/cu/ssw/ncwshares/t7103-courseoverview.html.

10 "Social Work - MSW," Hunter, accessed August 28, 2020, http://catalog.hunter.cuny.edu/preview_program.php?catoid=14&poid=1890&returnto=1246.

11 David Stoesz, *Pandora's Dilemma: Theories of Social Welfare for the Twenty-First Century*. (New York, NY: Oxford University Press, 2018).

opposed to anything that precipitated his removal to foster care). If you don't know how to read longitudinal studies, you won't be able to separate outcomes for kids who were poor from outcomes for kids who were abused or neglected. If you don't understand that drug use is not just something that people engage in because of a history of oppression, you won't be able to figure out how to help or whether a child can wait for that help to be effective.

Richard Gelles says it is inevitable that social-work schools would want to focus the social-justice issues. But at the outset of his courses, he warns his students, "You will face a situation where your clients are disproportionately from minority families, and they view you as a child snatcher, who is racist by definition. That will put a lot of burden on you." But classes on understanding identity and oppression are of limited use in preparing to work through these and other challenges CPS investigators face. What's more, they undermine respect for the role of CPS investigators in the child-welfare system. Jill Duerr Berrick, a professor of social work at the University of California, Berkeley, says the students "[she] train[s] and teach[es] have mixed feelings about joining this workforce. They will say, 'The only things I've read about this job are negative. I don't want to be oppressive. I don't want to take people's rights. I don't want to make bad decisions and I don't want to be castigated if I do.'"

At best, then, it seems social-work programs are teaching students modes of thinking that are largely irrelevant to CPS work. At worst, they are suggesting to CPS investigators that evidence is subjective, that all narratives should be considered equally, that a worker's own identity is the biggest factor in determining whether a child is in a dangerous situation, and that doing their job is to be "the oppressor."

But it's not just political correctness or postmodern philosophy that creates barriers to hiring the right people. Many child-welfare agencies do not do their own hiring; typically, a separate human-resources department administers tests and interviews for the positions available. John Mattingly, former commissioner of the Administration for Children's Services (ACS) in New York City, says that this approach to hiring is a holdover from Tammany Hall reforms designed to prevent the city commissioner from giving jobs to his relatives. But such policies are common elsewhere, too. The result is a disconnect between the candidates an agency wants and the ones human resources sends over.

Recent efforts to improve the CPS workforce will not sound revolutionary to observers in just about any other profession. The Annie E. Casey Foundation recently collaborated with two counties—one in Colorado and one in Ohio—to develop a "stronger child welfare workforce." Its report suggests agencies should "partner with HR," be "strategic and flexible in their approach to hiring and retaining the right people," use "competency models that identify key skills for certain job classifications," employ data to understand vacancy rates and the size of worker caseloads, and "build a positive work environment" more generally.[12]

These suggestions surely would improve CPS hiring (and retention), but in talking to various agency leaders and researchers, it seems that many of the problems with the system could be avoided if agencies simply focused on assessing candidates' competencies *before* choosing to hire them. The simple fact is that child-welfare agencies are failing to ask people with an interest in or aptitude for investigations to think about a career in child welfare, which leads to more problems down the line.

As Tracey Feild of the Casey Foundation points out, "You've got to find people who have the interest [in] do[ing] the investigation," people "who are not freaked out by going into uncomfortable situations, who have some tenaciousness about figuring out what [i]s going on." Quoting a consultant that the foundation hired to help with the Colorado and Ohio initiatives, she adds, "You may

12 The Annie E. Casey Foundation. *Five Steps to a Stronger Child Welfare Workforce.* (Baltimore: The Annie E. Casey Foundation, 2018, accessed August 17, 2020), https://www.aecf.org/m/resourcedoc/aecf-fivestepstoastrongerchildwelfare-2018.pdf.

be able to teach a turkey to climb a tree, but it's a lot easier to hire a squirrel."

Part of the problem, however, is that agencies cannot choose among candidates for an open position unless they have a surplus of candidates applying. Yet for too many agencies, the reality is much the opposite. Gregory McKay, the former director of the Arizona Department of Child Safety (DCS), says there was such a shortage of workers and so few applicants for vacancies that the agency adopted "a man-down philosophy." "You have thousands and thousands and thousands of cases," he notes, "and people quit or bow out." To fill the gap, the agency simply "push[es] another person in" with little to no training "to pick up right where [their predecessor] left off."

Because there is such a shortage of applicants, agencies often fail to distinguish between people who seek careers in child welfare because they are interested in counseling families and those who see their role as investigating whether a child has been abused or neglected. In fact, many agencies move people from position to position in order to avoid burnout. The thinking is that secondary trauma from investigating crimes against children can be mitigated by some time spent on more positive work, such as adoption counseling. But this kind of thinking assumes that everyone is a squirrel, so to speak. And given the applicant shortage, that is certainly not the case.

The real work of CPS begins with an investigation. John Mattingly described the typical experience of a CPS investigator during an event at the American Enterprise Institute in 2019:[13]

> *You're a 24-year-old woman. You have a degree in sociology with a history minor. You grew up in a suburban working-class or middle-class family and went to a school system,*

---

13 "The Forgotten First Responders: Recruiting and Training Child Protective Services." (*AEI*, 2019), https://www.aei.org/wp-content/uploads/2019/03/Transcript-The-Forgotten-First-Responders.pdf.

> *which was very much segregated one way or the other.... And you find yourself within two, three months on the job walking into a public housing apartment building, walking past the gangbangers who hang out in front, taking what you have to take from them as you walk by.*
>
> *You don't use the elevator if you're smart because the elevators are either broken or they're not safe at all. So you have to hoof it up the steps. You walk into a situation in a family that is only Spanish speaking....*
>
> *The report you got was that this mother was making her living by selling drugs out of that apartment and that the children periodically get bumped around by the drug users who are coming in. That's all you know. You don't know who made that report. You're not in a position [to learn much] because you have to get out there within 24 hours....*
>
> *When you come in, you are able to...talk to the mother because she does speak English, not terribly well but somewhat. She then tells [the children's grandparents], who just got into New York within the past 30 days, who you are. They snatch up their grandchildren and run out the front door....*
>
> *So you have to find a way to, first of all, make an initial assessment of this young woman; secondly, to get her to get the children back so you can speak with them; and thirdly, assess what you think [was] going on that night in that apartment.*

Assessing the conditions in the home, asking difficult questions of the adults and children present, gaining familiarity with any other reports of abuse or neglect made against the family, understanding risk factors like the presence of nonrelative males in the home—these are all necessary, time-sensitive steps an investigator needs to take to complete an assessment. Shockingly, however, many CPS investigators do not know how, or simply have not been adequately trained, to take such steps, even though conducting investigations is one of their core duties.

Another problem—one that Mattingly's example makes abundantly clear—is that CPS investigators routinely put themselves in harm's way to do their jobs but are not given the tools or training to protect themselves. In the fall of 2018, the *New York Post* reported that a fifty-five-year-old translator for the ACS in New York City was stabbed in the back by a grandfather after she and another worker interviewed him about the care of his grandchildren.[14] The translator had to undergo surgery after the attack. Another article from the *Chicago Tribune* found that between 2013 and 2017, at least a dozen Department of Child and Family Services workers in Illinois were seriously threatened or attacked while conducting an investigation.[15]

This threat to worker safety, coupled with the investigative nature of the job, does not immediately call to mind someone involved in child-welfare work. Indeed, according to Feild (again citing the consultant), the job description of a CPS investigator "correlates most appropriately to a CIA operative…because people may be deliberately lying to you, and you've got to figure that out."

Drawing on this observation, Cassie Statuto Bevan, who served on the US Commission to Eliminate Child Abuse and Neglect Fatalities, points out the disparities between the training required of a CPS investigator and that of another vocation that specializes in investigation: a police officer. Police academies require aspiring officers to complete at least sixty credit hours in order to graduate, which takes about six months. After graduating, recruits must receive another three to four months of on-the-job training before they can engage in any work as full-fledged officers.

In contrast to police academies, training at child-welfare agencies is typically closer to six weeks than to six months. In some state

14 Amanda Woods and Stephanie Pagones, "Man Stabbed ACS Worker for Suggesting His Grandkids Were Dirty: Cops." (*New York Post*, November 9, 2018), https://nypost.com/2018/11/09/man-stabbed-acs-worker-for-suggesting-his-grandkids-were-dirty-cops/.

15 David Jackson, "At Least a Dozen Illinois DCFS Workers Attacked, Seriously Threatened since 2013." (*Chicago Tribune*, November 17, 2017), https://www.chicagotribune.com/investigations/ct-dcfs-workers-met-20171117-story.html.

and county agencies, there is such a shortage of staff that investigators don't receive any significant field training before they are sent out to do their jobs. Bevan notes that the impact of this lack of training can be observed in Federal Child and Family Services reviews. The reviews, which are conducted by the US Children's Bureau to measure child-welfare outcomes among the states, show dismal results on various measures. The fiscal years 2015–2017 preliminary review, for instance, found that only in "68 percent of the applicable cases" was "face-to-face contact…made in accordance with state time frames."[16] And "[i]n 23 percent of the 1,247 applicable cases, safety-related services were not provided," meaning "children were left in homes with unaddressed safety concerns."

There's little question that we are recruiting the wrong people for CPS. So how should we think about it differently? An article posted on the website Child Welfare Monitor suggests a promising solution:

> *CPS Investigation should be a specialty in Masters in Social Work Programs. Students would learn advanced interviewing skills and how to assess the truthfulness of children and adults rather than, for example, believing children when they recant allegations with their parents in the room. Alternatively, CPS Investigations could be folded into the growing field of Forensic Social Work [social workers specifically trained to operate in the legal system]. In any case, a Masters-level specialization could be required in order to be a CPS worker, also adding a needed level of prestige to an important, difficult and hard-to-fill job.*

But experts in child welfare seem surprised—if not horrified—when I ask about adopting a model for CPS that is closer to that of police work. When I asked Professor Berrick whether it would help

16 "Child and Family Services Reviews Aggregate Report." (*Administration for Children and Families*, n.d.), https://www.acf.hhs.gov/sites/default/files/documents/cb/cfsr_aggregate_report_2015_2017.pdf.

to think about CPS work as more like the job of a law-enforcement officer, she responded, "I would find it startling to have a classroom full of students who have a BA in criminology." While she acknowledged her reaction might be a "gross generalization," she worried that those training for law enforcement would be seeking "adrenaline rushes," which "would be counterproductive" because "we're trying to dial it down, to get past [a given] emergency" as opposed to escalating the situation.

Some in the field acknowledge that CPS work might improve if agencies looked to law enforcement as a model of professionalization. Allison Blake, formerly the Department of Children and Families commissioner in New Jersey, believes that the state's Division of Child Protection and Permanency (DCPP) has not faced the turnover problems that other states have because New Jersey has a unionized workforce. She notes that "caseworkers were making a decent salary and had a decent benefits package and a lot of vacation [time]" even before a 1999 lawsuit questioning the agency's practices was filed, and although the unions "can be a thorn in your side," they establish a steady pipeline of workers into the agency.

But just as teachers' unions protect bad teachers and police unions protect bad police officers, so the unions for child-welfare workers protect ignorant, incompetent, and indifferent caseworkers. It is difficult to uncover the disciplinary actions taken against caseworkers for infractions or even the contracts that allow for a certain amount of bad behavior because, just as with other public-sector unions, there is a great financial incentive to sweep these matters under the rug.

In 2013, eight-year-old Gabriel Fernandez was fatally beaten to death in Los Angeles by his mother Pearl Fernandez and her boyfriend Isauro Aguirre. After months of torturing the boy in ways whose effects were visible to most everyone who saw him—burning him, starving him, shooting BB gun pellets at his face, hitting him with a bat and a belt buckle, etc.—the official autopsy declared he died of blunt-force trauma combined with malnutrition and neglect.

Gabriel's death exposed a broken system: Multiple reports were made by Gabriel's relatives, teachers, and even a security guard at a public-assistance office who simply saw him walk by, knew something was very wrong. But when the boy was visited and interviewed repeatedly by social workers as well as sheriff's deputies, they failed to note the multiple visible injuries on his body, and they also falsified reports about the case.

There were plenty of warning signs about Gabriel, but there were also warning signs that these caseworkers were not very good at their jobs. Unfortunately, their local Service Employees International Union (SEIU) protected them from any kind of consequences for poor performance. As Garrett Therolf, the former *LA Times* reporter who broke the story, reported in *The Atlantic*: "Under an agreement with the caseworkers' union, managers were forbidden to fire, suspend, demote, or even write negative comments about any of their workers once certain caseload caps were reached—and the department routinely exceeded those caps."[17]

This is outrageous, of course. As much as departments should lower the caseloads of child-welfare workers, the idea that they can't be held accountable for any of their actions until the state accedes to these demands is mindboggling. And the results are predictable. One of Gabriel's caseworkers, Pat Clement, was described as "profane, ill-tempered, and prone to yelling at clients," according to Therolf. A coworker called her a "ticking time-bomb." And her supervisor described her as a "burnout case." In fact, he had once "written a performance evaluation that scored her work as substandard, only to have his boss remove his criticisms and raise her score to 'competent.'"

After several visits to the home, including one after Gabriel wrote a suicide note and told a counselor he was serious about it,

17 Garrett Therolf, "Why Did No One Save Gabriel?" (*The Atlantic*, October 2, 2018), https://www.theatlantic.com/family/archive/2018/10/la-county-dcfs-failed-protect-gabriel-fernandez/571384/.

Clement reported "It is this [worker's] assessment that mother is overwhelmed with her own emotional pain, she is unwilling to continue counseling at this time.... There are no safety or risk's [*sic*] to the children's welfare at this time." She recommended closing the case.

Many public sector unions, most notoriously the American Federation of Teachers, are guilty of protecting incompetence. But even they don't prevent supervisors from giving their underlings poor reviews. The worst offenders may remain in "rubber rooms," continuing to pull in a salary even after they've been pulled out of the classroom. But these social workers were actually kept on the job, and no one was allowed make a peep about their performance no matter how much of a menace they were to the vulnerable children they were supposed to be watching.

In an unprecedented action, the four caseworkers and supervisors were charged with child abuse and falsifying records in Gabriel's case, a criminal prosecution that could have carried up to eleven years in jail. The charges were eventually dropped. Many child-welfare workers were outraged at the idea that they could be held criminally responsible for failing to do their job properly. But police officers can be held responsible in some cases for "failure to arrest" in cases of domestic violence, for instance; failing to remove a child being subject to this level of abuse seems analogous.

One could argue about whether the courts were the right about the criminal charges, but what about the union? Amazingly, seven years after Gabriel's death, the current Memorandum of Understanding between SEIU Local 721 Unit 723 and Los Angeles County includes the exact same provision it did when the boy was murdered, preventing supervisors from demoting, firing, or even writing a negative comment about workers if their caseload exceeds the departmentally specified maximum. Right now, the fates of children who already have been betrayed by the adults in their lives are in the hands of workers who cannot be held responsible for their actions.

The same union flexed its muscles again at the beginning of the pandemic and lockdown. The *New York Times* reported that "Under pressure from the Service Employees International Union...the rules governing [child welfare] oversight were relaxed throughout the state in March to protect workers from the virus. After lobbying from the union, Gov. Gavin Newsom dropped a requirement mandating in-person visits by caseworkers to some 60,000 children in foster care, as well as 14,000 children who remain with their own families after being recently abused or neglected. The policy was in place for more than three months, until Mr. Newsom... reversed it."[18]

During that time, the *Times* found that at least one infant died because workers did not follow up on a series of abuse reports. And his twin brother was saved only because the drug-addled mother posted on Facebook about the death of the first child. As Sarah Anne Font at Penn State University told me, "If child protective staff refuses to come to work, they should be fired. They're emergency responders. That's not acceptable."

But it is clear that this is not how they think of themselves. It is interesting that after a quarter-century of police forces training recruits to practice "community policing"—to work with families and become trusted figures in neighborhoods rather than simply breaking down doors and arresting people—the academics and policymakers in the child-welfare field still want to steer clear of a law enforcement model. Part of the reason is that many child-welfare experts and leaders do not think of parents who abuse or severely neglect children as criminals. They believe that parents, too, are the victims. They are victims of racism, poverty, and even the child-welfare system in some cases. And so, they can't really be held accountable for their actions. The goal is almost always rehabilitation. One could argue that rehabilitation should be the goal of

---

18 Garrett Therolf, Daniel Lempres, and Aksaule Alzhan, "They're Children at Risk of Abuse, and Their Caseworkers Are Stuck Home." (*The New York Times*, August 7, 2020, sec. U.S.), https://www.nytimes.com/2020/08/07/us/virus-child-abuse.html.

our criminal justice system too, but there are few who think that task should be undertaken by police officers.

Improving children's welfare is obviously the paramount concern, but aside from that, there are several other reasons why CPS agencies should look to law enforcement as a model. The first is workers' personal safety. CPS investigators are charged with knocking on doors of potentially violent adults and asking intrusive questions about their families. Even if the mothers (who are often the ones being interviewed) do not become violent, their husbands, boyfriends, or other male family members sometimes do.

Some agencies are taking note of the risks inherent in CPS work and acting on them. For instance, some investigators are given rudimentary training (often by retired police officers) in how to handle dangerous situations. Some agencies ensure that investigators go out to risky situations in pairs. Blake says that although her department did not have an official policy on weapons, she allowed her workers to carry mace.

Astonishingly, though, there are leaders in child welfare who think that these steps are not a practical step toward ensuring the safety of employees but another sign of racism and how we promote bias among workers. In an interview with *NewsNation*, Joyce James, former Assistant Commissioner of Texas CPS, explained that "without being conscious of it we have trained staff to not go to poor communities of color by themselves, to not go there at night.... The question is what do we already know about the community before we get there? What we know is that we are afraid to go there. It was a matter of how we have been socialized."[19] She suggests that these messages are leading to the removal of a disproportionate number of Black children. Never mind that there are plenty of poor white communities that child-welfare investigators should not visit alone or that the crime statistics in these neighborhoods certainly suggest caution is in order. In the service of demonstrating our commit-

19 https://www.youtube.com/watch?v=-NnzFJm8P_o.

ment to equity, we should encourage CPS workers to put their own lives in danger.

There are other areas where CPS might consider taking cues from law enforcement as well. It is not uncommon to hear complaints about the lack of a career ladder in child-welfare agencies. Some of these complaints are related to compensation, but in too many agencies, as soon as workers have a couple of years working with families and children under their belt, they are placed behind a desk to supervise others. Instead of putting its most experienced workers in supervisory positions, agencies need to have a position equivalent to that of a senior investigator or detective in law enforcement—veterans who continue to interview and work cases rather than simply supervising others.

Some agencies are taking the idea that law enforcement has something to teach CPS more seriously. Susan Morely came to New York City's ACS after twenty-one years of serving in the New York Police Department (NYPD), which included time in the Special Victims Division. She says that soon after she arrived, she saw that CPS investigators were "criticized for not doing things they didn't have the tools to do, for not knowing the criminal background of the people they were investigating or their domestic violence history." It became clear to her that these workers needed the same kind of access to information that law enforcement had. They also needed to improve their investigative practices.

Thanks to a partnership between the ACS and the NYPD, there are now 152 retired detectives helping CPS investigators on their most complex cases. CPS investigators are taking training courses through the NYPD, and police officers are being trained in some CPS work as well—in dealing with trauma, for instance.

Morely observes that "bringing law enforcement to help CPS wasn't the most popular idea.... If you were in a squad car and we told you CPS was going to help you, you'd be rolling your eyes." Now, based on questionnaires distributed to both groups, she says that police have more respect for CPS investigators and the complexity of their job. Her colleague David Nish, who handles workforce development for the ACS, says that CPS investigators are also "gaining respect for police and the intensive work they do."

In 2018, the ACS announced that it would open New York City's first-ever "simulated sites, where CPS will train in mock apartments, a mock courtroom, a mock detention center and interview rooms using actors and retired NYC family court judges."[20] Commissioner David Hansell notes:

> Our Child Protective Specialists are the first responders for New York City's children when they may be in danger, and they need the same state-of-the-art training experiences that other first responders have access to. Our new simulation centers will give future child-welfare workers a realistic sense of what it's like to conduct home visits during investigations, interview parents and children, and testify in court. Robust and realistic training is critical for ensuring that children across New York City are safe, which is why we've expanded training over the last year and why we're building these new sites.

Arizona has taken a similar approach. Though Gregory McKay warns that police officers are not always going to do a better job of assessing danger than a CPS worker or vice versa, he has expanded what was a small partnership between Arizona law enforcement and the DCS to one in which 120 former detectives are working with CPS. It has not been easy to find the right people for this position, however. Among other things, McKay notes that former police officers dislike the fact that they don't have the kind of authority they did as officers, as they cannot carry a gun and they do not have the power to arrest anyone. But they can use the investigative

---

20 Thomas Tracy, "EXCLUSIVE: Childrens Services Case Managers to Get Real-Life Home Visit Experience in Simulated Settings." (*Daily News*, November 25, 2018), https://www.nydailynews.com/new-york/ny-metro-acs-fun-house-training-20181124-story.html.

skills they gained during their time in law enforcement to improve children's safety.

To understand how foreign the idea of being a first responder may seem to many CPS workers, it is worth looking at what happened at the beginning of the COVID-19 pandemic, when a significant portion of CPS work came to a halt.

When the lockdown first happened, I spoke to Jessica Peck, a Colorado family lawyer whose practice centers on "kids in crisis." She was handling a custody dispute in which a child had credibly accused a third party of sexually abusing her while she stayed with her mother in Virginia. Generally, an investigator sees the child within seventy-two hours. But Peck received word that the local CPS had cancelled all forensic interviews. Putting off these interviews may not only mean leaving children in dangerous situations but also losing crucial evidence. "I'm worried about having cases dismissed or having people wrongly convicted," Peck said.

There is such a shortage of workers already in these positions that when more call in sick (or simply say they are worried about the risk of getting sick), the investigations can come to a standstill. Routine checks of children in foster homes were conducted on front steps rather than indoors, which meant that social workers never saw the inside of homes.

According to a March report from the *Washington City Paper*: "The virus has…throttled Child Protective Services' in-person welfare visits, reducing the number of social workers in the field from 57 to 33…. Those who are now teleworking say that, though it's a necessary safety precaution, video chatting with families makes CFSA's core work more difficult to execute, since virtual interviews offer limited windows into home life."[21]

When other crimes were reported during the pandemic, the police were not engaged in some kind of "tele-investigation" to

---

21 Morgan Baskin, "How the Coronavirus Pandemic Is Playing Out Inside D.C.'s Troubled Child Welfare Agency." (*Washington City Paper*, June 4, 2020), https://washingtoncitypaper.com/article/304423/how-the-coronavirus-pandemic-is-playing-out-inside-d-c-s-troubled-child-welfare-agency.

determine what happened. But we have created the expectation in law enforcement that their jobs are essential. The same cannot be said of many child-welfare workers. CPS investigators may not think of themselves as the kind of people who are running toward the fire while everyone else is running away, but child abuse and neglect are never put on hold—not even during a global pandemic. To ensure the health and safety of our children, agencies need to hire CPS investigators who are willing to put their own safety at risk.

Though the partnerships in Arizona and New York are promising, they still fail to address directly the issues plaguing the CPS workforce itself. McKay has tried to do so by forming partnerships with university programs in fields besides social work, including criminology. He tells me, "If you're recruiting people from social work programs, their ideology is one of rehabilitation, redemption, and mending people. You throw them into investigations, and you have a fundamental clash of ideals." What's more, university social-work programs have a steady stream of federal dollars coming in to train people in child welfare, and they don't always want to share that wealth with others.

David Stoesz has actually argued that the federal government has created a kind of child-welfare cartel. Washington only funds certain kinds of training programs. The people who graduate from those programs go on to serve and lead child-welfare agencies, which in turn apply for federal funds. Or as Stoesz puts it:[22]

> *[T]he child welfare cartel consists of the Children's Bureau, which diverts federal funds to schools of social work, providing stipends to students, who enroll in social work programs. In collaboration with schools of social work, lesadership academies for deans and directors, supervisors, and middle managers, further consolidate the centrality of the Children's Bureau in the cartel. While this arrangement might be justified as a*

22 Stoesz, "The Child Welfare Cartel."

> *systemic strategy to enhance child welfare, given social work's inadequate performance in professional education, the likelihood is that it will instead contribute to the inferior care that has typically been provided to maltreated children and troubled families.*

Recruiting a different kind of CPS investigator, therefore, may require bypassing the university system and appealing directly to the public. Like their New York counterparts, Arizona officials have also started talking about child protection as a category of first responder. With a video released in 2018, the state's DCS began explaining to the public exactly who these employees are and what they do. Some of the people in the video are actually former foster youth themselves. The video gives the public as well as potential CPS investigators a good idea of what the job entails. It also assigns investigators the title "secret superhero," suggesting that the department is trying to build more respect for their work.

The effort seems to have paid off. Turnover rates have fallen. But perhaps the most interesting sign that the agency is attracting more qualified people—and holding on to them—is the number of people wearing the department's new swag. No longer are investigators embarrassed to tell their friends and family that they work for the DCS; instead, they don hats and t-shirts proclaiming it. Just like police officers, firefighters, and emergency medical technicians, Arizona's DCS investigators have started taking pride in their jobs. This doesn't just mean that increasing numbers of qualified people will go into CPS work, but also that members of the public will be more willing to call CPS if they are worried about cases of child abuse or neglect.

The notion of CPS investigators as a form of first responder may not sit well with those who operate and teach social-work programs, who want child welfare to stop focusing on rescuing children. But for those who want to keep more children safe, the idea holds promise.

CHAPTER 8

MONEYBALL FOR CHILD WELFARE: HOW BIG DATA CAN HELP FIX THE SYSTEM

When schools across the United States closed in March 2020 as part of the lockdown measures, reports of child abuse and neglect plummeted. Pennsylvania and Ohio, for instance, saw at least a 50 percent drop in calls made to state hotlines, while some hospitals reported an increase in cases of severe child abuse showing up in emergency rooms.[1] This was not surprising, because teachers are leading reporters of abuse—their calls represent more than a fifth of the 2018 total—and it's hard to

1 Candy Woodall, "Child Abuse in Pandemic: As Hospitals See More Severe Injuries, 'the Worst Is yet to Come.'" (*York Daily Record*, May 11, 2020), https://www.ydr.com/story/news/2020/05/11/coronavirus-pa-hospitals-seeing-more-severe-child-abuse-injuries/3103045001/.; Hannah Catlett, "Ohio Department of Child Protective Services Concerned over 50 percent Drop in Child Abuse Reports." (*19 News*, May 1, 2020), https://www.cleveland19.com/2020/05/01/ohio-department-child-protective-services-concerned-over-drop-child-abuse-reports; and "Texas Hospital Sees Spike in Severe Child Abuse Cases Possibly Related to COVID-19 Stress." (*FOX6*, March 23, 2020), https://fox6now.com/2020/03/23/texas-hospital-sees-spike-in-severe-child-abuse-cases-possibly-related-to-covid-19-stress.

keep an eye on kids through occasional Zoom meetings.[2] Even those meetings were sporadic and not very well attended. Los Angeles reported that more than a third of children weren't checking in online at all. Besides waiting for the end of the lockdown to assess the damage, most officials found themselves with their hands tied. They could do little more than publicize child-abuse hotlines.

In April, Los Angeles County Sheriff Alex Villanueva proposed to let his deputies become more proactive, releasing a plan to "do welfare checks on our most at-risk kids with patrol personnel."[3] Following the death of six-year-old Gabriel Fernandez in 2013—deputies were found to have ignored clear signs that he was being tortured to death—the department may have learned an important lesson.

But the proposal hit a roadblock when Bobby Cagle, head of the Los Angeles Department of Children and Family Services, explained that "sending a uniformed law enforcement officer to a family's home without any articulable suspicion of child abuse or neglect would not necessarily improve safety for children."[4] He said that "such an action might increase stress on families and children, especially those in already marginalized communities, during one of the most stressful times most have ever experienced." Having police knock on the door of a family whose child had missed a school Zoom meeting might have been merited under these extraordinary circumstances. But it also likely would have run up against legal challenges.

The pandemic and the ensuing lockdown highlighted and exacerbated the biggest problem facing any child-welfare system. How do we know if kids are experiencing abuse and neglect when

---

2 "Child Maltreatment 2018."

3 Richard Winton, "We Do Not Want Another Gabriel Fernandez' Coronavirus Leads to 'Alarming' Drop in Child Abuse Reports." (*Los Angeles Times*, April 21, 2020), https://www.latimes.com/california/story/2020-04-21/coronavirus-child-abuse-reports-decline.

4 "The Sheriff's Dept. Offered to Check on At-Risk Children During Quarantine. L.A.'s Child Services Declined." (*California County News*, May 18, 2020), http://www.californiacountynews.org/news/2020/05/sheriffs-dept-offered-check-risk-children-during-quarantine-las-child-services-declined.

they are behind closed doors? Other crimes get reported by victims and witnesses. Child abuse often does not. And how do we find out what's happening without violating the civil liberties of parents?

One in three American children will be investigated by CPS before they reach the age of eighteen.[5] Some three million children are the subject of maltreatment investigations each year, and around 700,000 are officially classified as victims.[6] About 2,000 child fatalities are due to abuse or neglect by a parent or caregiver in the US annually, and about half of those are cases child-welfare agencies were aware of beforehand. It is easy for critics to say that we are getting too many reports to child-welfare agencies. But it may also be the case that many of the kids who need to be reported are not. And it may also be true that when they are reported, we are not processing and communicating issues correctly. As much as anything else, our child-welfare crisis is a crisis of information.

Fortunately, we live in the twenty-first century. And information is a problem that a lot of businesses, government agencies, and nonprofits have been working hard to solve for decades. Bookstores didn't used to know what customers would be interested in buying based on their previous purchases. Shoe stores didn't realize what was wrong when customers returned their products. Baseball teams didn't know which players were actually contributing the most to their team's wins or losses. Now, thanks to computer algorithms, they do. Unfortunately, the opposition to the use of predictive analytics in the field of child welfare is hampering our ability to get that information faster and use it more effectively. Opponents believe that this information will simply automate the racism that they believe already pervades the system. And so, counties, states, and even private philanthropies have been steering clear of giv-

5 Neil Schoenherr, "1 in 3 Children Investigated for Abuse/Neglect by 18." (Washington University in St. Louis, December 20, 2016), https://source.wustl.edu/2016/12/one-third-us-children-reported-investigated-child-abuse-neglect-age-18.

6 Courtney Collins, "How 'Big Data' Might Help Predict Which Children Are Most at Risk for Abuse." (*KERA News*, February 13, 2018), https://www.keranews.org/news/2018-02-13/how-big-data-might-help-predict-which-children-are-most-at-risk-for-abuse.

ing the financial support necessary for using big data to solve our child-welfare problems.

But the critics are wrong. This data allows us to make better decisions about when kids of all races are actually being maltreated. Data has historically served as a way to help minority groups overcome bias, and there is evidence that it can here too. If we want to keep more children out of danger—and stop intervening in the lives of families where there really aren't any problems—we'd be wise to bring child welfare into the modern age.

Our first line of defense against child abuse and neglect are the people who come into most frequent casual contact with children—friends, relatives, and neighbors. These are the adults who are most likely to get behind the closed doors, to see that a parent is regularly intoxicated or that there is no food in the refrigerator or that children are not being bathed or supervised. But for a variety of reasons, these sources are not enough. Relatives and friends don't want to report a family to the authorities. Neighbors don't want to get involved—either because of indifference or fear of retribution.

For the ones who do step forward, it is important that we do what we can to protect them. Unfortunately, there is a move currently afoot to ban anonymous reporting of abuse. The Homeschool Legal Defense Association, with the help of a coalition of others from a group called ParentalRights.org, is trying to change to the Child Abuse Prevention and Treatment Act of 1988 (which provides financial assistance to states for the prevention, identification, and treatment of child abuse and neglect), to encourage states to bar the anonymous reporting of child abuse or neglect. They believe that too many bystanders are using CPS as a way of persecuting mothers and fathers whose parenting choices they don't like, or who have some other vendetta against them.

The concern isn't unfounded. In 2017, Adam and Jessica Lowther's children were removed from their custody by New Mexico Children, Youth, and Families Department (CYFD) on the basis of a false sexual-abuse accusation by their daughter's kindergarten teacher who had met the girl only eight days earlier. The family spent $300,000 and six months trying to get their children back. One need only recall the McMartin preschool cases of the 1980s in Los Angeles or the similar Amirault cases in Massachusetts—false and fantastic accusations of sexual abuse that resulted in unjust prison sentences—to realize just how serious the consequences of a wrongheaded report might be.

But do we really want to stop neighbors from calling if they hear a child's screams through the wall? Or do we want relatives to risk the ire of their family if they think a niece or nephew is being left alone for days at a time? We allow people to anonymously report crimes all the time—no 911 operator hangs up because you won't give your name. We know people are worried about what happens if someone finds out they are a "snitch." We know people are scared to have any contact with police if they are in the country illegally. There are all sorts of reasons people don't want their name associated with a report of child abuse. It is the job of law enforcement and our court system to determine if the accusations are true. And there are penalties in place for anyone who intentionally makes a false report of any crime.

We also have another legal class of citizens who are required to report. Most states mandate that people in certain professions—doctors, members of law enforcement, public school teachers, and social workers, for instance—report suspected abuse or neglect. In recent years, though, with the spate of allegations of sexual abuse everywhere from Catholic parishes to gymnastic teams and elite private schools, some advocates have begun to push in the other direction—to force more people to report their suspicions.

Marci Hamilton, chief executive of CHILD USA and one of the attorneys leading the charge on behalf of sex-abuse survivors in the Catholic church and elsewhere, argues that every organization that deals with young people should adopt two rules. The first, she says, is that "if anyone has suspicions it is their obligation not just to tell their superiors but to call the authorities." The second: protect these whistleblowers from recrimination. In the wake of the scandal at Pennsylvania State University, the state expanded mandated reporter categories to include clergy as well as a long list of others (such as librarians) who regularly come into contact with children.

But more legal requirements for mandated reporting mean putting more people into potential legal jeopardy, both those accused of abuse and those who fail to report their suspicions. Penalties vary by state but in Massachusetts, failure to report by a mandated reporter can result in a fine of up to $5,000 and imprisonment of up to two and a half years. As Walter Olson of the Cato Institute notes, increasing the number of mandated reporters could "incentivize" people "to resolve uncertain, gray areas in favor of reporting." It will multiply "investigations based on hunches or ambiguous evidence which can harm the innocent, traumatize families, result in child protective services raids, and stimulate false allegations," he says.

Whenever any teacher or pastor sees an odd picture drawn by a first-grader or overhears an inappropriate-sounding snippet of conversation between twelve-year-olds, he or she will feel obligated to call the police or CPS or both. There is a case to be made that there have been too many instances—like Penn State or the Catholic Church—where people should have reported abuse to the authorities but didn't and that states should open the door wider for reports. But the real challenge remains how to sort through all those reports to determine what is worthy of an investigation and what is not. And it is only in recent years that child welfare has started to make a real dent in this problem.

When I moved to New York in the summer of 1998, the city was experiencing boom times: Jobs were plentiful, expense accounts were generous, and crime was down—way down. The *Wall Street Journal*, where I interned, was running columns by scholars at the Manhattan Institute and other think tanks extolling the virtues of "broken-windows" policing. The idea that cracking down on small quality-of-life crime violations—from graffiti to turnstile jumping—could have an effect on the likelihood that other more serious crimes would be committed was life-changing for the city.

In New York City, murders in New York City had reached an all-time high of 2,262 in 1990. Six years later, they had dropped over 56 percent.[7] By 2008, they were down nearly 77 percent, to 523, and all felony crime was down over 77 percent. The other factor in the change was the advent of a program called CompStat, a data collection and management system. After analyzing reams of crime data, police captains and lieutenants were quizzed by their superiors, in granular detail, about crime trends and plans to combat them.

The changes in police tactics as well as the change in information collection revolutionized how law enforcement was done in the city. And though you don't often hear about it now, the people who most benefited from these changes were people of color, living in the poorest neighborhoods in the city.

When it came to child welfare, though, the late 1990s and early 2000s were not as rosy. The agency overseeing the safety and well-being of children in New York City seemed to be lurching from one crisis to the next. In 2005, there were thirty fatalities of children who were under investigation by New York's child-welfare workers.[8] During the twelve years before that, the number went as low as twenty-two and as high as thirty-five. But it was the gruesome death of Nixzmary Brown in January of 2006 that seemed to push things to the brink.

The tabloids told her story for weeks: The seven-year-old was beaten frequently by her stepfather, bound to a chair with electrical cords and duct tape, while her mother and siblings stood by. As the *New York Times* reported: "Paramedics found her dead on the floor, most of her rail-thin body covered with cuts and bruises and black eyes in various stages of healing."[9] She was only thirty-six pounds

7 Heather Mac Donald, "New York's Indispensable Institution." (Manhattan Institute, *City Journal*, 2009,), https://www.city-journal.org/html/new-york%E2%80%99s-indispensable-institution-13196.html.

8 Josh Getlin, "Child Abuse Victim Again Galvanizes New Yorkers." (*Los Angeles Times*, January 18, 2006), https://www.latimes.com/archives/la-xpm-2006-jan-18-na-abuse18-story.html.

9 Andy Newman and Annie Correal, "Stepfather Is Convicted of Manslaughter in Beating Death of 7-Year-Old Girl." (*The New York Times*, March 19, 2008, sec. New York), https://www.nytimes.com/2008/03/19/nyregion/19nixzmary.html.

and appeared to have been forcibly submerged in a bathtub before being beaten over the head.

Nixzmary's parents had mostly stopped sending her to school over the previous six months. But on the rare occasions she would come, teachers reported the clear signs of abuse and neglect to authorities. The Administration for Children's Services paid several visits to the home but apparently determined that everything was fine. At one point shortly before her death, caseworkers were again sent to the house, but the stepfather refused them entry to the home, and they simply left.

Once you read the details of these cases, they stay with you—the helplessness of these children, the long-term nature of the abuse, the failures of the other adults in their lives to intervene. And it's easy to see the patterns of abuse in these cases—of mothers who stand by their men instead of their children, of the men living in the home who are rarely the biological fathers, and of a system that cannot seem to figure out what is going on behind closed doors despite numerous warnings.

I read all the accounts of the trial—and about all the other cases in New York of kids slipping through the cracks. And I listened to the promises of politicians who said that this would never happen again. "We as a city have failed this child," Mayor Michael Bloomberg told reporters.[10] "I want to assure all New Yorkers that a full investigation is underway. People will be held responsible for their actions in this tragedy."

He ordered the ACS to reopen numerous files. New York state legislators stiffened penalties to allow parents in such cases to be charged with first-degree murder—Nixzmary's stepfather was only convicted of manslaughter, claiming he didn't know that his beatings would lead to the girl's death. Efforts to publicize the city's child-abuse hotline were expanded.

But none of these efforts were revolutionary, as I found out later. If history repeats itself, the cycle for child welfare is actually

10 Getlin, "Galvanizes New Yorkers."

pretty short. In 1987, the death of Lisa Steinberg, a six-year-old Greenwich Village girl, led to outrage and some new child-protection policies. The 1995 death of six-year-old Elisa Izquierdo, who was beaten and starved, led to a sweeping overhaul of child welfare in New York. Officials authorized $600 million in additional funds to hike caseworker salaries, increase training and cut caseloads. (In 2016, the death of Zymere Perkins at the hands of his mother's boyfriend started this cycle all over again.)

In his 2017 book *Out of Harm's Way*, Richard Gelles offers a devastating account of how little effect bureaucratic reforms usually have.[11] More money, more staff, more training, more lawsuits brought against CPS, or the ever-popular convening of more "blue-ribbon" committees—nothing has really moved the needle on protecting children in recent years. In some cases, reform amounts to little more than changing the name of the agency.

The cases that provoke the most outrage—and should—are the kids who were already on the radar screens of child-welfare officials. "If CPS agencies cannot protect the children they already know to be at risk," Gelles asks, "whom *can* they protect?" For too long, we've been asking undertrained social workers to make high-stakes decisions about children and families based on patchy data and gut intuition. The result is a system riddled with the biases, inattention, bad incentives, error, and malice that plague all human endeavors, but especially massive government bureaucracies.

Gelles says, "Even the state-of-the-art assessment tools being used in New York are no better at predicting risk for a child than if you flipped a coin." He describes social workers' "expertise" as "simply inadequate" to the task of knowing when children should be forcibly removed from their homes, writing that these decisions inevitably "are influenced by the worker's personal characteristics, biases and experiences, which lead to a variety of problems concerning the reliability and validity of predicted risk."

11 Richard J. Gelles, *Out of Harm's Way: Creating an Effective Child Welfare System*. (New York: Oxford University Press, 2017).

Even if we improved the recruitment and training of social workers, the question would remain how to get better information to the people doing the job. The first important step was to collect the information about child-welfare cases in a systematic way. In 2006, New York instituted ChildSTAT, a program modeled on CompStat that collected detailed data on children who were being investigated by the Administration for Children's Services. By randomly reviewing a single abuse case with staffers each week, senior ACS officials, including the commissioner, seek to identify shortcomings.

For a variety of reasons, ChildSTAT was never going to be as effective as CompStat. John Mattingly, the commissioner who instituted the program under Mayor Bloomberg, told the Chronicle of Social Change that even if the data analysis was useful, the management system had to be different. "You can't run a child welfare agency based on police principles. Those guys would fire a captain on the spot if they didn't like how he described a case; you can't do that in child welfare."[12] (Another reason to consider the law-enforcement approach discussed earlier—maybe you should be able to fire someone on the spot at a child-welfare agency!)

That is not to say that it didn't help at all. Mattingly explained: "We started looking at the number of investigation cases opened up after a prior investigation had been closed. The larger the number of cases that were re-opened after you said no problem, showed you, you were wrong. That's how you can move an agency somewhat." But "somewhat" is the key word here. The leadership of the department was able to learn about some egregious problems with investigations, but otherwise, there was not a lot they could do with the data.

Until the 1990s, caseworkers' clinical judgment was the only thing they had to go on. In the late '90s, child-welfare agencies

12 "John Mattingly, Former New York City Child Welfare Boss, on the System's Past and Present." (*The Imprint*, July 31, 2018), https://imprintnews.org/child-welfare-2/john-mattingly-new-york-city-child-welfare-juvenile-justice/31766.

started using actuarial risk assessment models to determine which children were at a heightened risk of abuse. Structured Decision Making (SDM), which is based on these models, did improve matters to a limited extent. For one thing, it imposed some uniformity on the factors that social workers took into consideration when making decisions. According to the Children's Research Center, SDM was supposed to offer "clearly defined and consistently applied decision-making criteria" as well as "readily measurable practice standards, with expectations of staff clearly identified and reinforced."[13] Unfortunately, it did not produce the magnitude of improvement that Gelles and others had hoped for.

"The actuarial decisions are only as good as the data you have, and the child-welfare system had a limited portfolio of data," he recalls. Cities and states were collecting information on families through various agencies—child welfare, education, criminal justice—but it was difficult if not impossible for the different entities to share this information with one another, or for social workers to access it.

These state bureaucracies are often still living in the 1980s when it comes to technology. In an interview with *Bloomberg News*, Microsoft co-founder Steve Ballmer describes visiting a county department of mental health whose organizational system consisted of "hundreds of sticky notes in a variety of colors tracking things like different types of programs for various ages."[14] In 2015, he and his wife gave $9 million for the creation of a data-analytics system to connect Washington state's local child-welfare agencies and various nonprofits also serving those children. At first, it seemed like a success, but as the years went on, it became clear that maintaining its usefulness would require an additional investment

---

13 "Structured Decision-Making." (Child Welfare Information Gateway, accessed September 1, 2019), https://www.childwelfare.gov/topics/systemwide/assessment/approaches/structured-decision-making.

14 Dina Bass, "Ballmer Sees Software as Key Link to Reach At-Risk Schoolkids." (*Bloomberg News*, August 8, 2018), https://www.bloomberg.com/news/articles/2018-08-08/ballmer-sees-software-as-key-link-to-reach-at-risk-schoolkids.

of tens of millions of dollars. The agencies had neither the financial resources nor the staff to keep the system up to date.

Relatively few counties, let alone states, have been able to make that kind of investment in data and technology, let alone achieve "interoperability," ensuring the various public information systems could talk to each other. But that's what was needed to really understand and use the data to make predictions about the future.

Predictive analytics refers to the use of historical data to forecast the likelihood of future events. Thanks to powerful computers, statisticians in recent years have been able to develop models for understanding, for instance, the probability that a criminal out on parole might commit a crime again. In the area of child welfare in particular, proponents are enthusiastic about the prospect of getting better information about children at risk. There is so much we don't, and can't, know about what goes on inside of families that child-welfare workers are largely flying blind. But big data has the potential to tell the likelihood that a child will be subject to neglect or abuse.

"There are patterns, and if you get enough data and you run it through enough iterations, you will find the pattern in what appears to be chaos," Gelles says. This formulation will be familiar to those who have read *Moneyball*, journalist Mitchell Lewis's account of how big data allowed the Oakland Athletics baseball club to sign better players for less money and win championships against much wealthier teams.[15]

In fact, at the beginning of his 2016 book *The Undoing Project*, Lewis lightly mocks all the other uses people have found for predictive analytics in the years since *Moneyball* was published. "In the past decade or so, a lot of people have taken the Oakland A's as their role model and set out to use better data and better analysis of those data to find market inefficiencies," he writes.[16] "I've

15 Mitchell Lewis, *Moneyball: The Art of Winning an Unfair Game.* (New York: W.W. Norton, 2003).

16 Mitchell Lewis, *The Undoing Project : A Friendship That Changed the World.* (United States: W.W. Norton, 2016).

read articles about Moneyball for Education, Moneyball for Movie Studios, Moneyball for Medicare, Moneyball for Golf, Moneyball for Farming, Moneyball for Book Publishing (!), Moneyball for Presidential Campaigns, Moneyball for Government, Moneyball for Bankers, and so on."

But before we write off sophisticated number-crunching as yesterday's news, let's consider whether it could improve a field whose success or failure has life-altering, and even lifesaving, implications for children—one that has experienced very little improvement in the past few decades.

Emily Putnam-Hornstein has been steeped in data from the beginning of her career. In 2011, the same year she received her doctorate from Berkeley, she published a paper on predictors of child welfare in the journal *Children and Youth Services Review.* The question, which at the time seemed to Putnam-Hornstein like an interesting exercise but not anything with practical implications, was whether you could predict on the day a child is born the likelihood that he or she would eventually enter CPS.

Putnam-Hornstein was surprised to find that the answer was "yes," and "with a high degree of accuracy" to boot. Shortly thereafter, she was approached by New Zealand's Ministry of Social Development. When word about her work got around, there was an outcry. Citizens feared that the government's goal was to take children from their parents *before* the first report of abuse had been made. In fact, policymakers were trying to figure out how they could best deploy their home-visiting services, and they were interested in developing a proof of concept.

In 2012, working with lead researcher Rhema Vaithianathan, a professor of economics at Auckland University of Technology, Putnam-Hornstein developed a predictive risk-modeling (PRM) tool for children in families that receive public benefits. Among the data used are the age of mothers and the date of their first benefit payment, but there were more than a hundred other factors as well.

As Vaithianathan explained in *The Chronicle of Social Change*, "We see this train wreck in slow motion and no one is doing anything about it until that first call comes in. The question is do we have an obligation to do something?"[17] The ministry officials suggested that their data could be used to offer parenting programs to families with children at a high risk for abuse.

The backlash to the idea was immediate, however. Richard Wexler, executive director of the National Coalition for Child Protection Reform, suggested that using big data to determine which kids might be in danger resembles the plot of the movie *Minority Report*, in which police use psychic technology to figure out who is going to commit a murder and then arrest and convict the perpetrator beforehand. In an article on his blog called "Big Data is Watching You," Wexler, whose work has been cited by *The New York Times* and *The Washington Post*, wrote: "They are not proposing to rely on psychics in a bathtub. Instead they're proposing something even less reliable: using 'predictive analytics' to decide when to tear apart a family and consign the children to the chaos of foster care."[18]

Wexler cites a study by Emily Keddell of the University of Otago, which notes that 32–48 percent of the children in New Zealand who were identified as being at the very highest risk by the software turned out to be "substantiated" victims of child abuse. He decries what he sees as the unacceptably high "false positive" rate of such a system. "Think about that for a moment," he wrote. "A computer tells a caseworker that he or she is about to investigate a case in which the children are at the very highest level of risk. What caseworker is going to defy the computer and leave these children in their homes, even though the computer is wrong more than half the time?"

17 Darian Woods, "New Zealand Crunches Big Data to Prevent Child Abuse." (*The Imprint*, April 10, 2015), https://imprintnews.org/featured/new-zealand-crunches-big-data-to-prevent-child-abuse/10824.

18 Richard Wexler, "A Report from the National Coalition for Child Protection Reform on 'PREDICTIVE ANALYTICS' - THE DANGEROUS NEW FAD IN CHILD WELFARE." (*Big Data Is Watching You* [blog], 2016), http://bigdataiswatching.blogspot.com/2016/11/bigdata-is-watching-you.html.

Keddell, the paper's author, argues that the substantiation rate may not even be as high as it seems, because child abuse is often ill-defined, and defined differently in different localities. Plus, caseworkers are subject to bias, including from pressure by an algorithm. "Substantiation data as a reflection of incidence have long been criticized by researchers in the child protection field," she wrote.[19] "The primary problem is that many cases go [unreported], while some populations are subject to hypersurveillance, so that even minor incidents of abuse are identified and reported in some groups."

In 2015, the New Zealand program was shut down entirely. "Not on my watch," wrote Minister of Social Development Anne Tolley. "These children are not lab rats." She told the local press, "I could not believe they were actually even considering that. Whether it would have gotten through the ethics committee—I hoped it wouldn't."[20]

Putnam-Hornstein and her colleagues continued their work, developing new models informed by the pushback. In 2014, she began working on a proof of concept with the Department of Children and Family Services (DCFS) in Los Angeles County. Project AURA—the initials stand for Approach to Understanding Risk Assessment—looked at child deaths, near fatalities, and "critical incidents" in 2011 and 2012. Using data that were already being collected, including previous child abuse referrals, arrests, and substance-abuse histories, statisticians at a company called SAS created an algorithm and produced in each case a risk score on a scale from 1 to 1,000.

"In Los Angeles, we are data rich but analytically poor," Genie Chough, the director of government affairs and legislation at DCFS,

---

19 John Kelly, "New Zealand Analysis Should (But Probably Won't) Burst the Predictive Analytics Bubble." (*The Imprint*, May 23, 2016), https://imprintnews.org/blogger-co-op/new-zealand-analysis-probably-wont-burst-predictive-analytics-bubble.

20 Samantha Kirk, "Children 'Not Lab-Rats' - Anne Tolley Intervenes in Child Abuse Experiment." (*Stuff*, July 29, 2015), https://www.stuff.co.nz/national/health/70647353/children-not-lab-rats---anne-tolley-intervenes-in-child-abuse-experiment.

told me. AURA offered Chough and her colleagues the chance to make use of some of the vast quantity of information that was being collected on the families they served. According to Chough, when SAS compared the predictions with actual outcomes, the algorithm was 76 percent accurate. While not outstanding, that is significantly better than flipping a coin, and better than the findings from the New Zealand studies as well.

Nonetheless, Chough and her colleagues ultimately concluded that AURA was "fatally flawed." Since Los Angeles County used the private firm SAS, as opposed to a public university or some other open-source entity, to create the algorithm, it was not as transparent as they felt it should have been. The county attempted to validate the performance of the model, but researchers could not replicate it. Importantly, the data also could not be updated in real time. And with big data, the bigger and more current the inputs, the more accurate it is.

Putnam-Hornstein says this fact is not necessarily intuitive, even for someone trained to analyze data. "As a research scientist, I had always been taught to think about models that are developed for descriptive purposes and causal relationships," she says. But prediction risk modeling "is a different approach, a kitchen-sink approach. This is all the information we have at the time a call comes in. What can it tell us about future differences in outcomes? We are not looking at any one specific factor."

There is also information in big data that would make call screeners less likely to request an investigation of cases that don't merit one. One in three children in America will have contact with child services before the age of eighteen. That number suggests that agencies are wasting resources investigating cases that are highly unlikely to be substantiated. These false alarms significantly increase the caseload of child-welfare workers and make it difficult to focus sufficient time and energy on the cases that are most likely to need them. They also often justify further intrusions into family privacy.

While critics like Wexler worry about false positives, Gelles argues that the current system already produces plenty of the same. But right now, they're based almost entirely on the gut instinct of the caseworker visiting a home or the person answering the phone at a hotline.

There are two places in the US where predictive analytics have made their official child-welfare debut: first, Allegheny County, Pennsylvania, and, more recently, Douglas County, Colorado. The Allegheny Family Screening Tool was launched in August 2016. Some seventeen teams had answered a request for proposals put out by the county two years earlier, and Putnam-Hornstein and Vaithianathan's was selected. In March 2017, the county published its first report on their project.

The Department of Human Services "decided that the most promising, ethical and readily implemented use of [predictive risk modeling] within the Allegheny County child protection context was one in which a model would be deployed at the time an allegation of maltreatment was received at the hotline," the report explains.[21] The county receives roughly 15,000 calls to that line per year. Each one is currently given a score from 1 to 20 that determines its urgency and severity.

Marc Cherna, the Allegheny County Department of Human Services director, has served longer in that position than anyone else in the United States—since 1996. His agency is one of the few that haven't followed the pattern of a big child-fatality scandal followed by an ineffective cleaning of the bureaucratic house. Not to say things have always been great. As Cherna acknowledges, for the first several years he was there, "we were a national disgrace. We were written up nonstop. Kids were getting hurt."

In 2016, Allegheny County was in a particularly good position to experiment with predictive analytics, because it had a lot of data

21 Rhema Vaithianathan et al., "Developing Predictive Risk Models to Support Child Maltreatment Hotline Screening Decisions." (*Allegheny County Analytics*, March 2017), https://www.alleghenycountyanalytics.us/wp-content/uploads/2017/04/Developing-Predictive-Risk-Models-package-with-cover-1-to-post-1.pdf.

and because its data were accessible across different government bureaucracies. In 1997, Cherna consolidated several bureaus into one Department of Human Services, and the Richard King Mellon Foundation and seventeen other nonprofits created the Human Services Integration Fund "for projects that foster integration and support innovations in technology, research and programming that would be difficult or impossible to accomplish with public sector dollars." Several of the chief information officers of those groups agreed to help Cherna with a project that ended up merging thirty-two different data sets.

But there was another reason Allegheny County was the right place for this project. The Department of Human Services had built up a "high degree of trust" with the community, says Cherna. Scott Hollander, head of the legal advocacy group ChildVoice in Pittsburgh, confirms that assessment. Hollander, who has done similar work in Colorado and Washington, says what's different in Pittsburgh is "the willingness to try new things and not be afraid of failing. And there is a lot of discussion with stakeholders that doesn't happen elsewhere." For instance, when Cherna wanted schools to share data with child-welfare services and vice versa, Hollander and a number of his colleagues objected. "Hey, this doesn't seem right. The parents don't seem to know what's going on," Hollander says he told the agency. So Cherna asked Hollander and some of his colleagues, who work for a parents' rights group, to design a consent form that would be clear and fair.

Before the Department of Human Services put out a request for proposals for the predictive analytics project, they met with legal aid and civil liberties groups to discuss the implications for families. According to Hollander, the response "was a mixed bag." He recalls "people thinking this sounds interesting and you're trying to protect kids, but the factors you're describing seem like they could create biased decisions." "If you're looking at poverty and crime," he continues, "the police don't treat black and white people the same. You will echo the disproportionality that already exists in the current environment if you are looking at drug use, criminal activity, and whether there is a single parent as risk factors."

"The adage 'garbage in, garbage out' never holds truer than in the field of predictive analytics," writes researcher Kelly Capatosto in a report for the Kirwan Institute for the Study of Race and Ethnicity at Ohio State.[22] "Subtle biases can emerge when seemingly 'race neutral' data acts as a proxy for social categories." The result is that "data that is ostensibly used to rate risk to child well-being can serve as a proxy for race or other past oppression, thereby over-representing those who have suffered from past marginalization as more risky."

Putnam-Hornstein and her colleagues were sensitive to these concerns. When they began this work in New Zealand, they consulted extensively with leaders in the indigenous Maori community. Because native peoples are more likely to be caught up in the child-welfare system, they wanted to make sure this new tool was not having an adverse effect on them.

But Putnam-Hornstein argued that even—and perhaps especially—if you believe the deck is stacked against racial minorities, predictive modeling could be helpful. Let's say, for instance, that you believe the criminal justice system is biased so that the threshold for being arrested is lower for black men than it is for white men. That's actually a reason to include race in your algorithm: to help account for that difference.

This might sound like the soft bigotry of low expectations—are we really going to say a complaint is less serious if it's against a black man than if it's against a white one? But Putnam-Hornstein is right: Numbers can correct for bias.

The Allegheny Family Screening Tool was rolled out in August 2016. More than one hundred factors go into the algorithm—and race is not one of them. The system gives the call screener a score between 1 and 20 that describes the likelihood that the child in

22 Kelly Capatosto, "Foretelling the Future: A Critical Perspective on the Use of Predictive Analytics in Child Welfare." (*Kirwan Institute*, 2017).

question will be rereferred or removed from the home within two years, based on what is known from historical data. The screeners then assign an investigator to the cases with the highest risk scores.

More to the point, the algorithm is not just about removing kids from problem homes, a step nearly everyone agrees should be taken only as a last resort. "If we can figure out which children are the most likely to be placed in foster care when a call alleging maltreatment first comes in, the hope is that we can tailor and target more expansive and intensive services to that family at the outset, so as to prevent the need for placement," Putnam-Hornstein says. "Alternatively, it may be that there is nothing we can do to safely keep the child in the home. But at least we will make sure to investigate so that we can remove."

To avoid confirmation bias, when investigators visit the home, they are not told what score a family received. The results have been similar to those found in California: the model predicted with 76 percent accuracy whether a child would be placed in foster care within two years and with 73 percent accuracy whether the child would be rereferred—that is, whether child services would be alerted about that child again.

The county also looked at other measures to evaluate the accuracy of the tool. "We are keenly aware," Putnam-Hornstein acknowledges, "that by predicting future system involvement, we may simply be modeling (and inadvertently reinforcing) past decisions that were biased and/or wrong—placing children who could have stayed at home safely, and simultaneously failing to remove other children who are still being abused." So they also collected data from a local children's hospital. If the system is working correctly, you would expect that many of the children who come to the emergency room for cases of attempted suicide or self-harm—or as a result of other kinds of trauma that are associated with abuse—would be those who were previously given higher risk scores. And indeed, they are.

"Yes, the model is predicting placement in foster care among children referred for maltreatment," Putnam-Hornstein notes. "but the model is sensitive to children experiencing the most severe forms of more objective harm."

Two years later in April 2019, the researchers released the first impact evaluation of the Allegheny Family Screening Tool. The results were enlightening, to say the least. First, the authors noted that "Overall, the AFST did not lead to increases in the rate of referred children screened-in for investigation. Use of the tool appears to have resulted in a different pool of children screened-in for investigation."[23] In other words, the data suggests that it's not that too many children were being reported as possible victims of abuse or neglect. But many of the wrong kids were.

Indeed, the authors also found that "use of the tool led to an increase in the screening-in of children who were subsequently determined to need further intervention or supports. Specifically, there was a statistically significant increase in the proportion of children screened-in whose child-welfare case was then opened or, if no case was opened, were rereferred within 60 days." So it turns out that more of the kids who were being investigated with the new tool were the ones who really needed the help. Moreover, there was no increase in rereferrals for the kids who were screened out with the tool. Predictive analytics is helping screeners better figure out which kids are most in need of help.

Finally, the researchers found that "AFST led to reductions in disparities of case-opening rates between black and white children. Prior to the introduction of the AFST, case-opening rates for black children were higher than for white children. During the Post-AFST period, increases in the rate of white children determined to be in need of further child-welfare intervention, coupled with slight

23 "Frequently-Asked Questions by the Allegheny County Department of Human Services." (*Allegheny County Analytics*, April 2018, https://www.alleghenycountyanalytics.us/wp-content/uploads/2019/05/FAQs-from-16-ACDHS-26_PredictiveRisk_Package_050119_FINAL-8.pdf .

declines in the rate at which black children were screened-in for investigation, led to reductions in racial disparities."

In the more than a year since this finding was made public, it has received little to no attention. Richard Wexler has issued no apology. Kelly Capatosto hasn't published any kind of follow-up. And though there was plenty of coverage of the AFST when it first launched—the *New York Times Magazine* had a long article that included the voices of all of the critics—there has been little follow-up. To his credit, John Kelly, the editor of the *Chronicle of Social Change*, noted: "When it comes to stopping state-sanctioned violence—whether an unjustified police shooting or child removal—shouldn't we use the most advanced tools at hand? It seems to me that predictive analytics—which has been so maligned as the harbinger of automated racism—could actually be a key to eroding its hold."[24]

Frankly, no one should be surprised by this outcome. Data has often served as a way to help minority groups overcome bias. Take the SATs. Though it is these days more often decried as racist, the truth is that when college admissions offices came to rely on test scores more than on the individual impressions of their administrators, they were forced to admit more Jews. In 1925, Harvard's freshman class was nearly 30 percent Jewish. The next year, it fell to 15 percent and stayed about the same for the next two decades. It was not that anyone doubted Jews' academic qualifications. But their social characteristics were described as "different" and "peculiar."[25] The more colleges relied on softer standards, the more the anti-Semitic biases of the admissions officers came through.

The same thing happened with Asians. Asian enrollment at Harvard was 19 percent in 1992 and hasn't risen above 20 percent

---

24 John Kelly, "Can Predictive Analytics Root Out the Social Workers Most Likely to Break up Black Families?" (*The Imprint*, June 19, 2019), https://imprintnews.org/featured/can-predictive-analytics-root-out-removal-happy-social-workers/35650.

25 Jason L. Riley, "Harvard's Asian Quotas Repeat an Ugly History." (*Wall Street Journal*, October 8, 2019, sec. Opinion), https://www.wsj.com/articles/harvards-asian-quotas-repeat-an-ugly-history-11570575962.

since then, despite a significant rise in Asian applicants. Asian enrollment at Cal Tech grew steadily from 25 percent to 43 percent over the same period. Cal Tech's admissions process is race-blind. Harvard's is not. Harvard consistently rated Asian applicants lower on traits like "positive personality" and likability. The soft measures allowed the admissions officers' bias to come through. The test scores did not. In other words, if you are concerned about the presence of bias among child-welfare workers and the system at large, you should be more interested in using data, not less.

No one expects investigators to rely entirely on a score produced by a computer to make a determination about children's level of risk. But failing to have a basic understanding of statistics and how these models work means that some workers will simply reject these scores out of hand. Indeed, that happened with the Allegheny Family Screening Tool. As the authors of the 2019 report note, "there is considerable lack of concurrence with the AFST by call screeners, limiting the ability for a tool like the AFST to have effect on consistency."[26] When the tool was fully implemented, the county mandated that certain cases be "screened in," including, for instance, "any family that has had 4 or more referrals in 2 years without any of the referrals being formally investigated." But when the researchers looked at what happened, they found that "for the period December 1, 2016–November 29, 2018, only 61 percent of the referrals that scored in the 'mandatory' screen-in range were in fact screened in."

What part of "mandated" didn't they understand?

The future of PRM in child welfare is still an open question. Putnam-Hornstein wonders: "Two years down the road, it could really just be one more piece of paperwork they print up and attach to their case files. Maybe they don't trust the score and so they just ignore it. Or maybe the child-welfare workers don't do anything different in terms of interventions with the families."

26 "Allegheny County Department of Human Services."

But Gelles suggests things may go the opposite direction—that the score will come to be relied on more than it is in these pilot programs, impacting decisions even after the "hotline" stage. "If you're using this (a) to determine whether to remove a child from a home, or (b) to determine whether it's time to return a child to a home," he asks, "how are you not going to share that with the judge" tasked with making that call?

It could also be used to screen foster parents. That might begin to address the concerns of people like Wexler, who worry about the safety and well-being of children taken from their families by the state. And the data can also be used in a preventive context to help parents avoid contact with the child-welfare system. In September 2020, Allegheny County launched a voluntary program for new parents called Hello Baby, which offers families different levels of support depending on a family's risk factors. These can include home visits by nurses to learn how to better care for newborns, concrete goods, assistance with transportation, and connections to other community services.

But data analytics can also be used at other points in the child-welfare system. Take a program called Family-Match, launched in early 2018 by Adoption-Share, an online adoption network. Designed by Gian Gonzaga and Heather Setrakian, former senior researchers at the online dating company eHarmony, Family-Match aims to find adoptive homes that are good fits for children in the foster-care system.

Parents interested in adopting fill out a questionnaire asking them about what type of child they are looking for, as well as information about their own personalities, families, and parenting styles. Caseworkers fill out a similar form for the children (older children can help with their own forms) about their history, behavior, and personality. The information is then fed into an algorithm created by Gonzaga and Setrakian. Once a caseworker sees a family with a high "compatibility score," he or she will contact them to discuss next steps; the human element is still very much part of the process.

After the program operated in Florida for almost a year, the program made ninety-one matches (out of 800 children in the system), resulting in six finalized adoptions. And the matches were made, on average, in just over two months. Final adoptions can take place as soon as ninety days after the match. Under the old system, this population of children took an average of fourteen months between the time parental rights were severed and adoption, according to Florida's Department of Children and Families.

The program's database includes families from across Florida. In most states, caseworkers only know about the families looking to adopt in their own areas. And they might not want to recommend those families to others outside the district, lest they lose an option for placing children in their own community. But, as Gonzaga notes, if you pool everybody together, you can make better matches. This is not intuitive, and if you hire workers who have trouble seeing this, they likely won't use the program. Family-Match's compatibility score can also encourage families to consider a wider range of children than either they or a social worker might want to try, further expanding the opportunities for a good match.

The process of fine-tuning these algorithmic tools continues with the hope of finding out which children are at the highest risk, offering support to families before they need child-welfare intervention, getting investigators to the situations that are most urgent, and helping find good placements for children who have had to be removed from their homes. These tools can benefit all children, but there is evidence they are especially beneficial to children and families who most likely would be subject to bias. The promise of these methods is certainly large enough. As Vaithianathan points out, "It's implementable anywhere. The whole country could be using it because the data is already there."

CHAPTER 9

IT'S A HARD-KNOCK LIFE IN GROUP HOMES—BUT POSSIBLY BETTER THAN THE ALTERNATIVE

In 1994, House Speaker Newt Gingrich outraged Americans when he proposed cutting welfare payments to young single mothers and placing their children into orphanages if they could not support them. What was wrong with this man? As if it weren't bad enough to punish the poor by denying them government benefits, now he wanted to sentence their children to years in a Dickensian institution. The outrage provoked by Gingrich's proposals was instantaneous and intensified what was already a growing consensus against the use of orphanages—or group homes—by the child-welfare system.

Though these institutions never disappeared, their numbers have been shrinking as the pressure to close them has been growing. More than two decades later, in May 2015, at a hearing of the Senate Finance Committee, Orrin Hatch launched a broadside against group homes for foster kids. He told his colleagues that the facilities "are literally breeding grounds for the sexual exploitation of children and youth.... Traffickers know where these group homes are and target the children placed in them for exploitation."[1] He explained that the bill he was introducing "would refocus federal priorities on connecting vulnerable youth with caring, permanent families. This would be accomplished by eliminating the federal match to group homes for very young children and, after a defined period of time, for older youth."

Sexual exploitation and abuse are hardly the only danger to vulnerable kids placed in residential facilities. From overmedication and the unnecessary use of restraints to fighting among the residents and kids running away, the committee heard hours of testimony from former group-home residents who described the horrendous conditions they were forced to endure.

Less than three years later, Congress passed (as part of the 2018 budget bill) the Family First Prevention Services Act. Originally sponsored by Sen. Hatch and his colleague across the aisle, Ron Wyden of Washington, the cheers for this piece of bipartisan legislation were deafening. As a report in *USA Today* explained: "The law...prioritizes keeping families together and puts more money toward at-home parenting classes, mental health counseling and substance abuse treatment—and puts limits on placing children in institutional settings such as group homes. It's the most extensive overhaul of foster care in nearly four decades."[2]

To read such descriptions, it was hard to see why this didn't happen sooner. Who wouldn't want to see more kids able to stay at home? Who doesn't want to help struggling parents? And who wouldn't want to reduce the number of kids in these abusive institutional settings? The fact that the legislation was also budget neutral—by allowing foster care (Title IV-E dollars) to be used for "prevention services," states wouldn't need to rely so much on expensive congregate facilities—helped to seal the deal.

1 "Hatch Statement at Finance Hearing on Foster Care Group Homes." (The United States Senate Committee on Finance, May 19, 2015), https://www.finance.senate.gov/chairmans-news/hatch-statement-at-finance-hearing-on-foster-care-group-homes.

2 Teresa Wiltz, "When Trump Signed Spending Bill, He Signed into Law a Huge Overhaul of Foster Care." (*USA TODAY*, May 5, 2018), https://www.usatoday.com/story/news/nation/2018/05/05/foster-care-family-first-prevention-services-act-trump/573560002.

Legislators and advocates consistently repeated these talking points: more prevention, fewer institutions, same price. Even the experts, though, had some difficulty explaining how this would all shake out. If you prevent enough kids from entering the system, would that automatically reduce the need for institutional care? How soon would we see the effects? And what would we do in the meantime with the kids who were still coming into care but couldn't find space in an institution?

No sooner had the legislation passed than states started asking for temporary waivers from the federal government. They would need more time to comply. The prevention services for which states would now be allowed to use Title IV-E dollars had to be "evidence-based," but it was not clear which ones passed that test—the overwhelming number did not—and the federal government seemed to be dragging its feet in approving programs for reimbursement.

But the real and potentially catastrophic unintended consequences of Family First concerned congregate care. All over the country, kids were still entering foster care, only now there were fewer and fewer places to put them. A *Washington Post* report noted that across the country, "case workers and courts have been funneling children into crowded emergency shelters, hotels, out-of-state institutions and youth prisons—cold, isolating and often dangerous facilities not built to house innocent children for years."[3] "With few available beds in therapeutic care in Washington State," read an op-ed in the *New York Times*, "foster youth, especially those of color, are frequently forced to stay in hotels."[4] A Better Childhood filed suit against ten child welfare agencies in part because they house children in hotels, homeless shelters and institutions out

3 Emily Wax-Thibodeaux, "'We Are Just Destroying These Kids': The Foster Children Growing Up Inside Detention Centers." (*The Washington Post*, December 30, 2019), https://www.washingtonpost.com/national/we-are-just-destroying-these-kids-the-foster-children-growing-up-inside-detention-centers/2019/12/30/97f65f3a-eaa2-11e9-9c6d-436a0df4f31d_story.html.

4 Caroline Catlin, "Seattle's Foster Children Deserve Better." (*The New York Times*, December 30, 2019, sec. Opinion), https://www.nytimes.com/2019/12/30/opinion/foster-care-washington.html.

of state.[5] The nonprofit advocacy organization has documented placements with guardians outside the state and situations where youngsters with no criminal record are housed in prison conditions.

It was an outcome that our policymakers should have seen coming a mile away. It's not as if this was the first time that we had tried to reduce congregate care. Between 2000 and 2018, the percentage of foster kids in group homes actually dropped from 18 percent to 11 percent.[6] The low-hanging fruit—kids who could be placed elsewhere, with family or nonrelative foster parents—was already picked. This new legislation would force the remaining kids—the toughest cases by all accounts—out of group homes.

To meet the goal of family placements, state and federal agencies have for years mounted elaborate ad campaigns to recruit more parents. In some jurisdictions, nurses and counselors are offered specialized training and increased fees to take in children in need of medical or psychological care in order to keep them from congregate settings. States have tried to expand so-called therapeutic care as well.

In 2020, the Department of Health and Human Services embarked on a PR effort specifically to attract adoptive parents for teens in the foster system, a population for whom homes are often difficult to find.[7] Family First also encouraged states to recruit more foster parents (though it put no money behind the suggestion). But even with outsized efforts, most child-welfare programs can't fill the need for foster families. (In fact, the federal government doesn't actually know how many licensed foster beds states have now, and nothing in Family First will require states to provide those metrics to the feds.)

---

5 Associated Press, "Child Advocates Ask Judge Not to Dismiss Foster Care Lawsuit," NBC Washington, December 31, 2019, https://www.nbcwashington.com/news/local/child-advocates-ask-judge-not-to-dismiss-foster-care-lawsuit/2194791/.

6 "Children in Foster Care by Placement Type in the United States." The Annie E. Casey Foundation KIDS COUNT Data Center (The Annie E. Casey Foundation, accessed September 3, 2020), https://datacenter.kidscount.org/data/tables/6247-children-in-foster-care-by-placement-type#detailed/1/any/false/37.

7 Kyle O'Brien, "Ad Council Spots Show the Rewards of Adopting Teens from Foster Care." (*The Drum*, October 24, 2019), https://www.thedrum.com/news/2019/10/24/ad-council-spots-show-the-rewards-adopting-teens-foster-care.

But the authors of Family First seem unable or unwilling to acknowledge these efforts. The legislation notes that "a shortage or lack of foster family homes will not be considered an acceptable reason for residential placement."[8] So what exactly was the plan?

Some children have behavioral problems that torpedo adjusting to family life. According to a 2012 report from the Health and Human Services Child Welfare Information Gateway, "disruption rates"—meaning that a child is adopted and then "returned"—range from about 10 percent to 25 percent nationwide.[9] For older kids, the numbers tend to be higher. And some children, teens especially, don't want to be fostered or adopted by a family. They may have experienced multiple placements and prefer a group setting to trying to fit once more into a family unit.

Which makes you wonder: If the state has attempted to place kids in multiple homes and either they or their foster parents don't want to continue the placement, how many more times should we try? The answer seems to be: As many as it takes. Similar to the strategy of sending kids back to their biological parents after multiple prior removals, our approach to foster care fits the definition of insanity—trying the same thing over and over, expecting different results.

The incentives in terms of public relations and public dollars now are all on the side of reducing congregate care. Marie Cohen, author of the blog Child Welfare Monitor, pointed out that disconnect in a 2019 report from the Annie E. Casey Foundation.[10] The much-publicized study, wrote Cohen, "praised those jurisdictions with lower group home percentages" while "chastising those with higher rates." But "nowhere," noted Cohen, "did the authors men-

8 Pub. L. No. 115-123.

9 "Adoption Disruption and Dissolution." (Child Welfare Information Gateway, U.S. Department of Health and Human Services, Children's Bureau, 2012), https://www.childwelfare.gov/pubs/s-disrup.

10 Cohen, "Reducing Congregate Care Placements: Not So Easy, Not Always Good for Kids." (*Child Welfare Monitor*, April 15, 2019), https://childwelfaremonitor.org/2019/04/15/reducing-congregate-care-placements-not-so-easy-not-always-good-for-kids; "Keeping Kids in Families." *The Annie E. Casey Foundation* (The Annie E. Casey Foundation, April 2019), https://www.aecf.org/m/resourcedoc/aecf-keepingkidsinfamilies-2019.pdf.

tion the fact that eliminating too many congregate placements may lead to foster youth staying in offices, hotels, emergency placements, and abusive out-of-state facilities."

How did we know this was going to happen? In 2015, the California Legislature enacted the Continuum of Care Reform Act specifically to reduce reliance on group facilities and force the system to increase family placements. It didn't eliminate all group homes, but it designated such settings primarily as a short-term solution for youngsters certified as having a medical or criminal problem that required a restrictive environment. The state estimated that it would quickly move 65 percent of its group home population to families.[11] Instead, it found it was only able to transfer 35 percent. With fewer group beds available, it had to assign many of the children to medical and detention facilities even if they didn't require such settings.

Unfortunately, the Family First Prevention Services Act is modeled on California's program. It is also leading states away from congregant care, limiting the kinds of facilities that can be funded by federal dollars and by adding regulatory burdens to group placements. If we just run these places out of business, the thinking goes, states will have to come up with an alternative. Well, they have, and it's worse.

Now that we have completely overhauled our foster-care system in order to get rid of group homes, maybe it would be worth doing a closer examination of whether they're really as bad as policymakers and advocates claim. In fact, the evidence suggests that group homes have improved the lives of tens of thousands of children in the past and that they could help a certain population of children today if used wisely.

Back in the '90s, the ire provoked by Newt Gingrich's suggestion seemed wrongheaded to Richard McKenzie. An economist at

11 Justin Loudenback, "California's Sweeping Group Home Reform Falters Without Key Supports for Youth." (*The Imprint*, February 14, 2019), https://chronicleofsocialchange.org/child-welfare-2/california-group-home-reform-falters-without-key-supports-for-youth/33822.

the University of California at Irvine, McKenzie authored an article for the *Wall Street Journal* defending the institutions. "A funny thing has happened in the emerging debate" over orphanages, he wrote, "No one has thought to ask us orphans, the children who grew up in institutions, what we would prefer."[12]

McKenzie spent his formative years in the 1950s at Barium Springs, an orphanage in North Carolina. His parents were both alcoholics—his mother died when he was ten—and he was allowed to "run the streets," he recalls. He was shoplifting by the age of six, though he says he never got caught. The minister of the local Presbyterian Church told the head of Barium Springs that he and his brother "were great kids" and church members—neither of which was true, says McKenzie—and so they were brought to the orphanage.

When most people hear the word orphanage, they think about popular depictions like the drunken tyrant Miss Hannigan in Annie or Oliver Twist asking for some gruel: "Please, sir, I want some more." But that's not how McKenzie described it: It's true, he says,

> *Life in The Home (which is what we called it) was no picnic. When we were young, we got two baths and changes of clothes a week, regardless of whether we needed more. We went barefoot to school until late November (which, until it got cold, was a marked advantage). We went to bed in 'sleeping porches' that were totally unheated. We worked hard for long hours on the farm and in the shops, and we lacked a lot, not the least of which were the daily hugs other children take for granted and the requisite level of encouragement to read and study.*

But what was the alternative? McKenzie wrote:

> *If any of us had had a choice between growing up with Ozzie and Harriet or in The Home, each would surely have taken the former. However, we either didn't have parents*

12 Richard B. McKenzie, "An Orphan on Orphanages/Presbyterian Church Orphanage." (*News and Record*, December 10, 1994), https://greensboro.com/an-orphan-on-orphanages-presbyterian-church-orphanage/article_c70b917e-29e9-5ce6-a085-603ce868c1c8.html.

> *or left parents behind who were not worthy of the roles they had assumed. Those who think that private orphanages are 'extreme' solutions to the problems many children face do not appreciate the realistic options available to many children. Few of us would have entertained adoption, and virtually all of us today shudder at the foster-care option. The dominant emotion for those of us who return each year to homecoming [at the orphanages] is neither hostility nor regret, but sheer gratitude.*

When McKenzie's piece appeared thirty years into his professional career, he says he received more responses than to all of the other articles he had written combined. In an email to me, he wrote: "What surprised me was the number of contacts made by orphanage alumni who called or wrote to say, 'Right on!…And my home was better than yours.'" He was invited to attend several of their reunions.

In the years since, McKenzie has conducted extensive research on the alumni of these homes and written books about his and their experiences. In a survey of 2,500 orphanage alumni (with a whopping 62 percent response rate), he found that 85 percent looked back "favorably" or "very favorably" on their experience. "Only 2.3 percent of the alumni had hostile assessments," McKenzie wrote in an essay in the *Weekly Standard*.[13] "Moreover, the alumni reported that they had done better than the general population on almost all measures, including education, income, attitude toward life, criminal records, psychological problems, unemployment, dependence on welfare, and happiness."

His 2016 survey published by the National Center for Policy Analysis of 400 alumni from six orphanages in North and South Carolina found 80 percent reported "very favorable" experiences.[14]

---

13 Richard B. McKenzie, "The Success Story of Orphanages." (*Washington Examiner*, November 23, 2018), https://www.washingtonexaminer.com/weekly-standard/the-success-story-of-orphanages.

14 Richard B. McKenzie, "The American Dream Is Alive and Well – Among Orphanage Alumni!" (*National Center for Policy Analysis*, 2016), http://www.ncpathinktank.org/pub/the-american-dream-is-alive-and-well-among-orphanage-alumni.

And while 71 percent reported having grown up in lower-income class or poverty, 88 percent report living in middle class or above today. On a scale of happiness from 1–10, respondents reported an average happiness rate of 8.86. Eighty-two percent of these former home residents agree that they "have lived the American dream."

According to a 2020 report from the Children's Bureau, adults who had spent time in foster care as children had higher-than-average homelessness, unemployment, substance abuse, and incarceration.[15] While 31 percent of adult men in the US have attained a college degree, the same is true for only 5 percent of men who spent time in foster care. A third of the men lacked health insurance. Half the women had given birth by the age of twenty compared with only a quarter of the general population. And two-thirds of women who had spent time in foster care had been on some kind of public assistance.

Whether you attribute these outcomes to the child-welfare system or to the experiences that necessitated removing these kids from their families in the first place or some combination of the two, it is clear that these statistics paint the lives of former foster kids as a far cry from the American dream. And this suggests that maybe these group homes have not earned their reputation and that given the poor outcomes for kids who spend part of their childhood in foster care, it is time to reevaluate these institutions. McKenzie, for one, says he has become "very suspicious of the orphanage experts' expertise," and notes that the conclusions of his projects "defied the consensus view" on these institutions.

The consensus view has a long history. In his book, *The Invisible Orphanage: A Prehistory of the American Welfare System*, Matthew Crenson describes how the orphanages of the late 1800s were large, often dangerous places that took kids out of poor houses.[16] Some

15 Daniel Crary, "Unusual Study Details Woes Among Veterans of Foster Care." (*ABC*, January 22, 2020), https://abcnews.go.com/US/wireStory/unusual-study-details-woes-veterans-foster-care-68452492.

16 Matthew A Crenson, *Building the Invisible Orphanage: A Prehistory of the American Welfare System*. (Cambridge, MA: Harvard Univ. Press, 2001).

of their wards were eventually placed with other families, but many were also put on orphan trains to the Midwest, bound for a life of indentured servitude. Crenson notes that "as hard as it was to leave kids at the mercy of some adults, it was much worse to leave them at the mercy of 100 kids. Living in an orphanage meant either being a predator or a victim."[17]

By 1909, at the first White House conference on children, attendees agreed that "home life is the highest and finest product of civilization. Children should not be deprived of it except for urgent and compelling reasons.... Children from unfit homes, and children who have no homes, who must be cared for by charitable agencies, should, so far as practicable, be cared for in families."[18] At the turn of the twentieth century, progressives like Jane Addams began to campaign against these institutions and instead advocated for more aid to go directly to parents to keep them out of poverty to begin with. Crenson explains their view, "Rather than wait for things to go wrong in the family, why don't we make sure things don't go wrong in the first place? Why put kids in orphanages when their parents get tuberculosis? Why not prevent tuberculosis?" You can hear echoes of this argument in today's child-welfare discussion. If we put more money into prevention, these institutions wouldn't be necessary.

But the results of these discussions were hardly immediate. As Marshall Jones noted in his 1993 article for the *Social Service Review*, "the number of children in orphanage care did not decrease in the years immediately following the 1909 conference. On the contrary, from 1909 to 1933 the number of children in U.S. orphanages increased from 115,000 to 144,000 and remained high well into the war years.' It was not until after the war, 35 years after the conference, that the number of children in orphanage care finally dropped below the 1909 level."[19]

---

17 Dale Krieger, "The Rise and Demise of the American Orphanage." (*Johns Hopkins Magazine*, April 1996), https://pages.jh.edu/~jhumag/496web/orphange.html.

18 "Proceedings of the Conference on the Care of Dependent Children Held at Washington, D.C., January 25, 26, 1909." (U.S. Government, 1909).

19 Marshall B. Jones, "Decline of the American Orphanage, 1941–1980." (*Social Service Review* 67, no. 3 1993): 459–480, https://www.jstor.org/stable/30012508?seq=1.

During the second half of the twentieth century, orphanages began to close in large numbers because of government efforts to help families, as well as general economic growth. More parents could afford to care for their children at home. McKenzie also speculates that, as occurred with parochial schools, some of the homes in the South especially shut down operations rather than face racial desegregation after the *Brown v. Board of Education*.

But there were other factors as well, particularly financial ones. One was the slow decline of the churches that were the primary sponsors of these homes. Just as they had a dwindling pool of money to give to colleges and hospitals in the second half of the twentieth century, so the Baptists, Methodists, Presbyterians, and Catholics could no longer support such institutions—or at least not without government aid to supplement it. And that government aid often came with strings attached.

Their costs also rose. The professionalization of the field of child-welfare field, as well as a shift in the kinds of kids coming into these homes (from the merely poor to those who had experienced abuse, neglect, or other kinds of trauma at home), meant that homes were now required to spend more on both childcare and workers' salaries.

Jones describes how in 1960 the Children's Home of York, Pennsylvania, asked the Child Welfare League of America "to make a study of the institution and to recommend lines of development for the future."[20] The investigators "recommended that it either close or transform itself into a treatment-oriented program focused on the care of disturbed children." Jones summarizes the findings:

> *The CWLA report recommended that the old congregate building be abandoned and that six living units be constructed ($70,000–$80,000 per unit) or rented, each unit to contain eight to 10 children. The six living units together would require eight house parents, one for each unit plus two others*

20 Jones, "Decline of the American Orphanage."

> *to provide relief. In addition, the CWLA report called for six fully credentialed social workers: executive director, program director, director of casework, and three caseworkers. Further, the report recommended two possibly part-time professionals, a tutor and a recreation worker, and various professional consultants (psychiatrist, psychologist, pediatrician, and dentist). Finally, of course, the CWLA budget included lines for laundress, maid, maintenance man, clerical staff, fringe benefits, utilities, telephone, and the like. Throughout its report the CWLA emphasized "professional child welfare services" and "adequate salaries."*

It was not long before the homes that remained changed their structures, switching to a cottage-style model—with a smaller number of children assigned to a particular house mother in separate buildings. Many child-welfare professionals refused to send kids to these homes unless they saw that these professional standards were met. Though there were still too many children in these cottages to approximate a real family environment, they were set up to provide more individual attention, particularly for kids with emotional disturbances.

Though these changes made the homes marginally more palatable to social workers, it became the case that virtually any other option was preferable to institutional care. As Richard Barth, dean of the school of social work at the University of Maryland, wrote in his 2002 report "Institutions vs. Foster Homes: The Empirical Base for a Century of Action," "From the perspective of research on parenting and on efficacious mental health counseling, group care appears to have a low likelihood of being able to provide a powerful and positive intervention."[21] Barth acknowledges decades of research showing that children in institutional care "may expe-

21 Richard P. Barth, "Institutions vs. Foster Homes: The Empirical Base for a Century of Action." (School of Social Work, Jack Institute for Families, 2002), https://bettercare-network.org/library/principles-of-good-care-practices/transforming-institutional-care/institutions-vs-foster-homes-the-empirical-base-for-a-century-of-action.

rience less chance of abuse or neglect," something that may surprise Orrin Hatch and others who think these institutions are just hotbeds of maltreatment. But Barth concludes "placement in group care settings is not an essential component of child-welfare services systems of care for the vast majority of children" because "there is no substantial evidence to support the necessity or value of…these settings for most children involved with child-welfare services."

As with so much research in the field of child welfare, it is difficult to make apples-to-apples comparisons because we are not conducting randomized controlled tests on children. Depending on how a state is using congregate care and how many foster homes are available, different kinds of children with different kinds of challenges will be placed into group homes or family foster homes. Even McKenzie acknowledges that the homes when he was growing up were screening kids. They weren't taking in children who had engaged in dangerous behaviors or had exhibited any kind of significant psychological problems. This is why the local pastor had to lie to get the brothers into Barium Springs.

Today, though, there is a different kind of selection bias going on. Typically, only the worst-behaved children, the children with the greatest degree of emotional or developmental problems, or the children who have already been placed and removed from the greatest number of foster homes are the ones entering into congregate care. The fact that congregate care is a last resort for kids means that the poor outcomes of kids are baked into the cake. If you put a kid who has already been placed and removed from a dozen different homes into a group home and his outcomes are not great, well, who are you going to blame? The biological family that abused and neglected him? The foster homes that couldn't handle him? The social workers who kept moving him? Or the group home where he spent his last couple of years before aging out?

It is also difficult to measure the impact of group homes because these institutions take many different forms. The first is a kind of emergency shelter. When kids first enter foster care, if there is no family willing to take them in quickly, they can be sent for a period of days or weeks to such a shelter. The second kind is a psychiatric facility, meant for kids who have experienced a medical diagnosis that needs treatment by a trained professional. The third is a home for kids who have engaged in criminal behavior, a juvenile-detention facility. The fourth is a group home that is closer to a family setting, typically with two married parents living in a home with between six and ten children and taking care of them on a full-time basis, sometimes with a staff member or a respite couple. Often, there are several of these on a campus setting or that are overseen by one central organization. These homes are the modern-day equivalent of what McKenzie grew up with.

Barth's report suggests that the outcomes for kids in out-of-home care are poor when measured by their ability to develop interpersonal relationships, "including the chance to develop close relationship with a significant individual who will make a lasting, legal commitment to them."[22] They also have a less individualized educational experience because kids can't participate in extracurricular activities. And finally, he laments the higher level of reentry into the foster-care system and the lower rate of reunification with parents.

Of course, children who are placed in the first three kinds of residential facilities—an emergency shelter or an institution that caters specifically to kids engaged in criminal behavior or with severe emotional challenges are in these institutions because we have determined that there is no other place for them to go. Most foster families cannot handle these young people. The challenges that make them harder to place also make them less likely to reunify and less able to go to a regular school and participate in normal activities. But given that the goal is for these young people to spend as little time as possible in these settings, faulting

22 Barth, "Institutions vs. Foster Homes."

them for not developing more lasting interpersonal relationships seems absurd.

Barth also notes that worse adult outcomes among kids who have spent time in residential programs are also "because of its structure and the expectation that group care will take total responsibility for the child...group care often fails to provide real-life opportunities—like doing chores or preparing or purchasing food—that youth need to prepare for independent living."[23]

But again, the facilities that don't offer such opportunities are often the ones with the most severe limitations on young people. Not to be glib about it, but if kids are living in the equivalent of psychiatric hospitals or juvenile-detention facilities, then they are not making a lot of trips to the supermarket on their own or working with ovens and knives. On the other hand, the less restrictive settings are often specifically set up to do exactly that. In fact, before there were so many restrictions on child labor, McKenzie laments, many homes were able to be financially self-sufficient while at the same time teaching kids about farming or other skills.

With the increased regulation and professionalization of these homes, much of that was lost. Ronald Richter, the CEO of the JCCA, which oversees a residential care facility north of New York City, says, "We've legalized ourselves into a way of doing business that makes it difficult to serve children in a way they need to be cared for." Richter who was the commissioner for New York's Administration for Children's Services from 2011 to 2014 recalls heated conversations he used to have with Nicholas Scopetta, one of his predecessors in the job. Scopetta was raised in an orphanage in the Bronx and spent his life in the field of child welfare. As Richter recalls, he "felt like his life was saved by these nuns who cared for him and made him whole. He talked about it in such a compelling way and was offended by the demeaning way that, as he got older, child-welfare people talked about congregate care."

23 Barth, "Institutions vs. Foster Homes."

Richter understood Scopetta's sentiment. In his current job, he has worked to make congregate care better and argued for its importance as an option for some kids. JCCA also once looked like the homes that McKenzie describes. Richter says he has people on his board who grew up on the campus. "There are a lot of people who feel like this place saved their lives. They had a parent who was mentally ill. They say: It wasn't ideal or where I wanted to be, but it was better than trying to be a parent to my siblings."

Still, as Richter told Scopetta: There's no turning back the clock. "There aren't nuns giving of themselves today the way they were when you were growing up. There are unions and rules, and no one can touch a kid and it's not the same." As a result, Richter says that the only way forward is to make sure that residential communities like his are "specialized." For kids who come into the system initially and who seem to have real emotional or behavioral problems, it should be the job of one of these facilities to do a complete assessment. The state should require that the facility generate a full report and offer recommendations for treatment, placement, and even an educational plan. These programs should be working with parents and pediatricians and school districts to figure out how to proceed. The idea is not just to drop a kid off somewhere and make sure they're supervised until they can be sent back home or a foster home can be found.

The second reason to use residential facilities, says Richter, is for specialized treatment for longer periods of time. For kids who like to start fires, for instance, there is not going to be a foster home for them. For kids who have been involved in sex trafficking, he says, "you don't want them in the general population." For kids who are profoundly disabled or on the autism spectrum, residential facilities may be able to get them to the point where they can live in a foster home, but it may take a period of years. "They need 24/7 care to get to that baseline." For everyone else, Richter says, we should be able to find a foster home if—and this is a big if—we change the way we recruit foster parents.

But before we bury the idea of group homes as outdated, expensive, and inefficient, it is worth considering a few that are operating successfully. Take the Florida Sheriffs Youth Ranches, which was founded in 1957 and today operates four residential campuses across the state. Children between the ages of eight and eighteen are divided into cottages of ten children, each cottage with a full-time mother and father. The largest campus can accommodate fifty children. They generally start by attending school on campus (which is part of the local public school system) but can move to other local schools if their GPAs are sufficiently high. Being part of the public school system means students can participate in athletics and other extracurricular activities locally. They also have jobs on campus and, when they are older, off campus. The money they earn (which can be as little as $2.50 an hour for younger students) is placed into a bank account for them. The school teaches them how to save for the future and spend responsibly. Some students earn enough to purchase a car, which they can keep on campus.

There are other staff—including program assistants and medical professionals—on the campus, but the cottage parents are there full-time. There are relief parents who rotate among the cottages as well. When you ask people about their major concerns with residential care for foster kids, the first thing they often mention is "shift care" and that having people who are only there for eight hours at a time makes these environments unlike families.

The ranches are selective about who is admitted and will not take children who are a physical threat to themselves or others. They won't take kids with drug or alcohol dependence either. Most of their kids are actually not coming through the Florida child-welfare system but are recommended by private individuals or members of law enforcement. These kids have also been subject to significant trauma, though. For example, notes Bill Frye who is CEO of the ranches, one child came to them recently after having been sexually abused by his father and grandfather. The mother couldn't help and asked the ranch to take him in. Some children have been in the care of grandparents after their parents were incarcerated or died, but the grandparents became too old or infirmed to keep them.

The ranches have also tried to play a role in taking in kids who are removed from their homes by CPS. In recent years, they have offered to take in sibling groups to ensure that these kids don't get separated by different foster homes. Unfortunately, there is such reluctance to place kids in any kind of group-home setting that kids will be placed at the ranch only if every other type of placement has been exhausted, sometimes multiple times. Frye recently offered, free of charge, to take in a sibling group of four who had been removed by the state. Instead, the kids were separated into four different foster homes and then moved again into two different homes a few weeks later. Several years back, two brothers came to the ranch at the ages of twelve and thirteen. They had already been through twenty-four different foster homes. After several years at the ranch, the state came back and wanted to place them in a foster home again. They refused.

One source of the problem that the ranch experiences with state placements is that the ranch requires attendance at religious services. Students don't have to participate—they can even read a book—but they have to show up. Legally this is allowable, but it still makes child-welfare workers nervous. Frye says he sometimes wonders whether they should stop taking state kids and the 15 percent of their funding that comes from public sources. But then he worries about those kids who have been removed and have nowhere else to go.

The outcomes for the kids at the ranches seem better than for kids in congregate care and even for kids in traditional foster homes, with 90 percent graduating from high school. Having school on campus means that the ranch can closely monitor academic progress, but being a public school allows them to offer the other activities that make it seem like a more normal school experience.

Part of the ranch's success may be attributed to the long-term nature of the care there. Though some kids are on campus for less than a year, others stay for seven or eight. They do become close to the cottage mothers and fathers. These dedicated couples have walked the children down the aisle, driven across the country to help them after they've had trouble on their own, and offered them financial assistance during the pandemic.

There are a variety of other programs around the country that offer this kind of model—two cottage parents—but that generally host kids for a much shorter period of time. For them, the goal is to use the model of two full-time parents in a home to rehabilitate kids, get them used to normal life again (if they've ever been exposed to it before) in order to place them (permanently, they hope) in a family.

"These kids are the train wrecks of child welfare," says Eric Bjorklund, who runs Utah Youth Village, a therapeutic foster-care program that includes several group homes as well as forty foster homes serving about seventy-five children. He says the behavior he sees among some foster kids is almost "animalistic." They are angry and depressed and have problems connecting with adults. Some lack even basic hygiene skills. But Mr. Bjorklund sees it as his mission to help these children "become adoptable." Between 2016 and 2018, at least nineteen children have left Utah Youth Villages to be adopted into other families, and twenty-one more were placed with relatives.

To prepare kids to live in families again, Utah Youth Villages uses a behavioral intervention program called the Teaching Family Model. The model—which is also used at Boystown—involves positive feedback and age-appropriate motivation systems—behavior charts and small toys for younger kids and an elaborate point system and privileges for older ones. Developed by researchers in Kansas in the late 1960s, Teaching Family is one of the few effective and evidence-based foster-care intervention models.

A 2008 study, for instance, compared outcomes for youth in Boystown homes with those in treatment foster homes.[24] The authors found that group-care youth "were more likely to be favorably discharged, more likely to return home, and less likely to experience a subsequent formal placement. No differences were found in subsequent legal involvement or the likelihood of living in a homelike setting six months after discharge."

At first, the model can seem stilted. During a visit to a home here, I watched a parent named Darbie Pace periodically interrupt all conversation and whatever she was doing to give feedback on "skills"—like following instructions and greeting others appropriately—to the five foster siblings in her care. Family teachers begin their interactions with a positive, empathetic remark, then offer a specific correction, and, finally, a high five or other positive reinforcement. The ten-year-old girl in Ms. Pace's care smiled as she told me about the things she gets to do as a reward, like baking cookies. The three-year-old was working on not jumping into the arms of every adult he meets and instead telling them his name and shaking their hands.

"The Teaching Family Model teaches adults how to become loving and kind to children who no one else loves and thinks deserves kindness," Bjorklund explains. Utah Youth Villages runs several group homes where as many as six children or eight teenagers live with a family. The mother and father are full-time trained caregivers paid by Utah Youth Villages. They demonstrate for the young people behaviors and interactions that might take place in traditional families. They have dinner together every night, share chores, and hold family meetings.

About a third of the Village's funding for foster kids comes from its for-profit arm, which offers the Family Teaching Model for emotionally disturbed kids whose parents can afford to pay for behav-

24 Bethany R. Lee and Ron Thompson, "Comparing Outcomes for Youth in Treatment Foster Care and Family-Style Group Care." (*Children and Youth Services Review* 30, no. 7, July 2008): 746–57, https://doi.org/10.1016/j.childyouth.2007.12.002.

ioral treatment. It says something about the model's efficacy that parents would choose it in the free market.

A lot of foster care, Pace observes, is "just babysitting"—supervising "a kid watching TV"—rather than helping the children grow. The Teaching Family Model gives parents a script for their interactions and a way to measure progress. To be sure, it takes restraint on the parents' part. When situations escalate, teachers can't simply send kids to their rooms. They can give children negative consequences—a loss of privileges like watching television—but it is always in an empathetic tone: "You must be very frustrated to have broken that vase. How do you think you could express that frustration differently next time?" The parents sometimes sound like kindergarten teachers. But over the years, I've spoken to many foster parents who say that the children in their care have missed some major developmental milestones—a twelve-year-old may be operating on the level of an eight-year-old. What seems to an outsider like talking down to these kids is really a way of going back and teaching them things they never learned.

Only about five percent of parents actually make it through the training process for Utah Youth Villages because, says Charity Hotton, who supervises the recruitment process, a lot of applicants believe "that if you just love a child enough, everything will be OK." But they are bound for disappointment.

Hotton adopted her daughter, Kolony, when Kolony was thirteen. After bouncing around among different family members for more than a decade, Kolony spent two years in one of Utah Youth Villages' group homes and another year in a foster home. Kolony says she changed a lot during her time in the group home because of the "structure" and "routine" there. The parents spent a lot of one-on-one time with her. "I learned my feelings were OK, that I was not a bad person for being angry," Kolony says. But she also knows how to control those feelings. Now a bubbly high-school senior with a part-time job at a local bakery, she plans to go on a mission for the Mormon Church and then on to college (where she's being recruited to play rugby).

Thomas McCrae, who spent time in a Boystown Family Teaching Home in Washington, DC, after being in eleven different foster homes, says he didn't like the point system. It seemed artificial to him, not something that real parents would do. But the effect of living with a married couple and other kids has been powerful. "We had family dinners. There were five other boys. It was like having brothers that you would bond with and connect with and play basketball together."

His experience there, he says, "was the first time I could see what black marriage looked like. I learned how a man should treat a woman and how a woman should treat a man. They taught me how to build everlasting relationships." His foster homes were typically single women. But at the teaching family home, he says, "I was able to witness Uncle Phil and Aunt Viv," a reference to the couple on the sitcom *Fresh Prince of Bel-Air*. They were like my own black family sitcom of love."

McRae has finished college and is enrolled in a graduate program to get his master's in social work, but he still goes back to visit the couple in that home regularly. He considers them his godparents. Though he believes that group homes are not without flaws, he says that "a lot of residential programs have the potential to be great. They just have to find folks to operate them."

The same, of course, could be said of foster care. It works great as long as you recruit the right people. But family-style group homes may have other advantages. The couples receive extensive training and are carefully selected. Caring for these high-needs kids is their full-time job. Their sponsoring organization generally provides respite care and additional staff to help with their responsibilities.

For decades, congregate care has been dismissed as a placement of last resort. But by making it a last resort, letting kids migrate through dozens of homes before considering it, we are setting up these homes—and these kids—for failure. As with every option for kids in care, whether it's reunification, kinship care, foster families, or congregate care, the most important question is: What's the alternative?

It's a question that Richard McKenzie keeps at the front of his mind. He is often asked to speak to groups about his professional interests, but sometimes they ask about his personal story. "They like my rags to riches story," he says, "and sometimes applaud me for it." But he says the thing that he has difficulty getting across is that his success "is not in spite of his experience at the Home, but because of it."

CHAPTER 10

THE POWER OF FAITH: HOW RELIGIOUS COMMUNITIES ARE MAKING FOSTER CARE STRONGER

It's a cold Saturday morning in Greeley, Colorado. Megan Magel and I sit in her car, waiting for someone to open the back door of Journey Christian Church. Megan's trunk and backseat are filled with file boxes, snacks, extension cords, and a small sign that reads "Project 1.27 Training."

The executive pastor, Chadwick Kellenbarger, and his wife and thirteen-year-old daughter soon arrive. They're among the one hundred or so people gathering this morning to learn more about foster parenting. Project 1.27, which was launched by Robert Gelinas, a pastor, and is now run by Shelly Radic, a foster and adoptive parent, takes its name from the book of James 1:27: "Religion that God our father accepts as pure and faultless is this: to look after orphans and widows in their distress." But in the past decade, many churches—large evangelical ones, in particular—have adopted a more strategic approach to caring for the orphan. Pastors are trying to mobilize their congregations to take on this work.

Inside a large, multipurpose room at Journey, Megan, a licensed professional counselor who works as a family care manager for Project 1.27, directs Kellenbarger and me as we set up tables with eight or ten chairs each. At the room's front is a stage with a baptismal pool, a drum set, three large screens, and other set pieces for a large evangelical service. She plugs in the coffee maker and sets out a sign-in sheet. Shortly before 9 a.m., people stream in, bearing coffee cups and more snacks. Megan tells them to sit with "the ones who brought you." Each table soon consists of a foster couple (or, in one case, a single woman) and at least four other adults who have promised to support them, practically and spiritually, as they take in foster children. Some have brought their parents and adult siblings; others have come with their grown children, or coworkers, fellow church members, and neighbors. The foster parents and their supporters must be Bible-believing Christians, willing to sign their agreement to the Apostle's Creed.

Those volunteering as foster parents through Project 1.27 will have completed twenty hours' worth of training, though the state requires only twelve. This morning is the last part of their training. Sitting at my table are Jason and Michelle Watts, a middle-aged couple from nearby Loveland looking to become foster parents—again. For support, in addition to their eighteen-year-old daughter, Jaycee, they're accompanied by Greg and Sue, who belong to their Bible study group, and Greg and Sue's adult son and his girlfriend. This is not the Watts's first foray into foster care. Over the years, they have fostered eight children in their home. About a decade earlier, though, they adopted one of their foster children at age twelve and then decided to terminate their foster license. The boy had severe behavioral issues, doubtless a consequence of his nightmarish upbringing with his biological parents, which included being starved. As he hit his teen years, he had run-ins with the law. But Michelle and Jason remain hopeful about his future.

Now they're ready to open their home again. They haven't forgotten the pressures of fostering, starting with the logistics. When

Jaycee was younger, the family was constantly moving bedrooms around to accommodate different sibling groups coming to live with them, often on only a few hours' notice. Taking in a foster child disrupts the schedule of the whole house, Michelle notes—meetings every week with caseworkers, visits with biological families, doctors' appointments, therapist sessions, and lots more. She says that it usually takes her about two months to readjust each time a new child arrives—and one never knows how long those children will stay.

Jason and Michelle went through the state's basic training the last time they fostered, but they're impressed by how much they've learned from Project 1.27. The group watches an emotional video about being a foster child. In it, police remove a young girl and her baby brother from their home after her drunk father beats her mother; then the girl and the baby get moved into separate homes; she misbehaves, and her foster family punishes her harshly. In another scene, her foster mother offers her a dress, but it reminds her of one that her biological mother wore, and she screams. The video is not melodrama: it represents a fairly typical scenario.

Foster parenting is hard. National estimates suggest that about half of foster parents decide to stop during their first year.[1] Families are often ill-prepared for the challenges: the behavioral problems that many children exhibit, the medical concerns, even (and perhaps especially) dealing with the frustrating bureaucracy of the child-welfare system and family courts, as well as with the dysfunction of kids' biological families. One reason that foster kids go through so many placements—a group sued the state of Kansas on behalf of children with more than one hundred placements—is that many foster families can't handle the job.

"A lot of [foster kids] engage in really confusing behaviors, like, they love you one minute, and then they hate you the next minute," explains Charity Hotton of Utah Youth Village. "It's 'come here, go

1 "The Real 'Crisis' in Foster Care." (Foster & Adoptive Care Coalition, May 20,2019), https://www.foster-adopt.org/blog/real-crisis-foster-care.

away, I don't need you, but I'm going to demand that you do everything for me.' We have to prepare the family for the idea that, for a long time, this is not going to be a reciprocal relationship."

A "disrupted" adoption—meaning that a family after months (or even years) gives the foster child back to the state—is the worst of all outcomes. A child is initially told that he has found a "forever family," and then that family decides that they can't deal with him after all.

To change that situation, Project 1.27's leaders believe foster parents not only need better preparation; more of them are needed. Project 1.27, founded in 2004 and operating on a yearly budget of $430,000, is one of about a dozen "bridge" organizations across the country trying to connect churches with state and local agencies in the hope of recruiting and training more foster families. Arizona and Washington, DC, have 1.27 chapters; Georgia has Promise 686; Arkansas has the CALL; and Oklahoma the 111 Project. All belong to a movement, associated with the Christian Alliance for Orphans, called "More than Enough," with a goal to get at least one family in 10 percent of churches in the country involved in foster care. If they hit that target, they calculate, there'd be more than enough families to take care of all the kids in the system. And *more* than enough is the point, because not every foster child is right for every family, and caseworkers need placement options.

The people who are taking in our most vulnerable children and caring for them successfully are most often part of strong, tight-knit religious communities, usually evangelical ones. Four out of five people who foster have pointed to the support of their faith communities and churches as the reason for their success.[2] Churches and faith-based organizations have developed some of the largest, most innovative, and most effective programs for recruiting, training, and supporting foster and adoptive parents. More communities would do well to welcome these efforts and follow the lead of

2 Naomi Schaefer Riley, "Fighting Back on the War on Adoption." (American Enterprise Institute, May 28, 2019), https://www.aei.org/articles/fighting-back-in-the-war-on-adoption.

these committed families. Unfortunately, these are the very groups that are being targeted by social justice warriors in state and federal child-welfare agencies. They are being tarred as discriminatory and driven out of this work by people who are more interested in ensuring everyone supports the latest gender-identity theories than the notion that children should have a good home.

Still, groups like Project 1.27 continue their work. Megan talks about the sights and smells and sounds that can trigger foster kids to react. The smell of beer on a foster parent's breath may make a foster child think that she is about to be abused. One of the Watts's foster children lost his temper when asked to do the dishes. It turned out that someone in his biological family had smashed a beer bottle over his head when he was doing that chore. Choking up, Jason says that he wishes he had known more about the brains of the children he was caring for. "In all my interactions, I had no clue what was going on." Jason would wonder why these kids weren't listening to him, why they weren't doing what he asked. Now he understands that things that happened to them years ago remained like scars in their minds.

Another Project 1.27 foster mother, Noelle MacLeay, describes how the information she and her husband received about trauma changed how they've raised their fourth child, adopted from foster care when she was just six weeks old, after suffering abuse. "They taught us that though she will never remember, her body will never forget," says MacLeay. "When you talk to people in the world, they're gonna say, 'Oh, but she was a baby. It's fine.' And that's not true. Her brain is wired differently now because of that."

During the support training session, I watch Greg and Sue, who've volunteered to be part of the Watts's support network. They are moved by the video and by Jason's grief over the past but aren't sure what to say in the discussions that follow. Sometimes Sue offers a comment about her own children's willful personalities, always careful to say that she knows it's not the same. Greg awkwardly mentions a dog they once rescued, which would get upset whenever it saw a flyswatter. They concluded that someone must have used one to punish the dog.

They don't know much about Jason and Michelle's earlier experience with foster care—it was before the couples knew each other—but they do know the son who's been in trouble with the police and have offered to serve as a sounding board. Michelle says that this is an important part of the support that they need. They had a neighbor who would greet their daughters but shun their adopted son. They also had attended a church that was less welcoming toward foster children. "People would start conversations with us about our foster children because they wanted to gather information," Michelle says, not because they cared. "These are real people living in your home *as your children*, not just some kids you are watching." Their current church is smaller but much more supportive. Of its one hundred or so families, they can think of six off the top of their heads involved with fostering. It may seem like a small number, but when everyone knows someone engaged in this work, it can change the whole community.

Greg and Sue dutifully take notes. There is only one short break over four hours, but as I look around the room, everyone seems to be paying attention. No one is checking a phone, or even doodling on the information packets. Helping foster parents is something that these men and women take seriously.

At one point, the supporters are asked to think about the changes that a couple may experience when foster kids move in. "Our relationship just isn't a priority anymore," says Jason. "Or maybe it just feels that way." The last thing that churches want is for foster care to break up stable marriages. But the risk is real. Jason acknowledges that when things are not going well with a new child in the home, "isolation is my default response. I don't want my church family to know that there are problems."

Many foster families go through a "honeymoon period," where everything seems fine and the child is behaving well, Megan observes. But once a child starts to feel comfortable in a family, he or she may start acting out. This is when foster parents are more likely to isolate themselves—and when support teams should get involved. Do the foster parents need a babysitter? Do they need help with their other children? Do they need a meal? Each table is told to fill out a "support team roster," in which each person volunteers for specific responsibilities. From being "available to respond to the family in an urgent situation" to moving furniture or setting up outdoor play equipment to acting as "prayer team leader," there are tasks to engage everyone's talents and time. Megan tells me that most support teams establish a Facebook group or an email list so that everyone can be aware when the family needs a hand.

Each table is also encouraged to imagine how life changes for children already living in the home. Michelle says that she and Jason worried about how to prepare their biological children for hearing about the experiences of foster kids. Jaycee nods. "They told me things that happened to them, and I thought, Whoa!" Sue stops writing and looks up. Maybe she's thinking what most non-foster parents are thinking at this point. Would they be willing to expose their own children to the drama and pain that a foster child can bring into a home?

This is hard for some of the extended family in the room to grasp. Megan says that one couple's parents almost dropped out of the support training because they were so worried about the idea of their children bringing foster kids into their homes. I've often heard sentiments like this from foster parents, especially younger couples without their own kids yet. Shelly Radic, Project 1.27's president, tells me that a growing number of such couples are going into foster care. It used to be mostly couples who couldn't have kids of their own or empty nesters; not anymore. And this worries the couples' own parents. Do they know what they're getting themselves into?

In certain areas, Project 1.27 staff members are better able to help than a fellow churchgoer or neighbor. Noelle recalls how, during the week that the court was about to terminate parental rights for their older foster daughter (she had been living with them for a year and a half), a relative of the biological family, whom they had never heard from, came forward to contest the adoption. "Of course, I panicked," recalls Noelle. But her Project 1.27 caseworker counseled her to stay calm. At one point, it looked as though the courts would take the girl from them to go live with the relative, and Noelle and her husband told their biological kids that the child wouldn't be staying. In the end, she stayed.

This is the emotional havoc that foster care can wreak on a family. Families know that foster care is supposed to be temporary (except where families request that only children free for adoption be placed with them). Yet parents and foster children can (and should) get attached, and it's important not to minimize the sadness that the parents feel when a foster child leaves; but the loss can be better endured if they know that the child is going back to a stable home. It is becoming more common these days for foster parents to remain in contact with biological parents or other relatives who may take in a child, so they maintain some connection. And the more supportive adults that children have in their lives, the better.

The harder cases are those where a family has become attached to a child and worries that he or she is in danger of being abused or neglected again if returned to the biological family. Or the child is taken from the only home he or she has known for years and placed with relatives who suddenly appear. These are not infrequent occurrences. "You just have to hold on loosely, with open hands, and just love them, but be willing to let go as well," Noelle's husband reminds her. "And just have the faith that they're going to be okay and that they are loved, even if it doesn't look like it to us."

Sometimes what a family needs is faith, Noelle says. "There were times that we were just on our knees, and it breaks us. It's hard and it's painful, but we know that there's that faith of God being there for us and for her and for our bio kids that we've decided to drag along." She describes how hard it was to bring her foster daughters to visit their biological mothers: sometimes the women wouldn't show up, upsetting the kids. Nadia has asked her support group to pray for her foster daughter's biological mother because she doesn't feel able to do it herself yet. She has read the file on what the girl went through since she was a toddler. "I can't even talk about it because it makes me so upset."

At the end of the training, Megan asks each group to pray. Jason and Michelle stay seated, while others huddle around them, closing their eyes, putting their hands on the couple's heads and shoulders, and offering words of comfort and hope about the work they are about to take on.

The combination of evidence-based practical help and spiritual support for families has made organizations like Project 1.27 leaders in a foster-care revolution happening across the country, even in some places you might not expect it.

In Arkansas—one of the poorest states in the country and one with among the highest percentage of rural residents—one can see some of the most promising efforts in this regard. There are thousands of stable, middle-class families who have become aware of the problems plaguing their state's residents and have made a commitment to shelter, care for, and mentor kids at risk, to reunite them with their families if possible, and if not, to provide a permanent loving home for them.

In recent years, the foster care situation there had become unmanageable. In 2007, the number of kids in care in Arkansas was over 3,000, and it had grown to more than 5,000 ten years later.[3] A severe shortage of foster families meant that more kids were being placed in group homes or larger institutions. This was in no small part related to the state's high level of incarceration. The state

3 "Children in Foster Care in the United States." (The Annie E. Casey Foundation KIDS COUNT Data Center. The Annie E. Casey Foundation, accessed September 3, 2020), https://datacenter.kidscount.org/data/tables/6243-children-in-foster-care#detailed/2/5/false/871.

had the fastest-growing prison population from 2012 to 2016, and it had the highest number of children with an incarcerated parent in 2016.[4]

A group of churchgoers across the state took notice of the problem and, in 2007, launched a volunteer organization called the CALL, which stands for Children of Arkansas Loved for a Lifetime. Its staff encouraged pastors to talk more about foster care and adoption from the pulpit and began to offer training sessions for volunteers. Though the sessions were couched in religious teachings, they covered the same curriculum as the state. According to the Arkansan foster mothers I interviewed, they were also often more convenient and more welcoming to church members. All the training might be held over the course of a couple of weekends, instead of a few hours each week for several weeks, and it was offered in a greater variety of locations.

The number of kids in Arkansas's foster-care system has not changed much for the past couple of years. But at least the number of foster homes in the state that are certified and taking in kids has continued to grow. According to the *Arkansas Times*, it went from 1,601 in September 2016 to 1,821 a year later—a modest but crucial uptick that means the proportion of kids placed in family settings has increased.[5]

Many families, particularly in rural areas of America, are disconnected from civil society and religious communities. They don't have a social network of support. And their children are at the greatest risk for entering the foster-care system. Helping these children and reconnecting these families to each other and to their communities will take more than new public policies or an influx

4 "State Ranked 1st in Count of Kids of Jailed Parents." (*Arkansas Democrat Gazette*, November 23, 2017), http://www.arkansasonline.com/news/2017/nov/23/state-ranked-1st-in-count-of-kids-of-ja.

5 Benjamin Hardy, "DHS Report Shows Improvements in Arkansas Foster Care System, Worker Caseload." (*Arkansas Times*, September 6, 2017), https://www.arktimes.com/ArkansasBlog/archives/2017/09/06/dhs-report-shows-significant-improvements-in-arkansas-foster-care-system-caseworker-caseload.

of money. It will take ordinary Americans getting their hands dirty, working with parents and kids on the fringes of society.

The CALL, which operates in a whopping forty-four of Arkansas's seventy-five counties, is effectively a bridge between foster parents-to-be and the state bureaucracy. The organization says that it trains half of new foster families in the state and that families it has trained have cared for more than 10,000 children and provided permanent homes for 800.[6] Even in extraordinary times, their efforts seem to be paying off. The group did an online training for ninety-three families during the first month of the pandemic in April 2020.

The CALL's offices operate as central locations for a county's foster-care needs. Each one is made to feel homey, with brightly colored playrooms. County workers can bring children to the CALL if they've been removed from their homes in an emergency (which is less jarring than having a child wait in an office cubicle or a police station). Most have a "CALL mall," a thrift shop where foster families can pick up (for free) any clothes, diapers, formula, or toiletries they need for their kids. The freezer is stocked with dinners for foster families as well.

People are coming at the foster-care problem from a variety of angles. After college, Eric Gilmore and his wife (who had trained to be a social worker) volunteered to be houseparents for teens aging out of the system. (Houseparents typically are married couples who care for three or four kids at a time in foster-agency-provided housing). One young woman told him she had been in fifty different placements from the ages of twelve to eighteen. "The day after her eighteenth birthday, she was given a bag of clothes, one night's worth of bipolar medication, and a one-way ticket to some biological family members," Gilmore remembers. Stories like these shook him, and he and his wife launched Immerse Arkansas in 2010 to help older teens who were unlikely to be adopted.

6 "The Call." (accessed September 5, 2020), https://thecallinarkansas.org/about-us.

Immerse moved into the building of a former nightclub near the University of Arkansas. There, teens and young adults can do laundry, look for jobs online, and take life-skills classes. Immerse offers transitional housing, overseen by a residential adviser. Its staff will take these former foster youth to job interviews and talk to landlords on their behalf.

On Tuesday nights there is "the Gathering," in which current and former foster children can have dinner with mentors. There I met Dan Williams, a middle-aged civil engineer who has been paired up with a teenage boy for several months now. They go out to eat and talk about things like how to budget or how to interview for a job. "These are things that your own kids just know. You don't intentionally teach them," Williams says. But no one has done that for these kids. Williams seemed a little stuck on how to help when I talked to him, though—the boy, he tells me reluctantly, is in prison for the next few months. These organizations cannot fix every problem, but they have drawn more and more caring adults into the lives of these children and young adults.

Immerse Families is the result of a merger of Immerse Arkansas with a ministry at the Fellowship Bible Church in Little Rock. The ministry's four founders have all fostered and adopted. And one of them, Rachel Bell, told me that her friendships with the other three were an invaluable source of support in raising her two children, who have special needs and whom she adopted out of foster care. At the age of twenty-seven, Rachel was juggling eight therapy appointments a week for her children. "My friends were starting to have babies," she said. "But my kids weren't like their kids. My feelings weren't their feelings."

"For us," Bell says, "it was obvious that there was a primary need for families to have a connection with other families." The biggest culmination of these efforts is a weekend retreat for almost three hundred foster and adoptive mothers, fathers, and children—from infants to teenagers—in the Ozarks at the Youwannago Family Camp. Parents can attend some lectures and support groups—

needed for recertification by the state—while their children are supervised. But most of the time, families can hike, canoe, and go horseback riding together.

On the first afternoon, there is no fixed schedule: kids explore the playground and ball fields and ride inner tubes down the shallow creek. There is something almost utopian about the scene. About fifteen children—black, white, Asian, Hispanic—are playing a game of volleyball. There is a young boy, pushed by his mother in a wheelchair, basking in the warm sun, and a blind girl with a walking stick running up ahead of her father. There are children with obvious developmental impairments navigating the playground. But they are all surrounded by patient adults and older teens who are helping to ensure everyone gets a turn to serve the ball, that the child on a swing doesn't hit anyone, that everyone enjoys the afternoon. Frankly, it's hard to tell which child belongs with which family.

Here, these families seem to breathe a collective sigh of relief. One adoptive mother of a thirteen-year-old girl who spent her first eleven years in foster care says, "It's nice to be around people who get it. I can let this wall down." Most people don't understand why her daughter, who looks to be the size of an eight-year-old and has the communication skills of a toddler, cannot do something as simple as an Easter egg hunt without her mother holding her hand. But here, no one stares or asks too many questions. (In addition to the retreat in the Ozarks, there are also breakfasts, lunches, and dozens of other support events during the year.)

Finding homes for children who have been abused, neglected, or abandoned by their own families is a daunting problem. But the way that these organizations in Arkansas have come together to address different aspects of that problem—mentoring parents, caring for infants and children on a short-term basis, taking in kids who need a permanent home, helping young adults transition out of foster care—suggests a path forward.

Arkansas is a microcosm of the revolution that has been happening all over the country. The web of organizations serving kids and families in the foster-care system was on display at the Christian Alliance for Orphans, or CAFO, annual summit at the Southeastern Christian Church in Kentucky in May 2019. Thousands of people, representing hundreds of faith-based organizations attended—their missions ranging from the recruitment and training of foster parents to providing assistance for kids aging out of foster care.

Some organizations represented here—such as Focus on the Family and Bethany Christian Services—have been around for decades. Others sprouted up in recent years: Replanted Ministries offers postplacement support for adoptive and foster families. Patty's Hope provides counseling, training, and housing for biological mothers of kids in foster care. Reece's Rainbow advocates for children with special needs and awards grants to families who adopt them.

In 2004, thirty-eight people attended the first CAFO meeting in Little Rock. Jedd Medefind, the current president, says that attendees "realized they were working in isolation or even competition with each other and started to think they could do far more together." Some work directly with foster families, while other "bridge organizations" recruit and train church leaders to bring this work to their congregations. Pastors give sermons on foster care and adoption. Then an outside organization helps train volunteers. Another insight that the leaders gathered at CAFO regularly offer: Not every family can take a child into its home, but there are many ways to support foster care and adoption short of that.

In 2015, Adrien Lewis, a foster father, started an online platform called CarePortal. It allows churches to see requests from local child-welfare officials. They include calls for clothing, furniture, tutors, mentors, and a ride somewhere. They can even publish requests for people to open their homes to foster children. CarePortal now operates in twenty states and has served more than 40,000 children. Lewis sees Airbnb and Uber as a model for CarePortal, which he hopes will "change the way that local communities care for kids and families at risk."

In the same way that these organizations have taken lessons from the tech sector, so they are also interested in the science of attachment and trauma. Those who are unfamiliar with the evangelical community may find this surprising, but the leaders of these organizations have fully immersed themselves in the study of how to help traumatized kids. Many of these organizations now offer training in Trust-Based Relational Intervention (TBRI), a therapeutic, attachment-based model designed to help at-risk children. TBRI is also incorporated into the foster parent training for groups like Project 1.27.

The story of TBRI began about twenty years ago when David Cross, a psychology professor at Texas Christian University (TCU), developed a plan with his late colleague Karyn Purvis to help families who were struggling with kids they had adopted internationally. The stories of children who were adopted out of orphanages in Eastern Europe, China, and South America vary, but what many of them had in common was an almost complete lack of early attachment and developmental issues associated with large amounts of sensory deprivation. Stories of adoptive parents who visited these institutions almost always include shock at the silence in a room full of infants and toddlers. They learned not to cry because no adult had ever responded.

Adopted children arriving at their new homes were often out of control and sometimes violent. Cross recalls how the adoptive parents were "worn out" and were just looking for some kind of break. To offer relief, Purvis and Cross started a summer day camp for foster or adopted youth that sought to address their emotional and social needs. He says that it wasn't intended to be "therapy," but it did turn out to be "therapeutic." In the late '90s, "no one had answers for high needs kids," and there were even a number of high-profile cases in which adoptive parents tried to send adoptees back to their native countries or simply abandoned them to authorities here.

Cross and Purvis's summer camp led to remarkable improvements in children's behavior and social competency, but those gains proved to be short-lived. This set them off on a journey to develop a formalized program that could equip adoptive parents and professional caregivers with the ideas and practices to form healthy relationships with children who have experienced "relational traumas." That is, children who have been exposed to prolonged abuse or neglect and, as a result, face barriers to adapting to new environments and connecting with others.

Their program, which is detailed in the book, *The Connected Child*, came to be based on three core "pillars" stressing that new parents need to provide a safe and structured environment, build trust, and offer careful corrective training. Each pillar draws upon evidence-based elements used in therapeutic treatments for sensory processing disorder and post-traumatic stress disorder as well as cognitive behavioral therapy.

Purvis was the wife of a Baptist preacher, which often put her in touch with families engaged in adopting, but, as Cross says, "she always had one foot in faith and one foot in science." In 2006, Purvis and Cross published a formal study of outcomes associated with a later session of their summer camp that employed more refined trauma-informed protocols and activities.[7] They found that children experienced "reduced levels of salivary cortisol, reductions in child depression, and healthier attachment representations as assessed through family drawings." In a 2016 study on parents utilizing TRBI training, the program was shown to reduce physical aggression in children as well as produce "significant decreases on the Child Depression Inventory total score, negative mood score, and interpersonal relationships score for adopted children from pre-intervention to post-intervention."[8] Indeed, TBRI is one

7 Karyn B. Purvis and David R. Cross, "Improvements in Salivary Cortisol, Depression, and Representations of Family Relationships in At-Risk Adopted Children Utilizing a Short-Term Therapeutic Intervention." (*Adoption Quarterly* 10, no. 1, July 1, 2006): 25–43, https://doi.org/10.1300/j145v10n01_02.

8 Erin Becker Razuri et al., "Decrease in Behavioral Problems and Trauma Symptoms Among At-Risk Adopted Children Following Web-Based Trauma-Informed Parent Training Intervention." (*Journal of Evidence-Informed Social Work* 13, no. 2, June 14, 2015): 165–78, https://doi.org/10.1080/23761407.2015.1014123.

of very few programs designed to help this population that has been rated as "highly" relevant in child welfare by the California Evidence-Based Clearinghouse for Child Welfare registry.[9]

TCU now offers week-long training courses for TBRI trainers—others who will bring the techniques home to the professionals and foster parents in their local community. I attended one such training, dubbed "TBRI Fridays," at the Woodland Park Baptist Church in Hammond, Louisiana, about an hour north of New Orleans. It was sponsored by Crossroads NOLA, a foster care recruitment and training organization in New Orleans. For six hours, including a one-hour lunch break, foster parents, school counselors, psychologists, and volunteers for CASA (court-appointed special advocates) were given an introduction to what happens to children's brains when they experience severe trauma and what they can do to help. Youth who experienced time in foster care were found to have higher rates of post-traumatic stress disorder than combat veterans.

Kristen Carver, who leads part of the training, is the adoptive mother of three girls who were in foster care. She describes to the forty or so people assembled how she and her husband felt "isolated" because the girls were so "unpredictable" and violent in their behavior, which is not surprising. One of her daughters was actually in a foster home when she was an infant; she was placed in a back room, propped up against some pillows, and left in front of a television alone for twelve or fourteen hours a day.

Within weeks of starting to implement the TBRI program in her own home, she noticed significant reductions in the children's behavioral "meltdowns," including their tendencies to harm themselves and other people. They went from several tantrums a day for each child to maybe once a day and now much less frequently than that. Carver says that like so many of the families she meets now, she and her husband had reached a point of desperation. Of TBRI, she says, "It saved our family."

---

9 "Search Results," CEBC, n.d., http://www.cebc4cw.org/search/results/?keyword=TBRI&q_search=Go&realm=keyword.

Interspersed with slides about how a brain grows and develops are short videos of Karyn Purvis herself interacting with children. Cross calls her a "child whisperer," and she did have a certain way about her—firm but warm, and the kids seem to gravitate toward her. She is focused on "connecting not correcting." But that is not to say that she doesn't correct. Often, she has children ask for something or perform an activity several times until they can do it calmly and respectfully. She models the way that she hopes a child can, for example, ask to stay at the playground for longer and then asks them to try it. Instructions that are given are simple and short. Children are given two choices about how to proceed. More than that, and they can be overwhelmed.

But much of the program is devoted to helping the child form a bond with the adult. For instance, adults are often asked to imitate the movements of the child—a kind of "Simon Says," but with no words. Sometimes putting on a shirt of the same color or wearing matching bracelets or ribbons allows a child to feel not only that the adult is paying attention to them but that they are forming a connection with each other.

The TBRI trainers also remind adults to consider the basics first. Is a child hungry or thirsty? Kids who have been through severe trauma are often not capable of expressing their needs in the same way that others in their same age cohort might be. Indeed, their own bodies might be so "dysregulated"—a term that is used often in TBRI training--that they might not even know they are hungry or thirsty. Something as simple as having a child drink a cup of ice water may help them calm down.

Alex Brian describes learning about the "fight-flight-freeze" response through his TBRI training and how that helped him understand the behavior of his now four-year-old adoptive son when something would upset him. "Knowing why he is acting that way lets me know how to respond." Alex says his instinct would often be to say, "We've had this conversation 800 times. You need to respond to me respectfully." With TBRI he thinks, "It's been an hour and a half since you've had a snack. It's getting to be the end of your day. You're being disrespectful. I'm going to model it for you. I'll ask you to do it again."

TBRI has been adopted broadly by Christian communities around the country that have done a lot of international adoption and, more recently, have added foster care and adoption out of foster care to their missions. In all of these instances, people who may already be parents to multiple children of their own have had to rethink their approach. Cross says that Purvis worried about the church leadership not preparing parents for what it would be like to take in a traumatized child. "People said if you loved Jesus, you should adopt a child. And she challenged that message and said everyone can contribute, but not everyone has the tools to adopt."

Aaron Vogel, a New Orleans restaurant owner, already had four biological children when he and his wife took in their first foster child. But he says he has had to reconsider a lot, even the way he stands. With his kids, he is trying to project the image of a strong father, but these days, they are taking in children who have never had a father in their lives. And frankly, the men they have encountered have often hurt them. Vogel says he hangs back at first now when a foster child comes into their home, just asking a lot of questions and offering his help, never saying "this is how we do things around here."

As Purvis and Cross found, development in traumatized children has simply been halted at a certain point, and parents may need to speak to an eight-year-old the way they would speak to a five-year-old. Of course, the idea is to move them forward developmentally, but you have to start where they are. Melissa Breedlove, who does TBRI training for others now, says that she also parents differently since learning about the trauma that the children she fosters have endured. When a foster child comes into the home, bedtime has to be a whole different process. For one, many of them have never been put to bed before. "They just crash wherever they land. And so, it's a hard transition." There are many different steps to getting ready for bed, and they can't be rushed or skipped or a child will get very upset—even if a parent is particularly tired.

Anna Palmer, the founder of Crossroads NOLA, says that "when you understand attachment and its role in child development, you understand how important transitions are." Not only does that mean it's important to have fewer of them, but they also shouldn't be sudden unless it's absolutely necessary. Some of the families with Crossroads NOLA describe how workers will pick up a kid after school to bring them back to their family, and that foster child won't get a chance to say goodbye to siblings he's been living with for months or even years.

It is these interactions that have led Palmer and her team at Crossroads to believe that offering TBRI to a broader audience than just foster parents is an important step. It is now incorporated into training for new DCFS workers (two full days are required), and those who are already on staff can get continuing education credits for attending more in-depth sessions on trauma-informed care. Palmer estimates they have trained at least 2,000 professionals at their workshops with the support of grants from private foundations.

Brandy Young, who has worked for DCFS in the Covington region of Louisiana for thirteen years, says that TBRI was like a "missing puzzle piece," helping them to understand what was going on in the brains of the children they were trying to care for, and often in the brains of the parents who themselves had been in foster care. Despite the fact that she holds a master's degree in social work, she was never given the tools to handle someone who was coming from a place of severe neglect or abuse.

Around the country, Christian organizations like Crossroads NOLA, the CALL, and Project 1.27 have become committed not only to helping individual children but also to changing the way the entire system interacts with foster kids and families. The practical tools they offer, the community support they garner, and the spiritual and emotional help they give have the potential to transform well-meaning parents—people who are interested in helping at-risk children but don't really know what they're doing—into families who are well-equipped with both the information and resources to succeed. Unfortunately, these organizations are often underappreciated, if not downright demonized by the government agencies they are working to support.

CHAPTER 11

THE WAR AGAINST FAITH-BASED FOSTER CARE

In January 2019, the Department of Health and Human Services granted a waiver to Miracle Hill, a South Carolina foster-family agency, exempting it from a regulation requiring that federally funded agencies serve everyone, even if doing so violates the organizations' religious principles. The reaction was swift. "Let's call this decision what it is: state-sanctioned and government-funded discrimination," said Christina Wilson Remlin, lead lawyer for Children's Rights.[1] "It is despicable that this administration would authorize federally-funded state child welfare agencies to allow caring, qualified families to be turned away because they don't pass a religious litmus test," said ACLU lawyer Leslie Cooper.[2]

This was only the latest skirmish in a battle that will frankly have more significant, even life-altering, implications than whether bakers can be forced to make cakes for people whose marriages they

1 "South Carolina's Waiver to Discriminate." (*Children's Rights*, January 23, 2019), https://www.childrensrights.org/waiver-south-carolina-discrimination/.

2 Dick Mangrum, "ACLU's Take on the Trump Administration Action on South Carolina Request." (101.7 WGOG, January 23, 2019), https://wgog.com/aclus-take-on-the-trump-administration-action-on-south-carolina-request.

disapprove of, or even whether nuns should be forced to pay for other people's birth-control pills. Most foster-care agencies in this country are faith-based. If we shut them down, the half a million children in foster care right now and the hundreds of thousands who will come in over the next few years will have a much, much harder time finding homes. The strides made in the past decade by organizations like Project 1.27 and the CALL, not to mention countless other religious groups across this country, are one of the few bright spots in the dismal child-welfare landscape. That left-wing groups with radical sexual and secularist agendas have launched a scorched-earth campaign to undermine these organizations—and have successfully driven many religious agencies out of this business—should outrage every American who cares about the fate of at-risk children.

Indeed, it is not only the religious agencies that will be barred from operating, but soon, it will be religious people themselves. Or anyone with a vaguely traditional understanding of sexuality and gender identity. If you as a foster parent are not willing to support adolescents taking hormones or undergoing surgery because they have come to believe they were born into the wrong body, then you too will soon be unqualified to care for a child in need.

Like it or not, most foster families in this country take in needy children at least in part because their religious beliefs demand such an action. Religious agencies recruit these families, train them, and even certify them; they also offer emotional, logistical, and spiritual support for months and even years after placement. Religious foster families are among those most likely to take in children with special needs. Fostering a child or adopting a child out of foster care is such a life-changing commitment—one that tests even the most solid marriage and family—that most people would probably not undertake it unless they literally felt that God was telling them to do so.

Unfortunately, more and more of these agencies have come under fire because they do not adhere to state, local, or federal nondiscrimination statutes. Most states have adopted their own policies, apart from federal guidelines. In twenty-nine states as well as the District of Columbia, state statute, regulation, or agency policy prohibits discrimination in foster care based on sexual orientation or gender identity. On the other hand, eleven states explicitly permit state-licensed child-welfare agencies to refuse to place and provide services to children and families, including LGBTQ people and same-sex couples, if doing so conflicts with their religious beliefs.

This patchwork of laws has left many agencies in limbo and plenty afraid for their survival. Early in my work on this topic three years ago, I was planning to visit a successful faith-based foster agency in Florida. I was not going to write about their religious mission or their policies with regard to same-sex couples, but the leaders got cold feet and became worried that literally any coverage of their work would raise the agency's profile in the community and people would start to pressure them about their policies.

Many agencies saw the writing on the wall long ago. Shortly after Massachusetts legalized gay marriage in 2006, the Boston Archdiocese's Catholic Charities announced that it would no longer contract with the state to offer adoption services, lest it be forced to place children with gay couples.[3] Other religious agencies held on until laws that specifically targeted them were passed. In 2019, Catholic Charities in Buffalo ended its foster and adoption services because of a state law that would have required them to place kids with gay couples. The ACLU sued Bethany Christian Services in Michigan to get the organization to change its policy in this area. The state decided to settle with the ACLU, but then another religious foster-care agency, St. Vincent Catholic Charities, along with a former foster child and the parents of five adopted children with special needs, sued Michigan asking the court to allow faith-based organizations to continue contracting with the state.[4]

3 Colleen Rutledge, "Caught in the Crossfire: How Catholic Charities of Boston Was Victim to the Clash Between Gay Rights and Religious Freedom." (accessed September 2, 2020), https://core.ac.uk/download/pdf/62547978.pdf.

4 Jeff D. Gorman, "Catholics Launch New Volley in Fight Over Michigan Adoption Rules." (*Courthouse News Service*, April 16, 2019), https://www.courthousenews.com/catholics-launch-new-volley-in-fight-over-michigan-adoption-rules.

This case is currently on hold as the country awaits word from the highest court. On February 24, 2020, the US Supreme Court granted a review of the Circuit Court of Appeals' decision that had rejected the argument that agencies performing public child-welfare services have a constitutional right to discriminate. And that fall, the court heard the case. The arguments in favor of protecting the religious liberties of these groups have been well articulated by lawyers for the Becket Fund, among others. But it is the practical implications of closing these agencies that should concern Americans of every religious stripe and none.

Closing these agencies will be like closing Catholic schools—new ones may not appear, and the ones that do may not operate with the same care and commitment as the old ones. Sharonell Fulton, a foster mother who has taken in more than forty children with Catholic Social Services in Philadelphia asks, "What justice is there in taking stable, loving homes away from children? If the city cuts off Catholic Social Services from foster care, foster moms like me won't have the help and support they need to care for special-needs kids." If a foster agency like Miracle Hill—which serves 15 percent of the foster population in South Carolina—disappeared, it would have severe consequences for the state's needy children.

The "stable, loving home" argument should be familiar to advocates of gay adoption, who for years argued that it was wrong to deny children the chance to live in a good home solely because the parents were of the same sex. This argument slowly won support across the United States. Long before gay marriage was legalized, it was becoming more common for gay couples to adopt. "I think even many rock-ribbed evangelicals could agree that most kids would be better off raised by loving gay parents than by our incredibly screwed up foster care system," Megan McArdle wrote in *The Daily Beast* in 2013.[5]

5 Megan McArdle, "Can Gay Marriage Solve Our Adoption Problem?" (*The Daily Beast*, March 29, 2013), https://www.thedailybeast.com/can-gay-marriage-solve-our-adoption-problem.

Of course, that doesn't mean that every evangelical foster agency leader would want to be involved in placing a child with a gay couple—which is why they ran afoul of the Obama administration. But what faith-based and secular foster-family agencies have in common, or should, is an agreement that the needs of children come first.

The burn-it-all-down groups like Children's Rights and the ACLU not only claim that gay couples suffer the emotional harm of having been turned down by an agency—though there is no evidence that any one of these couples has been unable to find a different agency to suit their needs—but also that LGBTQ foster children are harmed by being placed with traditionally religious couples. And so, these same activist groups have also worked the system from the other end, pressuring state agencies to set restrictions on how foster parents and agencies must handle children's issues involving sexual orientation and gender identity.

The Illinois Department of Children and Family Services announced that it "will not tolerate exposing LGBTQ children and youth to staff/providers who are not supportive of children and youths' right to self-determination of sexual/gender identity."[6] According to DCFS, children have a "right to self-determination of gender and sexual orientation," and individual choices about "sexual orientation, gender identity, and gender expression" should be viewed as "developmental milestones, not problematic behavior." The role of adults is simply to "facilitate exploration of any LGBTQ matters through an affirming approach…by being open, non-judgmental, and empathic."

New York City takes a similar approach. According to the Administration for Children's Services website, the agency "is committed to providing all youth and families served by Children's Services and our contracted provider agencies a safe, healthy, inclu-

6 "Illinois Requires Foster-Care Workers, Parents to Support Transgenderism." (National Catholic Register, June 2, 2017), https://www.ncregister.com/daily-news/illinois-requires-foster-care-workers-parents-to-support-transgenderism.

sive, affirming and discrimination-free environment."[7] Children's Services workers must not "ignore safety or risk concerns when it is discovered that the foster parent...will not purchase clothing corresponding to the [Transgender/Gender Nonconforming] young person's gender identity [or] refuses to address the TGNC young person by preferred name/pronoun." Not only must foster parents promise that they'll refer to girls in their charge as "he" if that's what the child prefers, they must also buy dresses for their boys. Or they'll be considered a "safety risk."

Children's Rights also suggests that more states need to "require affirming placement and classification procedures; promote healthy gender identity development and expression; mandate affirming gender-responsive programming and activities while in care; and provide clear and ongoing training and competency requirements for staff.

According to California law, it is "the role of the child welfare agency...to support dependent children's ability to access medically necessary care, including gender affirming health care and gender affirming behavioral health services."[8] This includes not only treatments that "suppress the development of endogenous secondary sex characteristics," but also "interventions to align the patient's appearance or physical body with the patient's gender identity."

So if you are among the millions of Americans who do not think that you should place minors in therapies to suppress their hormones and irreversibly change their physical and mental development, let alone arrange for surgical interventions for children who say they feel like they were supposed to be born another gender, you are not qualified to be a foster parent. This kind of social engineering through the foster-care system is the last thing the system needs. It takes all kinds of foster parents to care for the children

7 "LGBTQ Policies." (NYC Children, accessed August 18, 2020), https://www1.nyc.gov/site/acs/about/lgbtq-policies.page.

8 "Foster Care: Gender Affirming Health Care and Behavioral Health Services." (American Academy of Pediatrics California, accessed September 3, 2020), http://aap-ca.org/bill/foster-care-gender-affirming-health-care-and-behavioral-health-services.

in our system. Some may be more comfortable with kids who have decided on a different sexual orientation or a different gender. But it should be the job of child-welfare workers to figure out the best fit for a child. And writing off loving parents because of their religious views is nuts. We need more people to volunteer for these roles, not fewer.

It would be worth taking a moment here to note that foster care is supposed to be a temporary arrangement. How would parents feel about their child entering foster care and then learning that a foster parent (with the support of a child-welfare agency) approved elective surgery for him or her? Advocates will claim that hormone treatments and sex-changing surgery are medically necessary and only done with the approval of doctors, but this is a very controversial area of medical practice. It is also worth noting that foster kids may be confused about their gender and sexuality, but they are also more likely to be suffering from co-occurring mental illnesses, including anxiety and depression. The fact that many foster children have been sexually abused doesn't help.

There is plenty of reason to be concerned that foster kids who say they are unsure of their gender identity may be taken advantage of by folks who have an agenda. Johanna Olson-Kennedy, the medical director of the largest transgender-youth clinic in the United States, one of the directors of a National Institutes of Health experimental study on early intervention in transgender youth, told an audience at the Gender Infinity Conference (an "Affirming Space to Empower Gender Diverse Individuals") in 2015, that "a not-insignificant" number of young people at her clinic "have actually done sex economy, sex work, for a place to live or something to eat," and that "a lot experience homelessness, precarious housing, and have been in foster care."[9]

Mitchell Laidlaw, an endocrinologist for Sutter Health who testified against the California law when it was being debated in 2018,

9 Madeleine Kearns, "The Tragedy of the 'Trans' Child." (*National Review*, November 21, 2019), https://www.nationalreview.com/magazine/2019/12/09/the-tragedy-of-the-trans-child/.

explained that when it comes to youth who identify as transgender, "the main problem is usually something else besides gender identity confusion." He notes that "doctors and psychologists have absolutely no way of diagnosing with certainty who is a true trans child and who has gender dysphoria confusion." Given that almost 70 percent of children who experience childhood gender dysphoria and are not socially transitioned eventually outgrow it, we need to be extremely careful about medical interventions for all kids, but especially for foster kids.[10]

Many religious foster parents will be driven out of the system by these kinds of regulations. Foster parents who adhere to a traditional faith, like any good foster parents, want to treat the children in their care as if they were their own biological children. And because they cannot in good conscience go along with such interventions, they may be forced to bow out of this enterprise entirely.

Maybe the creators of such laws believe that religious communities do more harm than good when it comes to foster children and that their backward views make them bad candidates for foster parents. Others seem to believe that faith-based communities can simply be persuaded to give up their old-fashioned convictions.

In 2019, a group of faith leaders and child-welfare professionals tried to release a "consensus statement" about foster care and adoption. The effort was led by a representative of the Annie E. Casey Foundation, who told me he believed that the people working in this area agree on "99 percent of issues" so they should be able to figure out a way to deal with the remaining 1 percent. The statement was a valiant effort, but the last draft of it before the participants gave up reads like a biblical text. Many parts of the statement clearly meant one thing to the "faith leaders" and another to the "child welfare professionals."

Take the statement: "We long to see children thrive in safe, permanent, and loving families." Well, of course, you do. But are you

10 Jiska Ristori and Thomas D. Steensma, "Gender Dysphoria in Childhood." (*International Review of Psychiatry* 28, no. 1, 2016): 13–20, https://doi.org/10.3109/09540261.2015.1115754.

willing to let families whose religious views you find distasteful provide homes for them?

Or what about "We believe that professionals, foster parents, and all others in the child welfare system should treat a child's sense of conscience, identity, and belief with sincere respect. At the same time, we believe foster and kinship parents should be free to express their sincere beliefs in respectful, non-coercive ways." What does it mean to sincerely respect a child's gender identity or sexual orientation? Does it mean that you have to accept it? Affirm it? Provide hormones to the child? Offer surgery?

There is a huge gulf on this issue. But while religious leaders are happy to "let a thousand flowers bloom" and encourage the founding and flourishing of agencies to cater to anyone who wants to provide a stable, loving home to foster children, the "child welfare professionals" want to shrink the field to the organizations whose policies and missions they approve of. Only they don't feel they will be shrinking it at all. Indeed, many of these advocates seem to believe they can simply lift the models that faith-based organizations have used and apply them in a nonreligious or even government-run context.

In the fall of 2019, Bob Bruder-Mattson, the president and CEO of FaithBridge Foster Care, came to the American Enterprise Institute in Washington to describe how we could begin to solve the country's foster-parent-recruitment problem. He explained how using demographic information provided by the state of Georgia, FaithBridge was able to analyze which kinds of families were most likely to succeed at foster care, in terms of both the number of children taken in over time and the number of years they were willing to do it, as well the quality of the care they were able to provide. By 2018, FaithBridge had served 1,178 children, 216 of whom were adopted. They had partnered with seventy-three churches and licensed 660 families.[11] They had also introduced more than 10,000 individuals to the needs of kids in foster care.

11 FaithBridge, unpublished data.

But before he presented the numbers, he showed a brief video explaining that the organization works toward "placing children into Christ-centered homes" and helps "families gain confidence to foster with people who are committed to doing life with them." FaithBridge and its partner churches see foster care "as the role of all, not the role of some." Finally, the video concludes: "we serve a much bigger God whose resources are without end. Who so loved the world that he gave his *something*, his only begotten son so that no one would be left alone."

After the presentation, Rob Geen from the Annie E. Casey Foundation approached me. He marveled at the presentation and the amazing work that FaithBridge had accomplished. And then he said, "We just need to find a non-private way to do this." It took me a moment to parse the phrase "non-private." But as the conversation went on, it was clear that he believed there was some way for government to replicate what FaithBridge was doing. I was gobsmacked.

For decades, as religious institutions have declined in popularity in this country, people have struggled to find a way to imitate them. How can we recreate the success of Catholic schools without all the Catholic moral teaching? How can we get people to volunteer at the same level if it's not through a church-run soup kitchen? How can we get people to donate money to worthy causes as if they were tithing to their church? How can we encourage young couples to marry and keep their relationships stable the same way that membership in a church or synagogue or mosque does? It is not that it is impossible to form a meaningful, lasting, and committed community in a secular context. It's just that it doesn't happen all that often.

There are still neighborhoods where people watch out for each other's kids and schools where parents volunteer. There are secular nonprofit groups that have great records of fundraising. But commitment to a religious institution is different somehow. It provides a framework for the way that people behave and relate to each other.

Living in a faith community requires a level of devotion, not just to God but to other people, that it is hard to find elsewhere.

And the idea that government or "non-private" entities could recreate this framework for foster care is absurd. Government can demand that people pay their taxes; it can require people to abide by some basic laws. It cannot force people to take a stranger's child into their home and care for him. It cannot force other members of the community to support their friends and neighbors in this work. Of course, government can and will continue to launch public information campaigns—since 2004, the Ad Council in partnership with HHS has produced more than $660 million worth of donated publicity to get more people to adopt—but there is a reason that these are simply not successful in the way that faith-based recruitment organizations have been.[12] There is no context for such efforts.

What is your responsibility to a child you've never met before? In principle, many people would probably say that they want to help, that every child deserves a loving home, that society should have a "safety net" for these kids. But when the rubber hits the road, only some families are opening their homes.

And some community organizations seem to be doing a better job than others. Foster-friendly churches, for instance, are usually multiracial, and foster parents say that it makes them and their children feel more comfortable. As Noelle MacLeay, who went through foster training with Project 1.27, notes, "Our youngest is biracial, and we're pretty white, you know. But there are other families here, so as she grows, she's not the only kid that doesn't match her family."

Foster-friendly churches are also aware that not all kids behave the same way. They don't banish loud or disruptive children, or even look at them funny. In the best cases, they have trained the church's staff to help with these unruly kids. Noelle remembers being "ter-

12 "National Campaign Showcases the Importance of Adopting Teenagers from Foster Care." (Press release, December 8, 2020), https://www.adcouncil.org/press-releases/national-campaign-showcases-the-importance-of-adopting-teenagers-from-foster-care.

rified" to drop off her first foster child in the nursery during the service (as she did with her older kids). She tried to explain to the woman running it: "Okay, she hits her head and will bite herself when she gets upset. Just come get me, and I'll come get her." The woman took the baby, hugged her, and said, "I've got this. I had a trauma baby too."

For those who would prefer that these faith-based organizations simply fold or who believe that these bastions of homophobia and bigotry can be replaced by a better model, it is worth asking how many institutions in Northeastern or West Coast liberal enclaves look like this? Are there a lot of other settings where you can feel comfortable bringing a child with special needs or who are loud and disruptive and know that people will not only make them feel welcome but also know how to help you care for them? I attend one of the largest synagogues in Westchester, and I can say that it is rare to find such children there, and there is no kind of childcare available for a child who will hit her head and bite herself if she gets upset. This is not a knock on my synagogue. But unless we can provide that environment, who are we to judge organizations that can?

In a world in which parents seem to be engaged in an ever-escalating battle over whose child has achieved the most academic, athletic, or social successes, where is the community that welcomes kids who look and act different, kids who have been abused or neglected and who can't behave calmly in any kind of social setting, let alone ace their SATs? These spaces are vanishingly rare.

When I tell friends in my community about these organizations and these churches—which are more common in the South and West—they often ask me whether the groups work in foster care simply to gain converts. I posed this question to Jedd Medefind of CAFO, who couldn't help but laugh a little. "If you just want to proselytize, you can go to the park and pass out tracts. Adopting or fostering or becoming involved in the life of a struggling family is far more costly than cheap proselytizing." He says the families and organizations represented at CAFO don't do what they do out of duty or guilt. "Being loved is the most transformative power on earth. The Christian gospel said our God welcomes us amidst our great need. We seek to reflect that same heart."

The vast majority of these new and innovative foster care and adoption organizations have sprung up in the evangelical world. The Catholic Church has been in the business of adoption and foster care since the nineteenth century, but there have been relatively few campaigns to recruit the people in the pews to take these children into their homes. Rather, it seems, that most Catholic parishioners have gotten in the habit of giving money to the cause but not thinking that they themselves are called to this work.

Kathleen Domingo, who heads the Los Angeles Archdiocese's Office of Life, Justice and Peace, told a local Catholic website that "the Catholic community has been very slow to get on board with fostering."[13] In the past couple of years, that has started to change. With the support of Archbishop José H. Gomez, Foster All, a local nonprofit, "has made more than 85 presentations at local parishes, signing up more than 300 people who expressed interest in foster care. Other parishes have hosted clothing drives or community breakfasts for children in foster homes." What are the rest of them waiting for? But the more that organizations like Catholic Charities are forced out of the work of adoption and foster care, the harder it will be to recruit, train, and support faithful Catholics who do want to do this work.

It's surprising to find that the Church of Jesus Christ of Latter-day Saints is not more involved in foster-care efforts. Unlike the Catholic Church, with its professional clergy and organizations devoted to caring for orphans, the Mormon church is led by volunteer laypeople. Why hasn't every ward in the United States assigned a "foster care" calling to someone in the congregation? Why haven't local bishops asked people to volunteer for foster care or adoption?

13 Nicholas Wolfram Smith, "Fostering Hope: L.A. Churches Part of Growing Foster Care Movement," (*Angelus News*, January 12, 2018), https://angelusnews.com/local/la-catholics/fostering-hope-l-a-churches-part-of-growing-foster-care-movement/.

Doug Andersen, a spokesman for the church, told me "the church can't be all things to all people. We can't weigh in on every issue." But some observers of the LDS Church suggested to me that after all the criticism it took for its role in passing California's Proposition 8 (which banned same-sex marriage in the state), the leadership wanted to stay as far away from issues that could land them in hot water again. As Andersen eventually acknowledges: "The legal environment has something to do with it." There are few organizations in this country with more committed members and more effective strategies for helping the most vulnerable than the LDS church. The idea that the Church is not doing this work because it fears that getting entangled in the foster-care system will put its mission at risk is a tragedy.

CHAPTER 12

RAISING THE BAR: GETTING MIDDLE-CLASS AMERICANS TO DO FOSTER CARE

Twenty years ago, a social worker from the Massachusetts Department of Children and Family Services called me to ask what I thought of my parents. I was a senior in college, my sister was a sophomore, and my mother and father wanted to adopt a child from foster care. Already in their midfifties, they were too old to take in a baby (not that there were many available anyway). But I hope it won't seem like bragging if I say they enjoyed raising kids tremendously and wanted to keep doing it.

They were deeply devoted, interested in every aspect of our lives. They provided us with everything we needed, if not everything we wanted. They cared immensely about our education. They both worked full-time, but their flexible schedules (my father was an academic, and my mother ran her own think tank) made them available to us whenever we needed them.

All told, my sister and I had a stable, happy childhood, and I explained that to the social worker. My parents had each mentioned to me separately that they regretted not having a third child. So here they were, financially comfortable empty nesters rattling around a big house with a nice backyard, exploring the possibility of taking in an older child from foster care.

They had talked to me about where they would send the child to school and other details. But they also confided that they were worried about welcoming a child who had the kind of emotional and behavioral difficulties typical of a child who had been in the system for a while. My sister and I had never been in any kind of trouble or faced any serious challenges growing up, and they felt that their parenting skills might not be up to the challenge. Could old parents learn new tricks? And what would be the risk to the child if they couldn't handle it?

I couldn't argue with them. I had never met a child in foster care. The only adoptees I knew were from China and the Philippines, and they had come here as infants. Who were my parents going to turn to if things got difficult? They were lone operators—with few close friends or family members living nearby and a small extended family. Nor were they martyrs. They gave to charity but were not the type of people who took on other people's problems and suffered in silence.

In other words, they were pretty typical upper-middle-class Americans. And as far as they had gotten in the process of adopting a child out of foster care, it started to seem overwhelming, and eventually things fizzled out. I do remember wondering at the time: If my parents—who had the financial means and the desire—couldn't do foster care, who could? Many of the would-be foster parents I have met since then wonder the same thing.

"I'll be there tomorrow at 10 a.m." That was the typical notice that Mark Daley, a foster father in Southern California would receive from a social worker about a visit to check up on the children he was fostering. It was the last day of the month, and social workers were supposed to have completed their rounds by then; so that's when she decided to come. Never mind that Mark and his husband both had jobs and would have to upend their schedules and the childcare they had arranged for their foster sons. This was not the social worker's concern. The following day, she arrived—ninety minutes late.

To be frank, most social workers are not used to dealing with families like Mark's. A former spokesman for Hillary Clinton's campaign, now operating his own communications business, which has tried to help Los Angeles County do a better job recruiting foster parents (through the use of focus groups and targeted digital marketing), Mark is part of a new "market segment" of people who are doing foster care. Whether they are gay couples, older single women who have decided to start a family on their own, or heterosexual couples with fertility problems, as a group, they tend to be educated professionals in a middle- to upper-class income bracket.[1] It is hard to tell how large this segment is because, despite complaining about serious shortages of foster homes, most states have not even done the most basic demographic research on who fosters, who is interested in fostering, or who is most successful at it.

Up until recently, social workers, guardians ad litem, and lawyers in the child-welfare system have dealt largely with lower-income families—not just families of the kids in foster care, but families providing the care. Even if the families aren't specifically offering foster care because of the small stipend they receive as a result—many certainly are—the stipend will significantly contribute to the family's bottom line. The result is a kind of chicken-and-egg cycle where the child-welfare system shapes itself to interact with lower-income, less-educated foster families (people who don't have jobs and, frankly, are used to tolerating government bureaucracy on a regular basis) then fails to attract or hold on to families with higher levels of income and education (who have busy lives and little time or patience for inefficient public systems).

1 https://activation.la2050.org/connect/tides-center-dba-childrens-action-network.

If race is the topic everyone wants to talk about in the child-welfare system, class is the topic we barely mention. Certainly, it sounds insensitive to suggest that we should be looking for wealthier families to foster children or adopt them out of foster care. Do we need Daddy Warbucks to provide children with a good home? Are material goods what really matters when helping vulnerable kids? Aren't lower-income families just as capable of providing love and support?

In principle, the answers to all those questions are obvious. It shouldn't matter how educated you are or how much money you make as long as you are committed to caring for kids in need. But families who are already living on significantly less than the average income may have trouble making ends meet when fostering children. Financial concerns are a major source of stress in all families but particularly in lower-income ones. Of course, it is possible to live paycheck to paycheck or to have no emergency savings available and still take in a foster child, but ideally, foster children would live in a home where parents are not constantly worried about the expense of a car repair or a medical bill.

Multiple sources have shown that households with unrelated foster children tend to have lower income and education levels than the general population. According to a 2008 study using the American Community Survey (ACS), the income in households with foster children is significantly lower than the average income in all households with children.[2] The mean income for all households with children ($74,301) is nearly one-third higher (31 percent) than the mean income of households with foster children ($56,364). Households with foster children are much more likely to be in the lowest income category (less than $20,000 a year) and much less likely to be in the highest income category ($100,000 or more a year).

The same pattern holds true for education. The education levels of households with foster children are lower than those for all

2 William P. O'Hare, "Data on Children in Foster Care from the Census Bureau." (The Annie E. Casey Foundation, June 2008), http://www.aecf.org/m/pdf/FosterChildren-July-2008.pdf.

households with children. Indeed, a "fifth (20 percent) of adults in households with foster children lack a high school degree compared with 14 percent for all households with children."[3]

To be clear, these averages are being pulled down by kinship care. It stands to reason that the extended family of children in foster care will be more likely to sit at the bottom rungs of the financial ladder and find themselves less educated as well. As we saw in Chapter 3, the fact that the kids were removed from a home and placed by the state with extended family also suggests that these kin foster families are not just typical family voluntarily stepping in to help before things get too bad. Many of them need the stipend that is provided from the state for kinship care.

According to a 2009 study using Illinois administrative data on foster families in the system between 1996 and 2002, "foster family wage income (mean is $35,587) was considerably lower than the median family income in Illinois (average median between 1997 and 1999 was $44,459).... The average family wage income among kinship families ($28,613) is significantly less than that among nonkinship foster families."[4]

A study conducted by researchers at Columbia University found that children living with nonrelative foster parents were only slightly less likely to be living in single-parent households than children living with their biological families. (21.1 percent vs. 22.9 percent).[5] Some of those single-parent households may be women who are financially secure and have just decided to start fostering later in life. But given that single-parent households are about twice as likely to be living in poverty as two-parent households, it seems likely that we are placing at least some of these foster kids into financially insecure situations. And that doesn't even get

3 O'Hare, "Data on Children in Foster Care."

4 Andrew Zinn, "Foster Family Characteristics, Kinship, and Permanence." (*Social Service Review* 83, no. 2, June 2009): 185–219, https://doi.org/10.1086/600828.

5 Jessica Pac, Jane Waldfogel, and Christopher Wimer, "Poverty Among Foster Children: Estimates Using the Supplemental Poverty Measure." (*Social Service Review* 91, no. 1, March 2017): 8–40, https://doi.org/10.1086/691148.

into the other problematic outcomes for kids who are living in single-parent homes.

One can argue whether a slightly higher-than-average income is enough to provide children who have already been traumatized with a stable home, but it is worth asking why wealthier families are so underrepresented among those providing foster care. Or, to put it another way, why aren't upper-class families doing their "fair share" of foster care?

The answer is pretty simple, according to Ronald Richter, former New York Administration for Children's Services Commissioner: "The only people who can be foster parents are people who don't work." He explains: "You could never be a foster parent who is a lawyer married to a doctor. You'd have to give up your career. You can have people who can afford to hire high-quality childcare who could never do it. It's just too hard." Richter believes that the system actually "incentivizes people who don't have a job. It's like we don't want children to end up in homes with resources. It's wrong, and we perpetuate it."

From foster-care training programs that are scheduled during workdays to last-minute visits from social workers to family-court hearings with no set time that are often postponed once everyone has arrived, the day-to-day inconveniences of becoming a foster parent are overwhelming. Richter cites friends of his—married men, a lawyer and health-care executive—who have a seven-year-old they've been waiting to adopt. The child has been with the couple since birth but has had different visitation arrangements, and the court cannot seem to make a final decision about whether to sever parental rights. As Richter explains, his friends' lives are "on hold." And so is the boy's. "It affects his learning and development, every aspect of his life. The system doesn't acknowledge you are talking about a little person." The couple have considered adopting another child (through a private adoption agency), but they can't do anything until this situation is settled. Says Richter: "It's torturous. Why would someone want to do this?"

Perhaps the thinking is that if you want to foster a child, you should be willing to engage in some sacrifice. Of course, these foster parents plan to do just that. When it comes to fulfilling the needs of the children, these foster parents will often go to any lengths. From handling behavioral challenges to medical needs to working with biological families for visitation, foster parents understand that these children will have demands that are far greater than most children. And they want what's best for them. But the system they are dealing with seems to be placing unnecessary obstacles in their way.

Even the initial inquiry made to a state agency about foster care can be frustrating. A 2005 study by researchers at Harvard's Kennedy School found that:

> By and large, agencies do not handle the first call well. The parents we interviewed found their initial contact with an agency to be the most difficult aspect of the process for two key reasons. First, many simply found it hard to get a worker to answer their call. They got lost in voice mail, were transferred from one person to another, and left messages that were never returned. Many focus group participants had to make several calls before getting an information packet or application form.... Second, many who did speak with someone were frustrated by the tone and content of their initial contact. These callers, who had little or no knowledge of the steps in the adoption process, made their first call to seek general information and ran into a system bent on preemptively weeding out those who aren't interested in hard-to-place children.[6]

I wish I could say that things have changed in the past fifteen years, but by and large, states are still handling this poorly. Overall,

6 Julie Boatright Wilson, Jeff Katz, and Robert Geen, "Listening to Parents: Overcoming Barriers to the Adoption of Children from Foster Care." (Harvard University, 2005), https://research.hks.harvard.edu/publications/getFile.aspx?Id=154.

state agencies are still behaving as if they are doing potential foster parents a favor by answering their questions. Calls by potential foster parents are viewed with suspicion, if not outright hostility. Again, there may be a chicken-and-egg problem. It is possible that a lot of the people calling are not the kind of people that we want fostering and the agencies want to discourage them from the get-go. But if you continue to provide this kind of "customer service," you'll continue to turn off more of the right people as well.

This attitude continues beyond the initial inquiry. Take, for instance, the questionnaire that is used by more than thirty-five states to screen candidates after they have talked to a social worker. An acquaintance of mine sent me a copy of SAFE (Structured Analysis Family Evaluation) when she heard I was writing about the child-welfare system. She and her husband had successfully raised one daughter who was now out of the house and were considering becoming foster parents. They had been through an initial meeting with a social worker that seemed to go well. But then they were given a document whose questions seemed to her both "intrusive and irrelevant."

She wrote to me:

> *Of course how one has disciplined one's children, or how often a couple fights, etc. are important and appropriate questions. What is not appropriate is asking me to rate the quality of my sexual relationship with my husband, and my early sexual and dating experiences. How about ranking my siblings in order of closeness? The quality of my parents' relationship, their views about sex, and an analysis of my parents' personalities also seems out of bounds. How about answering if my husband and I, my parents, or my siblings have ever been treated for an STD (question 56)—and tell me the relevance of whether any of my siblings has had cancer or been treated for mental illness.*

She suspected that many people decided not to pursue fostering simply on the basis of this questionnaire, "since this form is being filed with a government agency with no promise of confidentiality." She notes: "I think it's totally appropriate to ask about our use of alcohol, tobacco, medications, and even whether we currently use illegal substances. But the state of Maryland form asks if we have *ever* used an illegal substance. I'm supposed to tell that to the government?" She and her husband declined to answer the questions and have not been able to foster as a result.

So what is the reasoning behind a form that would end up pushing some clearly qualified foster parents out of the system before they had even gotten to their second meeting? The Consortium for Children, which produces the questionnaire, explains on its website that "there is a paucity of research concerning home studies. To date, there is not a home study model that has garnered the qualifications to be deemed 'evidence-based practice.'"[7] And that includes the SAFE study. They note that "the lack of research in this critical area of child welfare is startling because determining the suitability of Applicant Families for placement is one of the most crucial jobs in child welfare. The safety, permanence, and well-being of a child are dependent on a thorough and unbiased study of an Applicant Family."

Maureen Flatley, a consultant for the Consortium who has worked in the field of child advocacy for decades, explains that the point of the questionnaire is not to screen candidates exactly. It's not like there's a right or wrong answer for each question or that if you answer a certain number "incorrectly" your application to be a foster parent will be rejected.

Rather, she explains, the questionnaire will help social workers start more detailed conversations with the people applying to be fos-

---

7 John Mcmahon and Mellicent Blythe, "Recommendations for Building a Resource Parent Learning System for North Carolina." (UNC-Chapel Hill School of Social Work, March 2013), https://files.nc.gov/ncdhhs/documents/files/dss/training/Foster-Parent-Assessment-and-Training-Recommendations-March-2013.pdf.

ter or adoptive parents. "As the daughter of an FBI agent," she tells me, "one of the things I found shocking about the home study process was how little critical information was garnered, and how much was taken for granted as a result of a relatively superficial discussion."

She describes a case of a single, divorced man from Pittsburgh who "decided he wanted a blonde five-year-old from a Russian orphanage. The home study was three pages." Flatley says if they had asked more about his history, they might have learned that he had a poor relationship with his own daughter, whom he had molested. But they didn't, and then he sexually abused the adopted child.

Flatley describes how one can look at the top fifty stories of child abuse by adoptive and foster parents that have risen to the level of national reporting. In most of them, she believes the problem could have been averted if they had done a more thorough investigation. She says asking questions about the sex life of potential foster parents is also justifiable. While she understands that "questions about sex can feel intrusive they are appropriate on a number of levels. If a family is having problems in that regard, it may be a sign of the end of the marriage. And maybe the couple is adopting in order to mitigate the marriage problems."

Of course, by the standard that you just want to have a deeper discussion with parents about their backgrounds and parenting styles, you could justify asking them any question at all. Does one of your siblings suffer from mental illness or have they ever had hepatitis? Well, those questions could spark a useful conversation about how you would handle mental illness or other kinds of sickness as a parent. The question of which sibling you are closest to might lead to a conversation about how you would handle sibling rivalries in your home.

The fact that some of the questions have an almost Freudian air of suspicion to them also doesn't help. For instance, the SAFE questionnaire asked respondents to "Check the boxes that best describe your parents'/primary caretakers' attitudes about sexuality when you were a child." They include "Awkward discussing," "Open about sexuality," "Believed sex was sinful," "Sexually repressed," "Supported sex education." Even the way these questions are worded suggests a certain kind of bias in favor of parents with more liberal attitudes about sex. But why? Is there evidence that parents who were raised by people who believe sex is sinful are going to be better or worse as foster parents than those who don't? The fact that many foster kids have been raised in homes with very liberal attitudes toward sex may have contributed to the dysfunction they've experienced. Perhaps a home with more strict boundaries about sex might benefit them.

Flatley does not seem concerned at all about these intrusive questions discouraging potential foster parents. Indeed, she seems to think that *too many* people are trying to adopt and foster. She says she has "major problems with the orphan rescue movement" and worries that churches in particular are "ramping up people en masse to help kids without diving deeply into what that means." She suggests that this "has resulted in poor choices for children and an uptick in rehoming for children." This could be an argument for offering foster and adoptive parents more training and information about what's involved in taking in a child who has been traumatized. But whether it's an argument for trying to limit the number of people who even express interest is another story.

And let's be clear about exactly who is going to be taken aback by these kinds of questions, particularly when they're coming from the government or an agency working with the government. They will be people who are not used to having their personal affairs revealed to public officials. With the exception of filing income-tax returns, there are actually relatively few occasions where most middle-class Americans are asked to reveal personal information about themselves to the government.

But fostering and adopting are voluntary activities, and if a state agency is going to demand that people reveal all sorts of personal information, it should probably have a better explanation than the idea that it will spark a good conversation. Flatley's conclusion from her sample of high-profile cases is interesting, though it is important to note that cases of adoptions where children are abused severely enough to make national news is a tiny number. As we've noted, the median rate for reported maltreatment of children in foster care was 0.27 percent, about a quarter of the rate for the general population.[8] Frankly, we should be much more worried about the kids placed into kinship foster care, who may have regular contact with the mothers and fathers who abused or neglected them in the first place. But no one gives questionnaires to these family members.

The questionnaire is only one part of the process that suggests state agencies have not given much thought to whom they want to attract to foster care. Many of the regulations surrounding foster care make sense when they are applied to lower-income families or families who may only be doing foster care because they need the money. But they seem ludicrous if you were interested in attracting families who already have resources.

In 2007, Matt Bevin and his wife Glenna applied to be foster parents. His daughters had befriended an eleven-year-old girl at a local park. They learned that she was a foster child, and the Bevins inquired about adopting her. "We knew how to handle a bunch of kids," Bevin told *National Review* while he was running for governor of Kentucky. They already had five. Bevin was already a highly successful investor, and his wife was a stay-at-home mother.

"So we started the process. It went on and on and on." The couple sent in fingerprints, submitted to home inspections, and attended parenting classes. After more than a year, their application was rejected. "They said that five children were enough. We were told that it's better for her to be in an institutional environment than to be the sixth child in a family." Who would make such a decision?

If you consider that most of the people doing foster care are barely making an average income, if you consider that many of them lack a college degree and a significant percentage are in single-parent households, it is very easy to see why you would have

8 "Child Welfare Outcomes Report."

such a policy in place. Five kids are a lot, and why would you want to add one more to a financially unstable family? But when you have a family with plenty of resources, a parent who is home, enough money to afford extra childcare and any other services that a child who has lived through trauma might need, what is the point of such a rule?

The regulations about who can foster often seem nonsensical. In 2018, Bill Johnson applied to become a foster parent to his own grandson who was removed from his mother's care. The state of Michigan turned him down because they will not place a foster child in a home where there is a gun. Johnson is a former marine and longtime hunter. He and his wife own a fishing-tackle shop. He has several guns that he keeps locked up and one that he has a permit to carry.

Obviously, we don't want to place foster children in homes with illegal handguns lying around. And maybe if you're a social worker and this is what you're used to seeing, such a rule might make sense. Some child-welfare bureaucrats are simply uninformed or unfamiliar with life in rural America. Another longtime foster parent in Maryland recently wrote a story about how she was no longer allowed to take in children because she lived on a farm and kids might be harmed by equipment or falling in her barn.

One question is whether there is a more political motive behind this rule. Johnson says that child-services workers "told me flat out, 'You are going to have to give up some constitutional rights here if you want to keep that boy.'" Sandy Santana, executive director of the nonprofit advocacy group Children's Rights, told the *New York Times* that "becoming a foster parent is not a right, it's a privilege."[9]

This is certainly true. States impose all sorts of rules on foster families that are not imposed on other families—or certainly not enforced by government representatives showing up at their homes to check. Johnson sued the Michigan Department of Health

9 Sheryl Gay Stolberg, "Gun Rights and Foster Care Restrictions Collide in Michigan." (*The New York Times*, August 8, 2017, sec. U.S.), https://www.nytimes.com/2017/08/08/us/michigan-gun-foster-care.html.

and Human Services for violating his Second Amendment rights, but he lost, and the rule remains in effect. Similar rules have been challenged in Missouri, Arizona, and Illinois.[10] Texas passed a law recently to do away with restrictions on foster parents to securely store firearms.[11]

But if the ban on legally held and stored firearms were simply about safety, there are a whole lot of other features that would be banned from foster homes, like swimming pools. Citing 2010 Centers for Disease Control and Prevention data, economist John Lott wrote, "For all children younger than 10, there were 36 accidental gun deaths, and that is out of 41 million children [and] two-thirds…involving young children are not shots fired by other little kids but rather by adult males with criminal backgrounds."[12] By contrast, 609 children drowned that same year. Should we not allow families with pools to foster either?

There are clearly competing demands at work here. On the one hand, the state rightly wants to make sure that children technically in state custody are as safe as they can be. On the other hand, we are also trying to find good families for these kids to be with and make their lives as normal as possible.

In 2013, the House Ways and Means Subcommittee on Human Resources held a hearing about promoting "normalcy" for kids in foster care and passed legislation to encourage states in this regard.[13]

---

10 Alex Swoyer, "Missouri Foster Parents Challenge State Gun Law." (*The Washington Times*, January 22, 2019), https://www.washingtontimes.com/news/2019/jan/22/foster-parents-james-and-julie-attaway-challenge-m/.; Christie Renick, "Firearms and Foster Homes: Arizona Law Cancels Gun Regs for Caregivers." (*The Imprint*, February 26, 2018), https://chronicleofsocialchange.org/politics/firearms-foster-homes-arizona-law-cancels-gun-regs-caregivers/30027.; and Malia Zimmerman, "Illinois Gun Restrictions Unfairly Target Foster Parents, Lawsuit Claims." (*Fox News*, July 14, 2016), https://www.foxnews.com/us/illinois-gun-restrictions-unfairly-target-foster-parents-lawsuit-claims.

11 "Texas HB2363 | 2019-2020 | 86th Legislature." (LegiScan, accessed September 4, 2020), https://legiscan.com/TX/bill/HB2363/2019.

12 John R. Lott Jr., "Children and Guns: The Fear and the Reality." (*National Review*, May 13, 2013),https://www.nationalreview.com/2013/05/children-and-guns-fear-and-reality-john-lott.

13 "Hearing on Letting Kids Be Kids: Balancing Safety with Opportunity for Foster Youth." (Ways and Means Republicans, May 9, 2013), https://gop-waysandmeans.house.gov/hearing-on-letting-kids-be-kids-balancing-safety-with-opportunity-for-foster-youth.

Previously, if a kid in foster care wanted to sleep over at a friend's house, the friends' parents would have to pass a background check first. And a foster child couldn't accept rides home from school from a friend's parent for the same reason. Foster children were prevented from traveling out of state with their family or participating in sports. Sometimes they were prevented from using knives and kitchen tools, or even getting a driver's license.

David Wilkins, who was in charge of the Florida Department of Children and Families, told the subcommittee members during the hearing: "Our foster parenting population in our state has dropped over 15 percent over the last three years. …Upon surveying many of these parents, we were told that the frustrations are extremely high, and you heard some of the testimony there. Foster parents are burdened with paper work, court responsibilities, a list of job responsibilities, all centered around protecting the child, and the result is obvious. We are not letting kids be kids and we're not giving the parents the permission to parent. So, a culture change was needed in our state, and in essence to permeate the entire system with the information that normalcy in foster care is the most paramount of the goals."[14]

When middle-class parents who may already be successfully raising children of their own are faced with these kinds of regulations, they balk. And rightly so. These regulations make sense if you think there's a good chance that the people who are fostering are really incompetent parents (or worse) who are just fostering for the money. But if you are attracting stable families, who are part of stable communities, where you don't see a lot of drug use or violence or domestic abuse, then you might be able to think a little bit more about making a child's life normal instead of being concerned only about their minute-to-minute safety.

Instead of figuring out ways to recruit more stable and well-off families like treating applicants with respect, reducing some of the

14 "Hearing on Letting Kids Be Kids."

unnecessary paperwork, restricting the process to questions that actually have some bearing on whether they will be good foster parents, or holding information and training sessions at convenient times, some states have gone in the opposite direction—offering to pay families more to foster. As one Indiana advocate told a local public radio station: "When you ask someone to, for instance, take a baby home from the hospital and you give that foster parent $25 a day, many foster parents are paying more than that in child care because they're all still expected to work and hold down jobs."[15]

Many observers are shocked to find out how little assistance the government provides foster parents. According to a 2012 report from Child Trends, a nonprofit research group, per diem rates for foster parents of kids age 0–2 ranged from $8.09 in Nebraska to $27.45 in Maryland.[16] With these funds, foster parents are expected to pay for all of the activities that foster kids engage in.

Taking into consideration the actual cost of raising a child in different regions of the country, the report finds DC at the highest end, covering 145 percent of the basic cost, and Idaho at the lowest, covering only 39 percent.[17] States have moved to increase aid given to relative foster parents so that grandparents, aunts, and uncles are compensated at least as much as a stranger would be. If we are going to place kids with family, it certainly makes sense to give them as much help as they need.

But whether states should do more—financially speaking—to incentivize people to sign up is a more difficult question. The problem with this approach is that people who do it for the money are not ideal candidates. Foster children are also sensitive to the financial compensation strangers receive for caring for them. As Tracey

15 Brandon Smith, "Foster Advocates Call for Per Diem Increase." (*WFYI Indianapolis*, December 24, 2018), https://www.wfyi.org/news/articles/foster-advocates-call-for-per-diem-increase.

16 Kerry DeVooght and Dennis Blazey, "Family Foster Care Reimbursement Rates in the U.S." (*Child Trends*, 2013), https://www.childtrends.org/publications/family-foster-care-reimbursement-rates-in-the-u-s-a-report-from-a-2012-national-survey-on-family-foster-care-provider-classifications-and-rates.

17 DeVooght and Blazey, "Family Foster Care."

Feild, the director of the Annie E. Casey Foundation's child-welfare strategy group, told the Associated Press, "Kids know the difference between a job and not a job."[18] When I talk to young adults who spent time in foster care, I am struck by how focused they are on the money. Even a decade later, they can remember exactly how much the parent was given and how much of that money was actually used for expenses related to their care.

Foster care is supposed to be as much like living in a normal family as possible. We want children who have been abused or neglected—and certainly traumatized by whatever happened in their biological home and the fact that they were removed from it—to have a sense of stability. They are supposed to feel as if there are adults in this world who genuinely care about their well-being and are not simply engaged in this work because it is a quick way to a paycheck.

It is hard to say how many foster parents are motivated by money and to what degree. Lisa Harper, a counselor for the CALL, an agency in Arkansas that helps churches recruit and train foster parents, recalls people in her community doing foster care when she was growing up. She says,

> *Growing up, my aunt did fostering… but I don't think I even understood the concept then—the gravity of what she was doing or what all that entailed. In my adolescence, it was just these children who didn't have a home that my aunt was taking care of. I think there was a connotation that I had of foster parents based off of how I saw them engage and that was just that this was someone that the state was paying you to watch the child. There was no real caretaking involved. It was just a house, a meal, another adult that these teens had to follow orders from.*

18 Tereza Wiltz, "Foster Parents Have Become Professionals in Some States." (Pew, February 20, 2019), https://www.pewtrusts.org/en/research-and-analysis/blogs/stateline/2019/02/20/foster-parents-have-become-professionals-in-some-states.

Of course, there are egregious cases in which foster parents are not simply treating foster children as part of a financial transaction but are also neglecting the children and squirreling money away for themselves. Alex Brian, who adopted a son out of the foster-care system in Louisiana recently, told me that he was initially reluctant to do foster care but when he went to an informational meeting at the urging of his wife, "it really opened my eyes to some of the needs." When I interviewed Alex at a church he pastors, he told me that the people in that meeting "were asking questions that were really unsettling. You know, a lot of questions about money in relation to children." For example, someone asked: "Okay, so if I take a kid with a disability, how much money do I get then? Okay, if I take two kids, is that like a multiplier or do you just add it up?" Some of the questions Alex found "heartbreaking." Like "Okay, so if I take in a foster kid, do I have to put them in the same area of my house as the rest of my kids or can I keep them kind of separate?"

It seems like you might not have to go through a hundred-question survey about people's relationships with their siblings or what their parents thought about sex to figure out these are not ideal candidates. Why are informational meetings about foster care filled with these people? It's clear that they want the money.

Offering more money could backfire and result in worse care for children. The logic is similar to what has happened with blood donation. Studies comparing blood donation (for which donors were not compensated) and plasma donation (for which they were) have shown that the latter yielded a much higher percentage of tainted donations. Researchers speculate that donors were more motivated to cover up their diseases and past risky behavior if they were donating for money. Offering foster parents more money could end in the same result—except that unlike plasma, which can be tested for contamination, foster parents are difficult to screen.

Another option would be offering different in-kind payments. In Florida, a group called One More Child offers free housing to foster families that want to take in more kids than their home may allow. These families still go through the organization's regular training process and live on a campus with other foster families, but they often find that with housing costs covered, one parent does not have to work to make ends meet. Because kids in sibling groups are some of the hardest children to place, the offer of a larger house can encourage parents who are already fostering for the right reasons to increase their capacity.

Faced with the choice between trying to attract foster parents by offering them more money and trying to attract foster parents who already have enough money, the answer should be obvious. We need an "internal culture shift," as Daley puts it. This group of what he calls "family planners"—which includes LGBT couples, couples with infertility issues, and older childless women—have the resources and "want to see impact on someone's life and impact on their own life" from taking in foster kids. According to the 2018 American Community Survey, married male couples (who have fewer biological options for producing children than same-sex female couples) earned about 15 percent more than married heterosexual couples.[19]

Instead of financial compensation, it would be worth considering what foster families themselves identify as things they most need—and barriers that stand in their way. In general, foster families are very clear about the things that frustrate them and rarely mention money. Surveys of foster parents have shown that the lack of engagement in decision-making around a child's future is a leading cause of dissatisfaction or stopping fostering altogether.

National estimates suggest that 30 to 50 percent of foster parents quit within one year of volunteering their services.[20] For example, a recent *Boston Globe* investigation found that 2,000 Massachusetts

19 "2018," Census.gov, n.d., https://www2.census.gov/programs-surveys/demo/tables/same-sex/time-series/ssc-house-characteristics/ssex-tables-2018.xlsx.

20 Ron Haskins, Justin Kohomban, and Jennifer Rodriguez, "Keeping Up with the Caseload: How to Recruit and Retain Foster Parents." (Brookings, April 24, 2019), https://www.brookings.edu/blog/up-front/2019/04/24/keeping-up-with-the-caseload-how-to-recruit-and-retain-foster-parents/#:~:text=Estimates percent20show percent20that percent20between percent2030.

foster families "have stopped accepting foster children in the past five years—almost as many as the total number of foster families currently in the system."[21] Many foster parents cite lack of support and guidance from caseworkers as reasons for leaving the system. A report from Oregon noted, "The burdens on existing foster parents hurt recruitment as well, because they are the primary recruiters for new foster parents."[22]

Virginia foster parents have complained to me about caseworkers placing children in their home without mentioning food allergies or asthma and failing to inform them about a child's history of sexual abuse, even though other children in the home could have been in danger as a result. The lack of communication is something the families interviewed by the *Boston Globe* mention as well; they were not told about the children's trauma, different medical issues, or even things that might comfort them.

It may sound crass, but what financially well-off foster parents want is better customer service. They want to have their phone calls answered. They want to deal with knowledgeable professionals. They want the best advice in a timely way for how to support the children in their care. They want social workers and courts that are respectful of their time and their other responsibilities, including their other children. They are happy to give their own money to pay for kids' clothes and toys and extracurricular activities and even bigger ticket items like mental health counseling, especially if it means less paperwork. They want to be able to treat their foster children the same way they would treat any child, ensuring that they are able to fully participate and enjoy life with a family.

Government bureaucracies are not exactly known for treating people with respect. For one thing, there is little incentive to do so.

---

21 Kay Lazar, "For Foster Parents, Chaotic State System Makes Job Even Harder." (*Boston Globe*, April 13, 2019), https://www.bostonglobe.com/metro/2019/04/13/foster-families-dcf-failing/1SlwDvK7MLDCyFaLVi9ZeP/story.html#:~:text=Some percent202 percent2C000 percent20families percent20have percent20stopped.

22 John Sciamanna, "New Survey Shows Decreased Supply of Foster Homes." (CWLA, n.d.), https://www.cwla.org/new-survey-shows-decreased-supply-of-foster-homes.

Either you pay your taxes, or you'll be fined—the IRS agent doesn't have to be kind to you. If you want your driver's license, you'll stand in line for hours at the DMV, just like everyone else, even if the system is outdated and the people are rude. But foster care is different. We want people to volunteer. We want kids in the most stable and loving families available. We want people who are not asking whether they can put a foster kid in a separate part of their home. Even the staunchest proponents of the free market would argue that there are other ways to compensate people beside money—like with respect or recognition.

It is time for states to undertake a complete "secret shopper" assessment of their foster-care recruitment system to find out what happens when someone calls for information and tries to sign up for training. They should look at their questionnaires and ask first whether they have appropriate policies in place to ensure the responses are confidential. They should weigh the necessity of individual questions in terms of providing useful information, as opposed to just "starting a conversation."

They should weigh blanket policies on, for example, the number of children that are allowed to be in one home and consider the resources in that home to care for the child. States need to be able to weigh the risks of placing a child in a stable family who happens to live on a farm against the risks of a child being near farm equipment.

States should start using focus groups and other marketing techniques to understand the demographic profile of their ideal foster parents and what those people need in order to sign up and stay in the system for the long haul. Agencies should be doing exit interviews with every foster parent who quits to find out what went wrong. All of these would be much better uses of the state's funds than adding a few more dollars to foster-care stipends.

It is possible that the state bureaucrats will never be good at treating people well, though there are certainly exceptions to that rule. There are some private organizations that are doing the best work for foster-care recruitment, including the focus groups and demographic research, but states still need to be willing to collect and share data for them to be effective.

And the federal government should be willing to incentivize this kind of research and change in recruitment methods. The Family First Prevention Services Act pays lip service to the idea of recruiting more qualified foster families but does not offer any funding to do so. Good foster parents don't magically appear, and though they are willing to sacrifice a lot, we should not expect them to be martyrs. As Mark Daley says, "it's time to treat foster parents as if they are a community asset."

It is certainly true that many middle-class Americans have no contact with child welfare, and they have no idea what is involved or how badly they are needed. So, where we are going to find the army of middle-class Americans who are willing to do foster care? CASA volunteers are a good place to start.

According to the numbers provided by the national CASA organization, there were more than 93,000 volunteers in the program in 2018, who served a combined 5.5 million hours.[23] Volunteers are required to do about thirty hours of training before they start and another twelve hours of in-service training per year. A third of volunteers stayed with one child for two to three years. And a quarter were with the same child for more than four years.

This kind of sustained relationship can have a tremendous impact on kids in the child-welfare system. And the volunteers are the kind of adults who have the time and the wherewithal to help. Among the volunteers, 39 percent had a bachelor's degree and another 23 percent had a postgraduate degree.[24] Again, being educated is not necessary to aid children in need, but when it comes to helping them navigate a complex court system—not to mention

23 "2018 Annual Report." (National CASA/GAL Association for Children, 2018), https://nationalcasagal.org/wp-content/uploads/2019/09/CASAGAL_2018_AnnualReport_Final_Spread.pdf.

24 National CASA/GAL Association for Children, n.d.

school systems and family issues—an education helps. There is a big difference between serving as a CASA and serving as a foster parent, but being a CASA often serves an entry point to fostering or adopting. The more they see the system up close, the more they realize how much they are needed.

CHAPTER 13

WHAT'S HOLDING US BACK? CHANGING THE LAWS AND THE POLITICS OF CHILD WELFARE

The country could be doing something to improve child welfare, but the growing national political consensus is taking us in exactly the wrong direction. On the left, there is an increasing number of advocates and policymakers who don't see a need for foster care at all. They see it as systemically racist and largely unnecessary, a punishment leveled against the poor. They are primarily concerned with family preservation and reunification and kinship care. Adoption, when it is absolutely necessary, should prioritize race-matching. On the right, meanwhile, there is a growing chorus of libertarians and religious conservatives who are worried that the child-welfare system has become a tool of government overreach designed to harass homeschoolers or folks who just want to give their children more independence. The right believes that government has a secularist agenda that punishes people of faith for their parenting decisions. The left believes that laws about drug use are selectively enforced against poor and minority families. And they are largely in agreement with libertarians who think our drug laws are useless and needlessly punitive. Almost no one is interested in enforcing timelines for terminating parental rights or giving more power to child-welfare agencies or courts to change parental behavior.

It was not always thus. There used to be a sensible center on the issue of child welfare, and it is worth understanding what that looked like, how it disappeared, and what, if anything, we can do to bring it back.

By the time Mary Landrieu arrived in Washington in 1997 to begin her first term as a Democratic senator representing Louisiana, she already had a longstanding interest in the issue. As a teenager, she had befriended a homeless boy and served as a kind of advocate for him from the time she was fifteen until she was twenty-two. "That began my journey in understanding even as a teenager, how broken our foster-care system was," she says. As the mother of two adopted children and the wife to a man who was adopted as a child, Landrieu was more familiar than most of her Washington colleagues with the plight of the most vulnerable children in America.

There were three big problems that Landrieu saw with the child-welfare system in the '90s. The first was that foster care was "a life sentence." The "foster-care system," she tells me, "was supposed to be a temporary healing place for children…but the data showed that once you got into the foster system, you never really got out." The second problem was that the "quality of foster parents was not what I would consider adequate or appropriate." Though she notes there were "certainly some wonderful people in the system…it was not where we needed to be." Finally, she notes that there was "a strong bias against adoption," particularly against transracial adoption.

Landrieu made common cause with a number of her colleagues on both sides of the aisle. There were other senators like Landrieu who were personally touched by issues of adoption and foster care. Olympia Snowe, Republican from Maine, was orphaned by the time she was ten and raised by an aunt and uncle who struggled to support her and her five cousins. Kay Bailey Hutchison, Republican from Texas, adopted two children. Other members of the group committed to reforming child welfare in the late '90s and early 2000s included Democrat Jay Rockefeller of West Virginia and Republican Mike DeWine (then senator from, now governor) of Ohio.

But changing child welfare from a perch in Washington, even with bipartisan support, is difficult. There are always going to be more urgent or high-profile issues or issues that affect a wider swath of the population. Landrieu says she gives a lot of credit to her former colleague Sen. Charles Grassley: "It's hard when you're chair of the finance committee to say to your staff, 'Okay, I realize there are a hundred people standing at my door, every single solitary one of them wants a tax credit. But today I'm working on a foster care bill. There's no one standing at my door, no foster care kids waiting. They don't have a lobbyist, but today that's what we're doing."

The beginning of federal involvement in the child-welfare system can be traced back to 1912 when Congress created the Children's Bureau, which was aimed at reducing infant mortality and child labor, though less with the way that children were treated by their parents or caregivers. But with the 1935 passage of the Social Security Act, the federal government began large contributions (at first only $1.5 million annually) "for the purpose of enabling the United States, through the Children's Bureau, to cooperate with state public-welfare agencies in establishing, extending and strengthening, especially in predominantly rural areas, public [child] welfare services… for the protection and care of homeless, dependent, and neglected children, and children in danger of becoming delinquent."[1] By 1958, the program was allotted $17 million, and the funds were no longer restricted to rural areas.

1 "Child Welfare Legislative History." (Committee on Ways and Means House of Representatives Green Book, 2012), https://greenbook-waysandmeans.house.gov/2012-green-book/chapter-11-child-welfare/legislative-history.

States were also required to match the funds that the federal government was providing.

The 1960s brought more federal support for research into the best child-welfare practices through the Department of Health, Education and Welfare (which eventually became the Department of Health and Human Services). Washington also required that states develop plans to assure that each child in foster care "received proper care and that services were designed to improve the child's home so he or she could return there or be placed with another relative."[2] By 1967, the federal government required that any states that did not already do so provide foster-care assistance as part of their Aid to Families with Dependent Children programs.

During the 1970s, the federal government started to pressure states to do more on the prevention side of things. In addition to the passage of the Child Abuse Prevention and Treatment Act in 1974, the new Title XX program of the Social Security Act included "preventing or remedying neglect, abuse, or exploitation of children and adults unable to protect their own interest, or preserving, rehabilitating or reuniting families."[3]

The Adoption Assistance and Child Welfare Act, passed in 1980, required that states show "reasonable efforts" to prevent a child's removal to foster care and to reunite a child who has been removed with his family.[4] By 1985, the federal government was also providing funds to help children youth in foster care aged sixteen and over to transition successfully into adulthood. Each new allotment of funds came with its own set of requirements both for the execution of programs and the reporting of results.

But exactly how much power the federal government had to enforce these rules has never exactly been clear from a practical perspective. And there have been legal questions as well. In 1983, several children in the Illinois foster-care program sued the director

2 "Child Welfare Legislative History."
3 "Child Welfare Legislative History."
4 "Child Welfare Legislative History."

and the guardianship administrator of the Illinois program under a statute that provides remedy when private citizens are "depriv[ed] of any rights…secured by [federal] laws."[5] The lawyers for the children argued that Illinois had failed to make reasonable efforts at preservation and reunification required under the Adoption Assistance and Child Welfare Act.

As the authors of an article in the journal *Social Work* on the impact of the decision noted, "One critical feature of the act was that the federal government's only enforcement authority for addressing a state's failure to comply was the elimination or reduction of payments to the state."[6] But as with other mandates, Congress is either unaware of the extent to which these laws are being flouted or doesn't have the will to withhold funds to enforce compliance. The question in the lawsuit was whether a private citizen could compel the state to follow federal guidelines. And the answer from the court was no. The Supreme Court held in *Suter v. Artist M.* that AACWA "only required that a state have a plan for the administration of adoption and foster care programs in order to receive federal reimbursement, not that the plan be correctly carried out."[7]

One response to this decision was that the federal government offered states more flexibility in carrying out the requirements of Title IV-E and IV-B. In the aftermath, HHS offered waivers to up to ten states for certain aspects of their plans. But at the same time, Congress (led in this effort by Landrieu and her colleagues) passed legislation that further restricted state child-welfare policies. The Adoption and Safe Families Act put in place a clear timeline to ensure that kids in foster care could not be left there for too long. They also passed the Multi-Ethnic Placement Act, which barred discrimination on the basis of race or ethnicity in the placement of children in foster care or for adoption.

5 Rudolph Alexander and Cora L. Alexander, "The Impact of Suter v. Artist M. on Foster Care Policy." (*Social Work* 40, no. 4, 1995): 543–548, https://www.jstor.org/stable/23718387?seq=1.

6 Alexander and Alexander, "Suter v. Artist M."

7 "Suter v. Artist M. " Oyez. (accessed September 4, 2020). https://www.oyez.org/cases/1991/90-1488.

With each law passed, Congress built in some degree of flexibility, though. Yes, the Adoption and Safe Families Act requires states to file a petition for the termination of parental rights when children have been in foster care for fifteen of the past twenty-two months. But as we have seen, the "reasonable efforts" provision means that states often don't abide by the rule because judges or social workers deem that parents haven't been offered appropriate services, for instance. And so, the flexibility has often meant that states have simply ignored the provisions. Meanwhile, the money put into child welfare has continued to grow.

For the 2019 fiscal year, federal spending on child welfare reached $9.8 billion, with most of that coming through Title IV-E of the Social Security Act.[8] Title IV-E primarily supports foster care and adoption assistance, programs that would have been unrecognizable to legislative leaders in the first half of the twentieth century. About $730 million of the federal total comes from Title IV-B—the Stephanie Tubbs Jones Child Welfare Services (CWS) program and the Promoting Safe and Stable Families (PSSF) program—which offers grants to promote child and family services, including programs like substance-abuse recovery.[9] Other smaller federal programs include money authorized by CAPTA, which was enacted in 1974 to improve CPS and fund state and local child-abuse treatment and prevention initiatives.

According to a 2016 survey, states spent about $30 billion on child-welfare services, with about 56 percent coming from state and local funds and the remainder provided by the aforementioned federal programs, along with a few others.[10] In other words, the federal government should have a lot of leverage over child-welfare agencies in states, but it does not.

One reason for this is that policymakers cannot agree on what a quality child-welfare system looks like. As Landrieu notes, "It's

8 Emilie Stoltzfus, "Child Welfare: Purposes, Federal Programs, and Funding." (Congressional Research Service: *In Focus*, August 1, 2019), https://fas.org/sgp/crs/misc/IF10590.pdf.

9 Stoltzfus, "Child Welfare."

10 Stoltzfus, "Child Welfare."

almost like fashion...one year everybody's wearing bell-bottoms. In the next ten years, everybody's wearing straight pants. The same thing happens in child-welfare policy, you know, for one decade, adoption is a big deal. And then the next decade...reunification of families and then the next decade it's prevention." As each idea comes into fashion, Congress attempts to tie a different set of strings to the money. If states and tribes accept Title IV-E money, they are implicitly accepting the rules put forth by the Department of Health and Human Services and the oversight of Congress.

But Congress has few mechanisms for ensuring that these rules are followed. The 1994 Amendments to the Social Security Act authorize HHS to see whether states are meeting the requirements in titles IV-B and IV-E using Child and Family Services Reviews (CFSRs). All fifty states, the District of Columbia, and Puerto Rico completed their first review by 2004 and their second review by 2010. After each round, no state was found to be in substantial conformity in all seven outcome areas and seven systemic factors. By the third round, which began in 2015, things did not look much better.

A report on twenty-four states evaluated noted that they "met few of the performance standards established by the Children's Bureau.... Two states achieved substantial conformity for Safety Outcome 1: Children are, first and foremost, protected from abuse and neglect."[11] No states achieved substantial conformity for the "Children have permanency and stability in their living situations" or "The continuity of family relationships and connections is preserved for children." Only six states achieved a rating of strength when it came to the diligent recruitment of foster families.

Despite these dismal results, no one wants to cut funds that are aimed at helping the most vulnerable kids in this country. Child welfare is already one of the lowest priorities in most state's budgets.

11 "Child and Family Services Reviews Aggregate Report." (*Administration for Children and Families*, n.d.), https://www.acf.hhs.gov/sites/default/files/documents/cb/cfsr_aggregate_report_2015_2017.pdf.

Social workers are notoriously overworked and underpaid. There never seem to be enough services to help families in need. Family courts are overwhelmed. But surely, as Landrieu notes, there has to be some federal accountability. She says she prefers "carrots," like incentives for states to process more adoptions more quickly. But "sometimes sticks may be necessary. Yes, it does seem counterintuitive to withhold money, but we do it for highways, we do it for education."

The way the federal government distributes money certainly has a deep impact on how states spend it. Advocates have long noted that if you pay for something, you get more of it. And since the federal government reimburses states for days that children spend in foster homes, the thinking is we get more kids in foster homes. There's less incentive to provide them with what can be costly services at home.

It's possible that we are paying for the wrong thing. One alternative would be to pay for kids to have more options. That is, we could be rewarding states for the recruitment and training of quality foster parents. The federal government should be willing to pay for so-called empty beds so that when kids do come into the system, we have a lot of good alternatives available for them.

States have long demanded that the federal government provide them with more flexibility in how they are allowed to spend their IV-E funds so that they can do more to help families before children need to be removed. The Family First legislation passed in 2018 certainly did that, shifting more of the funds toward preventive services and away from group homes. But so far, Family First is looking like another piece of federal legislation that will be largely ignored by states, many of which have already been granted waivers from it.

The best-case scenario is that it will end up being like No Child Left Behind. Though that piece of education legislation has not shown much of an effect in improving American student achievement, it has at least had the effect of forcing states to give the federal government more accurate data about educational outcomes—disaggregated by race and other demographic factors. If the federal government can at least force states to submit more accurate data about child welfare that can be compared across state lines, it might go a long way toward ensuring greater transparency and accountability. Then it could adopt the model of rewarding states that show progress on measures like safety and permanency.

Almost a quarter-century after Landrieu's arrival in Washington, it seems like the things that were improved weren't improved that much. The number of reports of child maltreatment has increased. The number of kids in foster care has gone up and down and up again. But the number of children who are officially classified as "nonvictims" but have been victimized has risen by 400,000. Adoptions have ticked up, but there are still around 20,000 children who age out of foster care every year.[12] Any improvements that are going to happen will have to either involve the federal government's decision to enforce the rules on the books or states' decisions to change their child-welfare agencies and family courts of their own accord.

It's also worth noting that any new useful legislation is unlikely to pass in our current political environment. If anything, the consensus is becoming that foster care is useless, if not harmful, and that substance abuse driving the high numbers of kids at risk is unimportant, if not harmless.

In the absence of meaningful legislation and enforcement from the federal government, the best hope is for states to act. Any effective reform will have to involve not only governors, who direct state child-welfare agencies, but also the legislatures that control the purse strings of state courts. They are the ones with the power to ensure that courts are well-staffed, that judges are well-trained, and that children's cases are decided in a timely manner that keeps in mind the best interests of children, not just adults.

12 "Extending Foster Care Beyond 18." (NCSL, July 28, 2017), https://www.ncsl.org/research/human-services/extending-foster-care-to-18.aspx.

Unfortunately, the momentum seems to be moving in the opposite direction. Some advocates seem to think that the termination of parental rights is a matter undertaken too quickly. A bill introduced in 2020 by Democratic congresswoman Gwen Moore of Wisconsin would have the Department of Health and Human Services "pause" the timeline for foster care completely. The Preserving Family Bonds Act, which was passed by the New York State Legislature in 2019 but later vetoed by the governor, would have let birth parents whose rights have been terminated by the court apply to visit their children.[13] They would have been entitled to a hearing to argue that their continuing contact is in the child's best interest. New York offers among the longest paths to permanency from foster care of any state in the country, with foster care lasting thirty months, on average.

Even assuming, though, that judges can move things along, the question remains whether they are making reasonable decisions for the kids they are supervising. Judges rely on the information presented to them by caseworkers and lawyers. And many will say that the information and expert opinions they are getting are not very good.

It is not uncommon, on the other hand, to hear caseworkers blaming family-court judges for kids' prolonged stays in foster care or poor decisions about reunification. When I interviewed an ACS spokeswoman a few years ago about why there were such high levels of abuse while kids in ACS custody were visiting their biological parents, she told me that "decisions about visitation are made by family court judges," not her agency. Well, yes, but those judges are being advised by caseworkers, who report to ACS.

There is seemingly no end to this blame game. But from a legal perspective, it is family court where the buck is supposed to stop. The judges are the ones making final decisions. If agency workers are not fully investigating the circumstances or not presenting all

13 Latoya Joyner, Pub. L. No. A02199A (2019).

the information or not considering all the possibilities for placement and how those will affect a child's long-term welfare, then family-court judges have to press them harder on those matters.

If judges are often operating without all the information that they need to make decisions, at least part of that is their own fault. It's particularly shocking to see how often judges do not ask for the input of foster parents in deciding what's in the children's best interests. Especially given the high turnover rate of social workers and others laboring in the child-welfare system, one might think it particularly important for the judge to hear the views of a longtime foster parent or the relative caregiver.

ASFA technically gave foster parents the "opportunity" to testify at family-court hearings and suggested that foster families be notified of hearings regarding children in their care, but under the law, judges were not required to do either. A 2005 report found "inconsistent notification of caretakers and providing [of] opportunity to be heard."[14] Cassie Statuto Bevan, who worked as staff director for the House Ways and Means Committee and helped draft the 1997 law, told me that "the states and courts were ignoring the opportunity [for foster parents] to be heard that was in AFSA."

Bevan worked to amend language as part of a 2006 law that mandated that any "case review system" must include procedures that assure the foster parents "are provided with notice of, and a right to be heard in, any proceeding to be held with respect to the child."[15] Nothing has ever been done to enforce the provision, and it is rarely honored. Bevan said the act remained unfunded and "no HHS [Health and Human Services Department] guidance was issued and no oversight on the provision was rendered." Not surprisingly, then, a 2018 report by the federal Administration for Children and Families found that only "five states received a 'strength rating'" for a "process for foster parents, pre-adoptive par-

14 "52 Program Improvement Plans." (Presentation, Administration for Children and Families).

15 "42 U.S.C.," govinfo. (accessed September 4, 2020), https://www.govinfo.gov/content/pkg/USCODE-2010-title42/html/USCODE-2010-title42-chap7-subchapIV-partE-sec675.htm.

ents, and relative caregivers of children in foster care to be notified of, and have a right to be heard in, any review or hearing held with respect to the child."[16]

Of the scores of foster parents I've interviewed about family court in the past two years, almost none were aware that they had a right to speak in court or to be notified of any hearings that would change a child's placement. Even when they have been informed of the obligations that the court has to keep them in the loop, they may still find themselves shut out of the process.

These end-runs around the law are infuriating. To give judges the benefit of the doubt, one reason that many of them are wary of hearing from foster parents is that they don't have the time and resources to assess their credibility: Are they bad-mouthing the biological parent because they want to adopt the child? Are they praising the biological parents because they are relatives?

Some wonder whether foster parents have a financial incentive to make negative assessments of biological parents so they can keep the kids. In fact, most states offer subsidies for foster care that are higher than their subsidies for adopting a child out of the foster-care system.[17] But most states have a shortage of foster parents, so nonrelative caregivers in it for the money can almost always get another child placed in their home as soon as one is removed.

About half of states have provisions similar to the 2006 law that allow for foster parents, pre-adoptive parents, or relatives providing care to apply to be parties to the case. But these provisions are not automatic and do not have any meaning unless the judge enforces them.

A couple of states have gone further, including Colorado, which allows "foster parents who have had a child in their care for more

16 "Child and Family Services Reviews Aggregate Report." (*Administration for Children & Families*, U.S. Department of Health and Human Services, n.d.), https://www.acf.hhs.gov/sites/default/files/documents/cb/cfsr_aggregate_report_2015_2017.pdf.

17 Barbara Dalberth, Deborah Gibbs, and Nancy Berkman, "Understanding Adoption Subsidies: An Analysis of AFCARS Data." (*ASPE*, U.S. Department of Health and Human Services Office of the Assistant Secretary for Planning and Evaluation, January 2005), https://aspe.hhs.gov/system/files/pdf/73686/report.pdf.

than three months and who have information or knowledge concerning the care and protection of the child [to]...intervene as a matter of right following adjudication with or without counsel."[18] The law was initially challenged but eventually upheld by the state's Supreme Court.

Georgia passed a law that would require the courts to "make specific written findings of fact regarding participation by the caregiver of a child, the foster parent of a child, any preadoptive parent, or any relative providing care for a child."[19] It also would allow these caregivers to call witnesses—including doctors, therapists, and teachers—to testify regarding their observations about the child. By requiring the court to solicit the input of the foster parent or relative caregiver, though, the law places the onus on the judge instead of on the parents or their lawyers. This could move things in the right direction.

Some advocates worry that such laws could flip the script, suddenly providing foster parents with undue influence over the process. Melissa Carter, executive director of Emory University's Barton Child Law and Policy Center, is concerned by the "idea of injecting another party to influence or bias" the proceedings. "At the end of the day when you offer an alternative like a foster parent, it's too easy to then devolve into a comparison between parents"—with the natural parent or parents at that point already found lacking by the system. Carter suggests allowing foster parents to speak at nonadjudicatory hearings, where the termination of parental rights, for instance, is not at stake.

The conditions under which foster parents are heard need to be worked out. But they are a vital source of information for the child-welfare system, and it's time we stopped ignoring them.

18 Colo. Rev. Stat. § 19-3-507(5) (1997).

19 "Georgia HB906 | 2019–2020 | Regular Session." (LegiScan, accessed September 3, 2020), https://legiscan.com/GA/bill/HB906/2019.

CONCLUSION

PUTTING CHILDREN FIRST

On the rare occasions when Americans pay attention to issues of child abuse and neglect, it is because of shocking headlines. David and Louise Turpin, for instance, were found to have imprisoned and tortured twelve of their thirteen children, starving them and at times chaining them to their beds. The abuse went on for years without any reports to authorities, partly thanks to the fact that the kids were being "homeschooled." Americans also took note of the case of Jennifer and Sarah Hart, who drove off a cliff into the Pacific Ocean, murdering their six children adopted out of foster care. The idea that these kinds of horrors could take place without anyone suspecting something was wrong is deeply disturbing and makes us wonder what else are we missing. But these high-profile cases also give us a false impression about what's really going on in the child-welfare system.

There are surely cases of foster and adoptive parents who mistreat the children in their custody, sometimes severely. There are surely families using homeschooling as a way to cover up child abuse. Similarly, we know there are teachers and neighbors who make up allegations of child abuse either out of ignorance or malice. And there are social workers and judges who railroad innocent parents, separating them from their children without real evidence they have done anything wrong. Our system should work harder to prevent all of these crimes.

But these are not the cases that fill the towering files at child-welfare agencies or overwhelm the dockets of family courts. The vast majority of cases of abuse and neglect in this country are not cases of parents going to extraordinary lengths to hide their actions. They are the cases that we know about.

They are not the cases of hardworking parents trying to do their best only to have children removed from their care because they can't make rent. They are the cases of parents whose behavior is driven by alcohol or drugs or mental illness to such an extent that they cannot adequately supervise or protect or care for their children.

They are not the cases of busybody neighbors reporting mothers for running into the A&P while their children remain in the car or parents who let their kids walk to the park alone. They are the cases of children who are reported to authorities by teachers concerned about students who show up to school without having eaten in days or without wearing a coat in winter. They are the cases of neighbors who hear screams through apartment walls or who see young children left alone for days or nights at a time.

They are not the cases of white social workers who believe that black parents don't know how to raise children and remove them because of racial bias. They are the cases of social workers from all racial backgrounds who offer families a long list of services from drug rehabilitation to housing vouchers to family counseling and then—only after months or years have passed—do they ask a judge if they can remove a child in danger. But just as often they return those children after a short time.

The most common and most serious problems with our system occur with the children who are already on our radar screen. Child-welfare agencies and family courts are among the most incompetent and inefficient public bureaucracies in the country; the people they touch are the most vulnerable; and their ability to change the lives of those people is the greatest. The combination is deadly.

Sometimes the investigation is not done quickly. Sometimes it's done incompletely or incompetently, failing to consider any or all of the evidence. Then it is put in the hands of social workers, lawyers, guardians ad litem, and judges, who are making decisions about placement too slowly or without all the information or by considering the best interests of the parents rather than the children. Sometimes these decisions are weighted by considerations of racial disparities or social justice rather than the only thing that should matter—the safety and well-being of that particular child.

The reason these kids suffer is rarely the result of an evil parent deliberately planning and covering up the torture of a child. Rather, there are parents who cannot or will not take care of their children, and an entire child-welfare system is bent toward protecting, not children, but adults by virtue of their victimized status, kinship, race, or tribe. Children who are in danger in this country are treated instrumentally to promote the rehabilitation of their parents, the social welfare of their communities, and social justice for their racial and ethnic groups. Their most precious developmental years are lost in bureaucratic and judicial red tape.

Conservatives are not wrong—more than anything, the things that drive abuse and neglect in this country are the disintegration of the family and the scourge of drug addiction. As far back as 1997, the Heritage Foundation noted: "The underlying dynamic of child abuse—the breakdown of marriage…—is spreading like a cancer from poor communities to working-class communities."[20] Having two sober married parents in a home—regardless of their economic status—offers an enormous amount of protection to children, particularly young children.

1 Patrick Fagan, "The Child Abuse Crisis: The Disintegration of Marriage, Family, and the American Community." (The Heritage Foundation, May 15, 1997), https://www.heritage.org/marriage-and-family/report/the-child-abuse-crisis-the-disintegration-marriage-family-and-the

But for many children, that ship has already sailed. They are living in homes with single mothers and a rotating cast of boyfriends. They have little, if any, contact with their fathers. If their mothers weren't already using drugs when they were born, they have started since. And the dysfunction that comes with the addiction and the often-co-occurring mental illness has made it impossible for these mothers and fathers to stay in their homes, to hold down a job, to keep the electricity and water running, and to ensure that their kids are fed, clothed, and able to attend school.

Liberals are right too. To help these kids will require a massive reform of our child-welfare agencies, an influx of financial resources, and better stewardship of the money we already spend. We need to attract more qualified candidates to child-welfare agencies, and we need to spend more time training them in the job we expect them to do. Agencies need resources to ensure that they use the latest technology and data analytics to get a better handle on the problems of abuse and neglect.

And they need to be honest with the public about exactly what is causing investigators to conclude that abuse or neglect is occurring in a home. Agencies should consider eliminating the category of neglect altogether and force caseworkers to choose a clearer reason—substance abuse, mental illness, lack of running water, etc.—for removing a child. More transparency will create a virtuous cycle—people will be more willing to report their concerns to authorities they trust and more likely to be foster parents or support fostering in their community.

Bureaucracies cannot raise children. But if these bureaucracies don't function better, children's lives will be ruined or lost. We need to overhaul our family court system, getting a higher level of professional into family law. Family court needs to works more efficiently and with the goal of ensuring the child's best interest, regardless of whether that means they can stay with people who are their biological relatives, let alone whether their caretakers will look like them.

And we need to shift the way the law—and our culture—views foster children. For decades, advocates have attempted to change child welfare through lawsuits. But the results have been mixed at best. Children's Rights, a watchdog group that grew out of the ACLU, has filed class actions in almost half the states in the country. The group's mission is to "hold governments accountable for keeping kids safe and healthy" by pursuing "relentless strategic advocacy and legal action," and it has won its share of battles.[21] But whether children are safer or healthier as a result remains open to question.

Most states facing these legal actions have settled, resulting in federal consent decrees. These decrees usually mandate spending more money and shrinking caseloads—arrangements that agency employees are happy to facilitate. As with class-action lawsuits against school districts, the remedy in child-welfare lawsuits is always more money. But money does not necessarily lead to better outcomes in either arena. Some of the settlements may actually make things worse. In 2020, Kansas agreed to settle a lawsuit against its child-welfare system, consenting to grant substantial oversight authority over its restructuring to a prominent advocate, Judith Meltzer.[22] Meltzer is head of the Center for the Study of Social Policy (CSSP), which has just launched the upEND Campaign. Its goal: ending children's removal from families entirely because foster care is racist.[23]

Given their priors, it's unlikely Meltzer and her colleagues will devote much effort to recruiting more foster parents. Making foster care sound evil and racist will discourage volunteers. Pressure to abolish foster care will result in worse outcomes for children because it will reduce the pool of potential foster parents. The

---

2 "Children's Rights." (Children's Rights, n.d.), https://www.childrensrights.org/.

3 Laura Bauer, "Settlement Could Take Kansas Foster Care from 'Shockingly Broken' to Model for Nation." (*The Kansas City Star*, December 15, 2019), https://www.kansascity.com/news/politics-government/article244104907.html.

4 "New Movement Seeks to UpEND the Child Welfare System and Create Anti-Racist Supports for Children and Families." (Center for the Study of Social Policy, accessed September 1, 2020), https://cssp.org/about-us/connect/press-room/new-movement-seeks-to-upend-the-child-welfare-system-and-create-anti-racist-supports-for-children-and-families.

remaining volunteers will be the least qualified and most likely to be doing it for the small amounts of money that they receive.

There is, however, a more promising legal avenue to get children who are caught in the system the help they need—recognizing a child's legal right to a family. A noteworthy amicus brief filed in the case by an Arizona-based group called Generation Justice in the *Fulton v. Philadelphia* case before the Supreme Court floats this idea: "As the parties seek the balance between the right to religious free exercise and the interest in freedom from discrimination, this Court should not lose sight of what may be the most critical matter at stake—the children's profound interest in forming familial bonds..... Impeding access to quality foster care, a gateway to timely adoption, hurts children."

In 2020, James Dwyer, a law professor at the College of William and Mary, filed a federal lawsuit with a similar rationale on behalf of a two-year-old who had been fostered by a couple he knows. The couple had cared for the child since he was born, but he was removed to live with a grandfather, who was previously deemed unfit because of his long criminal record. Dwyer suspects that race played a role in this decision—the child is black, the mothers are white. (The black caseworker scolded the mothers at one point for not using beads in the child's hair.)

Dwyer argues in the brief that "at some point, a child's interest in continuity of placement must become sufficiently strong that it receives the same substantive due-process protection that the federal courts give to adults' less vital interests in maintaining and receiving recognition for their intimate relationships. Basic respect for the humanity, personhood and fundamental need of a child requires this."

In addition to the fact that foster kids lack an effective means of appealing their cases--higher state courts are deeply reluctant to overturn family court decisions—Dwyer argues that children have a "liberty interest" under the 14th Amendment that has not been properly considered by the courts yet. While conservatives are generally loath to discover new rights in the Constitution, federal civil-rights lawsuits may be necessary in order to do what is best for foster children. Moreover, as the Generation Justice brief argues, there is reason to think that the crafters of the 14th Amendment likely had family bonds in mind and not just the other rights of a citizen. As one member of Congress noted at the time, the states ratified "the universal understanding of the American people" that free individuals have "the right of having a family, a wife, children, [and a] home."

In other words, as former New York ACS head Ronald Richter says, "Children are not chattel. They are not pieces of furniture you can just move around," Or, as the Generation Justice brief has it: "The victorious North's desire to protect people's ability to form familial bonds did not disappear with slavery."

What would it mean if we took seriously the idea that the child-welfare system exists to put children first and that children should have a right to form familial bonds, whether they be with biological family or nonrelatives who care for them? It would mean that we need to provide vulnerable kids with abundant options for safe, loving foster and adoptive homes. It would mean that rather than trying to run evangelical foster and adoptive organizations out of business because they don't adhere to the latest ideological trends, we would ask why there aren't more of them.

It would mean asking where the Catholic, Mormon, Jewish, and Muslim communities are and why they aren't following the lead of their evangelical peers. Why aren't they recruiting CASA volunteers? Why aren't they mentoring biological families who are trying to reunify with their children or helping provide material, emotional, and spiritual support for people who are doing foster care?

It would mean persuading more ordinary, middle-class Americans of all faiths and no faith to step up. It is easy to throw up our hands and stay away from these systems and the people they serve. But the more that we stay away, the worse the systems become. There is no one left with the time, the inclination, and the ability to care for and advocate for these children. And the systems simply adapt accordingly, running roughshod over children's best interests and simply trying to accommodate masses of dysfunctional adults.

What would it mean for a child to have the right to form family bonds? It would mean reorienting the child-welfare system away from bloodlines and skin color—as if those are the factors that ensure a child is fed, clothed, educated, supervised, and loved. It would mean understanding the implications of faith and class on this debate. Having money does not make you a more loving parent. But a stable source of income means that you can spend more time worrying about the needs of the traumatized child in your house and less time on where your rent check is coming from or how you're going to pay for groceries. Faith also does not make you a better parent. But it does mean that you're more likely to want to foster in the first place and that you will be more likely to have the relationships and support that will make fostering or adopting a child from foster care more successful.

What would it mean to orient the child-welfare system around the best interests of the child, to allow that child to form new family bonds when a family of origin cannot love and protect that vulnerable human being? Let me offer one last story.

Ansley was born premature with drugs in her system and, for months, the doctors seemed to think that was the problem. Sara Pendleton spent every day in the hospital just holding Ansley because the girl would cry in pain for hours if she were put down. Ansley's biological mother refused to be involved but would not relinquish custody. Sara had spent time with dozens of substance-exposed babies in the NICU, and she knew that there was something else wrong with Ansley. But she was not allowed to get a second opinion or take the child out of state to consult with specialists. Neither the medical system nor the legal system would let her advocate for Ansley.

Sara was "only" a foster mother.

By the time doctors correctly diagnosed the toddler with a rare genetic condition called Costello's Syndrome, her health had deteriorated. The medical procedures that she underwent resulted in a massive coronary incident that left her in a vegetative state. For five and a half years, Sara and her husband cared for Ansley, though her condition was terminal. Sara propped her in front of different brain-stimulating images throughout the day. Sara picked colors Ansley seemed to like (yellow) to decorate her bed and her wheelchair, and played music she wanted to listen to. One year, she took Ansley to the New York City Ballet. She says that even if she couldn't see it, she could sense the lights and the color of the place. Ansley didn't have a seizure for the entire three hours that she was at Lincoln Center, an unusually long span. A year after her death, Sara still feels guilty for not doing more.

She wrote on Facebook a "memory" of Ansley from 2014: "If you have a child who needs you extra, there's a reason for it. Let them take all your time. Give them the extra snuggles. Don't leave them if you know they don't handle being left. It never lasts long. The ones who need more from you usually have a good reason. I don't regret the years of my life spent glued to her side. They were worth every sacrifice. (SHE was worth every sacrifice)."

What would it mean for our child-welfare system to be oriented around the best interests of children? It would mean that every child would get the kind of love and protection they deserve.

ACKNOWLEDGMENTS

It would be easy to put off writing a book during a pandemic, but thanks to my supportive colleagues and friends, I had no excuses. I'd like to express my gratitude to Robert Doar for encouraging me to pursue this area of research and for bringing me to the American Enterprise Institute to carry out this project. Both in person and virtually, my fellow fellows have challenged my thinking and, I hope, made my arguments sharper.

Emily Putnam-Hornstein and Sarah Anne Font have provided me an enormous amount of guidance through the murky waters of academic literature on this subject. That level of statistical analysis and dry humor is hard to find in one person, let alone two. Marie Cohen and Cassie Statuto Bevan have also given me innumerable insights into how the child-welfare sausage gets made. The other members of AEI's Child Welfare Innovation Working Group have informed and challenged me on so many of these issues and I'm deeply grateful for their friendships.

Ronald Richter is one of the first people who explained the child-welfare system to me, and he has spent countless hours talking to me since. His tireless advocacy for vulnerable children and his willingness to engage people on all sides of these debates are an inspiration.

I have been overwhelmed by the deep devotion of so many foster and adoptive families and the people and organizations who are helping to support them. Jedd Medefind, Shelly Radic, Lauri Currier, Anna Palmer, and so many others have welcomed me into their communities and shared their stories of heartbreak and triumph. I cannot thank them enough.

Thanks to Adam Bellow for his belief in the importance of this subject and for sharpening the manuscript. Kristi Kendall and Alice Lloyd have provided me with invaluable research help and new ideas for thinking about this topic.

Now about that pandemic. I want to thank Emily, Simon, and Leah for being so good at entertaining yourselves that I could find the time to write this book. Though being at home all the time may not have been your first choice, it has been my great joy to spend these hours and days watching you grow into such insightful, funny, and loving human beings. And to Jason, of course, there's no one I'd rather be in lockdown with.

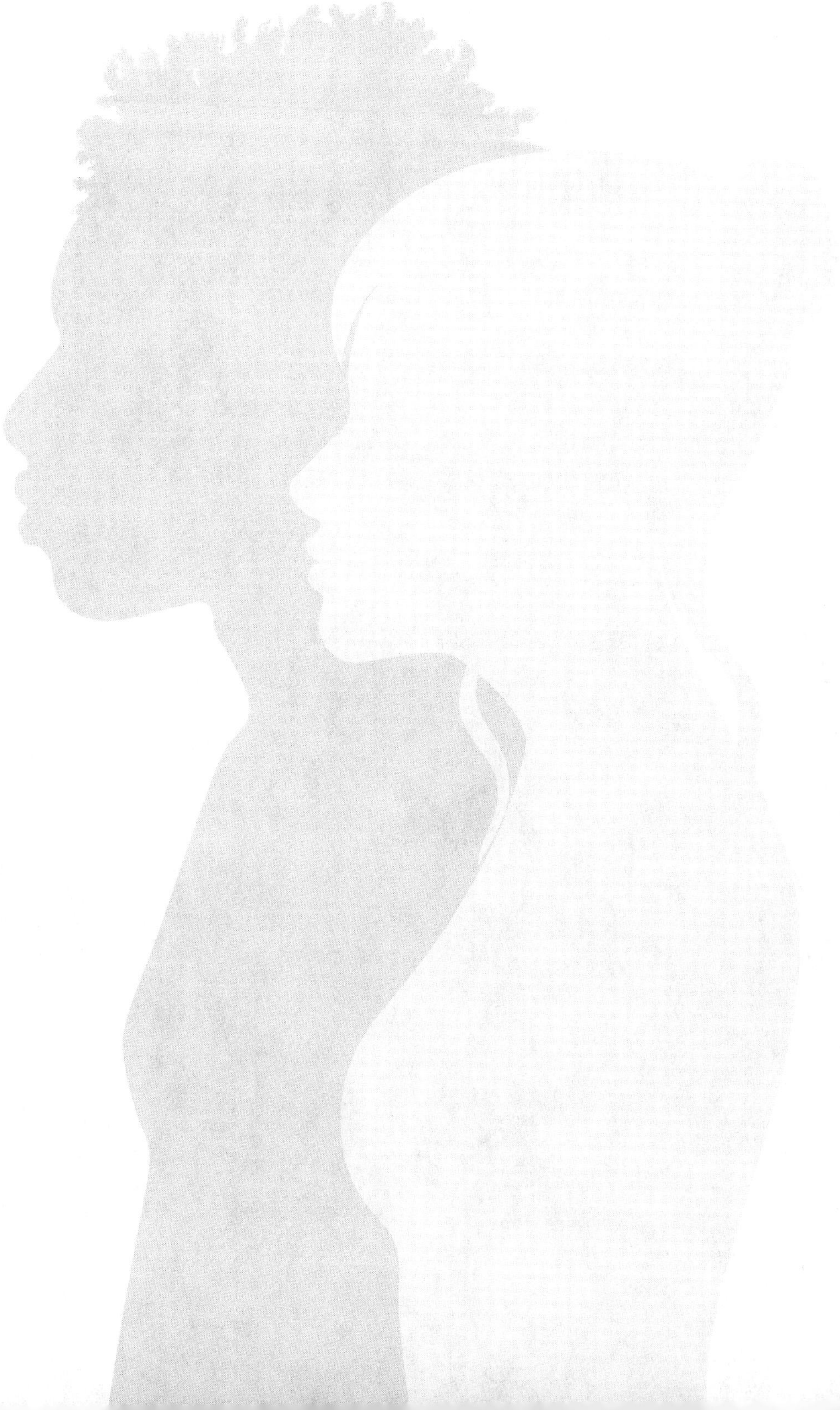